L
Abou

The only book-sized guide devoted *exclusively* to boarding
(All others include numerous *day* schools)

40 Important Facts and Figures

Set out in simple, concise form on a separate page
for *each* of the 231 boarding schools
throughout the *entire* country
that have over 60 boarders

The Various Types of Schools

Coed—boys—girls—PGs—Military
Junior boarding schools—very low cost schools
Schools for those with learning differences
Secondary schools with boarders under 9th grade

Unique Statistical Tables

(covering the 110 larger schools)

School size—percent of day students
No. of states represented—no. of foreign students
Financial aid—alumni support—dress code
Library volumes—SAT scores—College admissions
Endowment—required church attendance—community service
Schools offering: hockey—golf—crew
riding—squash—skiing—sailing—swimming

Handy Location Maps

New England—Mid Atlantic—Southeast—West—Midwest

To Order:

(If not available at your local bookstore)
Send a check for $16.50 (includes mailing costs)

To: *The Boarding School Guide*
56 Paces West Drive, NW
Atlanta, GA 30327
(404) 261-2682

THE BOARDING SCHOOL GUIDE

Facts and figures on 231 leading schools throughout the United States

Compiled and edited by
Kiliaen V. R. Townsend
Educational Consultant

AGEE
PUBLISHERS
INC.
Athens, Georgia

This book was produced by Agee Publishers, Inc., Athens, GA. The maps were produced by Preston Rose Printing Co.

Library of Congress Catalog Number: 89-84769

ISBN: 0-935265-18-X

Cover picture: Julia Farnham, St. Mark's (MA) '89
Carter Townsend, Deerfield Academy (MA) '91

Dedication

To My Two "Preppy" Sons —

Van, a graduate of the Westminster School in Atlanta, Georgia, Williams College and Middlebury's Breadloaf School. Formerly a teacher at Darlington (GA) and now at St. Mark's (MA) since 1984. An exchange teacher at Radley College in Oxford, England for the year 1988-1989.

And Carter, a graduate of the Lovett Lower School in Atlanta and the Eaglebrook Junior Boarding School (MA), who is now attending Deerfield Academy (MA).

Acknowledgements

First of all, my wife, Rena, has been indispensable not only for all her typing but for permitting me the time to undertake this project. I'm sure she has often felt neglected, but her "sunny" disposition saw us both through to the finished product.

Phil Smith, long-time Director of Admissions at Williams College, has been invaluable with his advice and counsel.

Everett Gourley, respected retiring Director of Admissions at the Asheville School, has also been particularly helpful and encouraging.

Not to be overlooked are the numerous other boarding school admission directors and headmasters that I have had the opportunity to know. There are too many to name, but they have been a great source of information as well as an inspiration for me to try to do something that will possibly be of some help in the splendid job they are doing for their schools and the youths of this country.

Contents

Introduction

This guide covers 231 schools throughout the entire United States that have at least 60 boarders and a student body from a number of different states as well as foreign countries. Each of the individual pages devoted to these schools (pages 52 through 278) contain 40 or more pertinent facts and figures which are important for a student and the parents in narrowing the selection to the handful of schools that should be visited.

Despite the general opinion, northeastern states do not have a monopoly on boarding schools. True, there are 80 in the six New England States (pages 14-15), but 151 of these 231 schools are located in 32 other states, including 44 in the mid-atlantic region (map on page 12), and 45 in the southeast (map on page 13). The midwest has 32 boarding schools (map on page 17) and the far west 30 (map on page 16).

There are choices of urban, suburban, and rural settings as well as sizes ranging from 60 to 1200 students (see pages 28-29 and 50-51).

These 231 boarding schools offer an extensive cross-section of available options. They provide for just about every conceivable need in education, including generous financial aid for 15 to 50% of the student body.

There are schools for the average or above average student as well as for those with learning differences (pages 51 and 255-274), and ages accommodated range from 6 to 20 (see pages 20-24).

There are coed (page 18) as well as all boy and all girl boarding schools (page 19). There are very low cost schools for students with special qualifications, such as only one parent, etc. (page 228-232), and there are military schools (pages 51 and 233-254). A great many schools offer a post graduate year (page 24).

Also included are junior boarding schools that accommodate youngsters below the 8th grade and run through the 9th grade, after which most go on to a secondary boarding school (pages 20 and 51, also, pages 275-278).

Omitted from this guide are a relatively small number of other boarding schools, most of which are predominantly day schools or have few boarders or cater to a small geographical area. Their omission in no way reflects on their particular merits as boarding schools (see page 50 for partial listing).

231 Boarding Schools in 38 States

C = COED, B = BOYS, G = GIRLS

Connecticut
(23 Schools)

AVON
CANTERBURY
CHESHIRE
CHOATE
E. WALKER
FORMAN
GUNNERY
HOTCHKISS
INDIAN MTN.*
KENT
LOOMIS
MARVELWOOD
MISS PORTER'S
POMFRET
RECTORY*
RUMSEY*
ST. THOM MORE
SALISBURY
SOUTH KENT
SUFFIELD
TAFT
WESTMINSTER
WESTOVER

PENNSYLVANIA
(14 SCHOOLS)

CARSON LONG
CHURCH FARM
GEORGE
GRIER
HERSHEY

Massachusetts
(32 Schools)
(See other map for location of these 99 schools)

ANDOVER
BERKSHIRE
BROOKS
BUXTON
CAMBRIDGE
CHAPEL HILL
CONCORD
CUSHING
DANA HALL
DEERFIELD
EAGLEBROOK*
EAGLE HILL
FAY*
FESSENDEN*
GOV. DUMMER
GROTON
HIGHCROFT
LANDMARK
LAWRENCE
MACDUFFIE
MIDDLESEX
MILTON
MISS HALL'S
NORTHFIELD
ST. MARK'S
STONELEIGH
TABOR
WALNUT HILL
WILBRAHAM
WILLISTON
WINCHENDON
WORCESTER

N. H. & VT.
(15 Schools)

BREWSTER
CARDIGAN*
DUBLIN
EXETER
HOLDERNESS
KIMBALL UNION
NEW HAMPTON
PINE RIDGE
PROCTOR
PUTNEY
ST. JOHNSBURY
ST. PAUL'S
TILTON
VERMONT A.
WHITE MTN.

New York
(15 Schools)

DARROW
E. WILLARD
GOW
HOOSAC
KILDONAN
KNOX
MASTERS
MILLBROOK
NYMA
N. COUNTRY*
NORTHWOOD
OAKWOOD
STONY BROOK
STORM KING
T-PAWLING

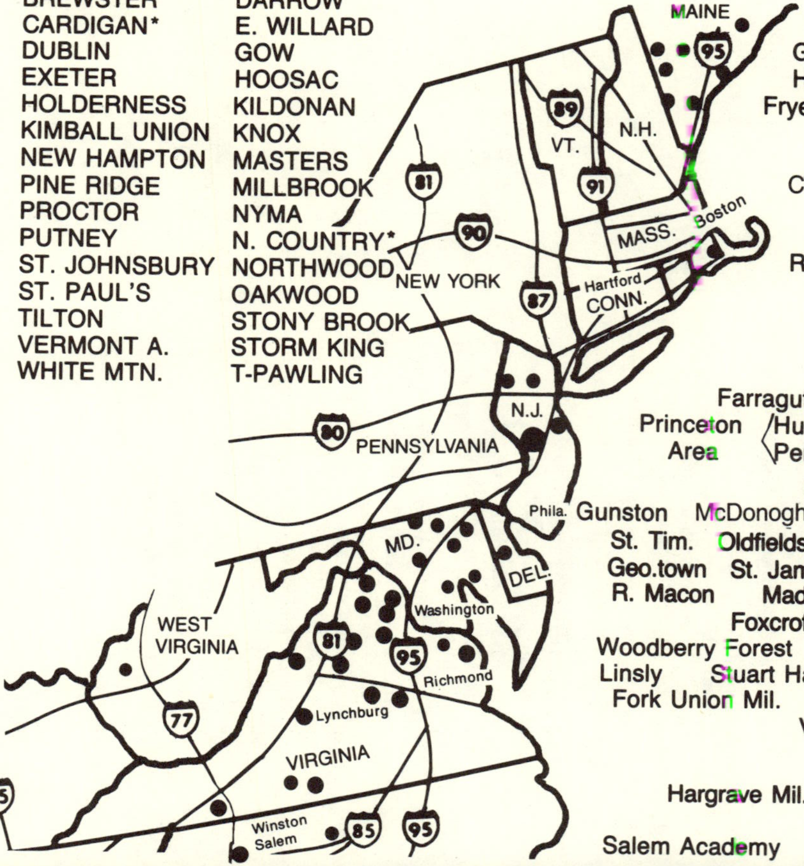

Maine Central
Gould Kents H.
Hebron Hyde
Fryeburg Bridgton

N.H. & VT. (15)
CT. (23) MA(32)

RI: Portsmouth, St. George's, St. Andrew's

New York (15)

Farragut Purnell Blair
Princeton Area: Hun, Pennington
Lawrenceville
Peddie

Pennsylvania (14)
Gunston McDonogh W. Nottingham
St. Tim. Oldfields Garrison Forest
Geo.town St. James St. Andrew's
R. Macon Madeira Episcopal
Foxcroft Christchurch
Woodberry Forest St. Margaret's
Linsly Stuart Hall Blue Ridge
Fork Union Mil. St. Catherine's
Virginia Episcopal

Hargrave Mil. Chatham Hall
Oak Hill
Salem Academy Oak Ridge Mil.

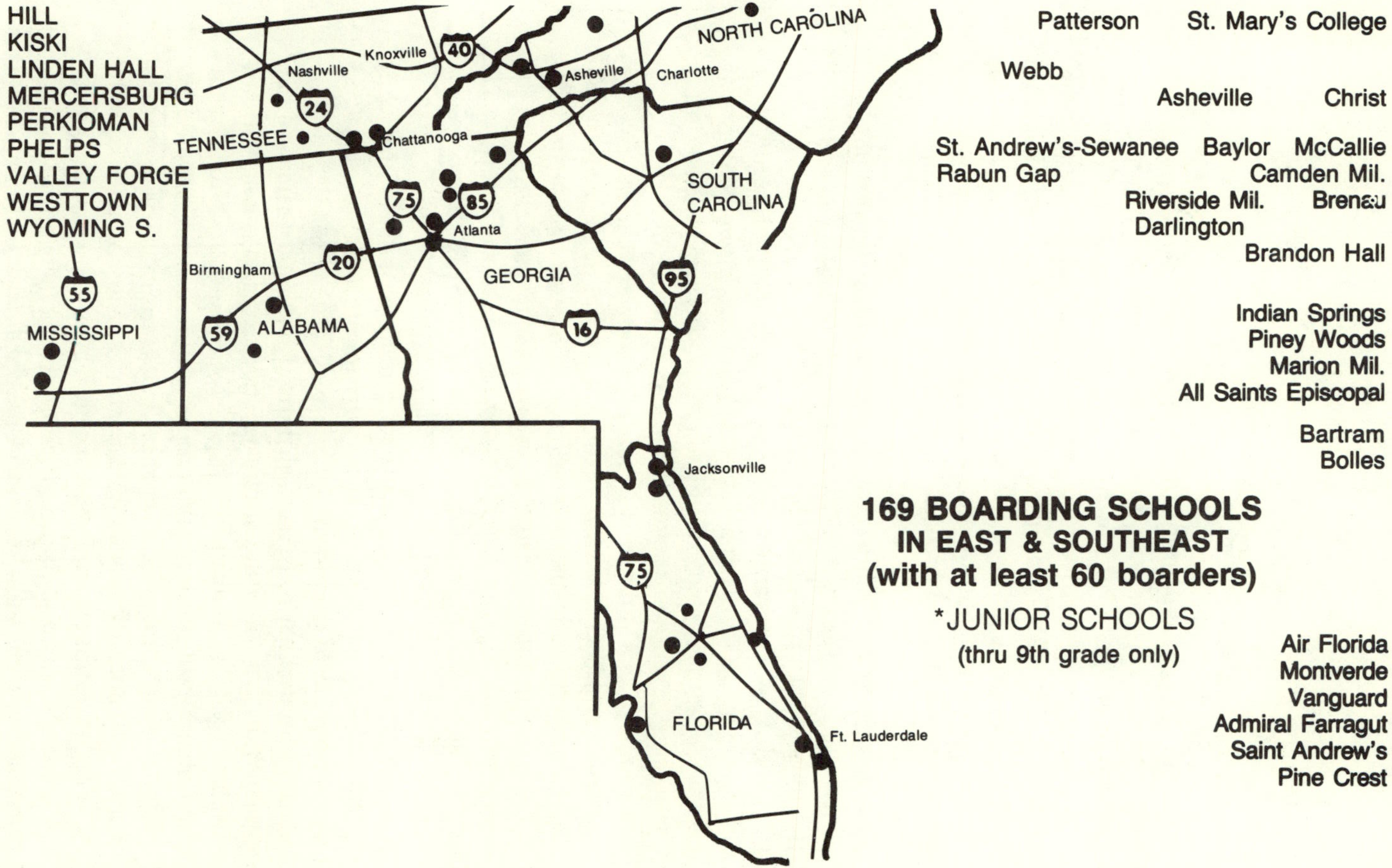
HILL
KISKI
LINDEN HALL
MERCERSBURG
PERKIOMAN
PHELPS
VALLEY FORGE
WESTTOWN
WYOMING S.
Patterson
St. Mary's College
Webb
Asheville
Christ
St. Andrew's-Sewanee
Baylor
McCallie
Rabun Gap
Camden Mil.
Riverside Mil.
Brenau
Darlington
Brandon Hall
Indian Springs
Piney Woods
Marion Mil.
All Saints Episcopal
Bartram
Bolles
169 BOARDING SCHOOLS
IN EAST & SOUTHEAST
(with at least 60 boarders)
*JUNIOR SCHOOLS
(thru 9th grade only)
Air Florida
Montverde
Vanguard
Admiral Farragut
Saint Andrew's
Pine Crest
NORTH CAROLINA
SOUTH CAROLINA
TENNESSEE
GEORGIA
ALABAMA
MISSISSIPPI
FLORIDA
Knoxville
Nashville
Asheville
Charlotte
Chattanooga
Atlanta
Birmingham
Jacksonville
Ft. Lauderdale
40
24
75
85
20
95
16
55
59
75

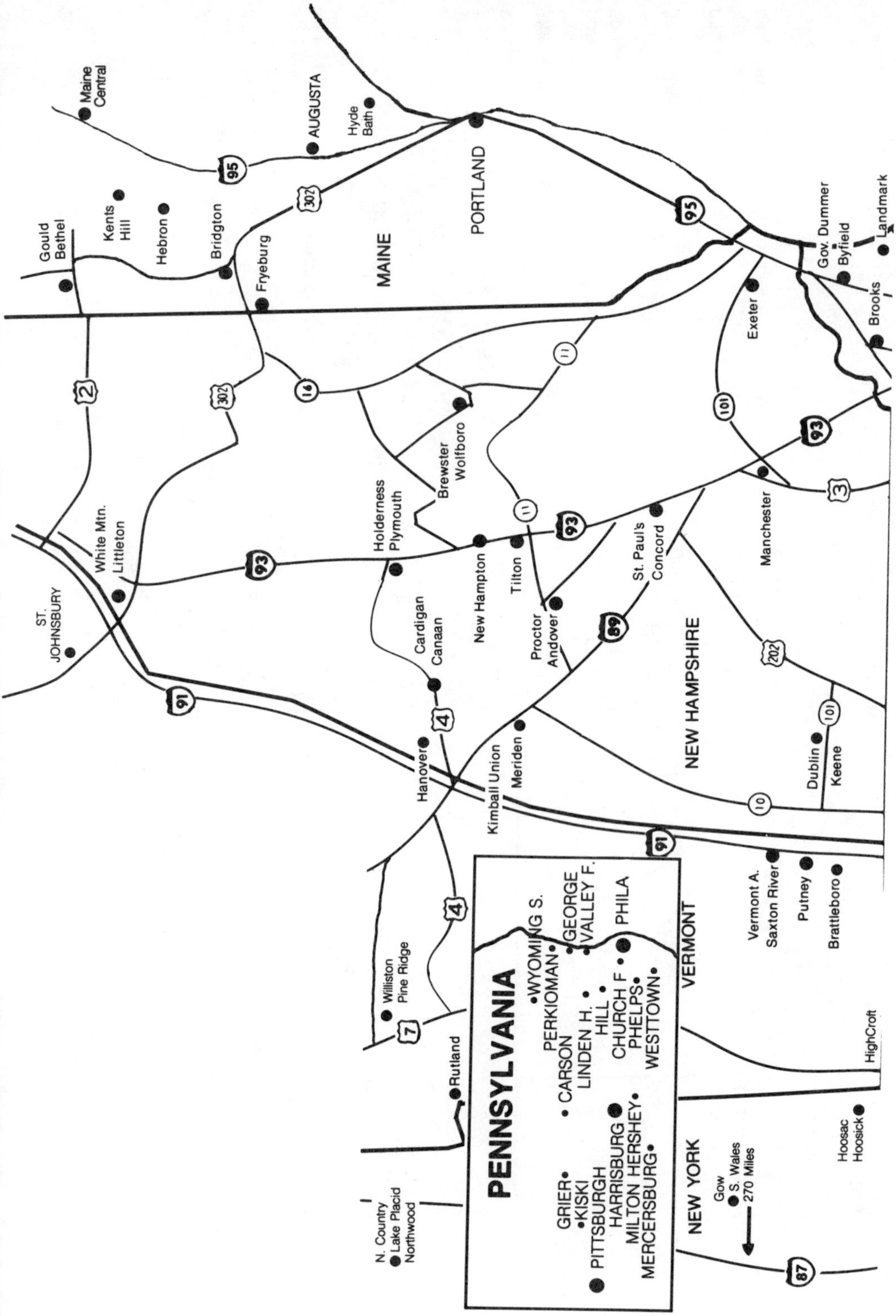
MAINE
NEW HAMPSHIRE
VERMONT
NEW YORK
PENNSYLVANIA
Maine Central
AUGUSTA
Hyde
Bath
PORTLAND
Gould
Bethel
Kents
Hill
Hebron
Bridgton
Fryeburg
Gov. Dummer
Byfield
Landmark
Brooks
Exeter
ST. JOHNSBURY
White Mtn.
Littleton
Holderness
Plymouth
Brewster
Wolfboro
New Hampton
Tilton
St. Paul's
Concord
Manchester
Cardigan
Canaan
Proctor
Andover
Hanover
Kimball Union
Meriden
Dublin
Keene
Vermont A.
Saxton River
Putney
Brattleboro
Williston
Pine Ridge
Rutland
HighCroft
Hoosac
Hoosick
N. Country
Lake Placid
Northwood
Gow
S. Wales
270 Miles
GRIER
KISKI
PITTSBURGH
HARRISBURG
MILTON HERSHEY
MERCERSBURG
CARSON
LINDEN H.
HILL
CHURCH F
PHELPS
WESTTOWN
PERKIOMAN
WYOMING S.
GEORGE
VALLEY F.
PHILA
95
302
2
16
11
93
101
3
89
202
10
91
4
7
87

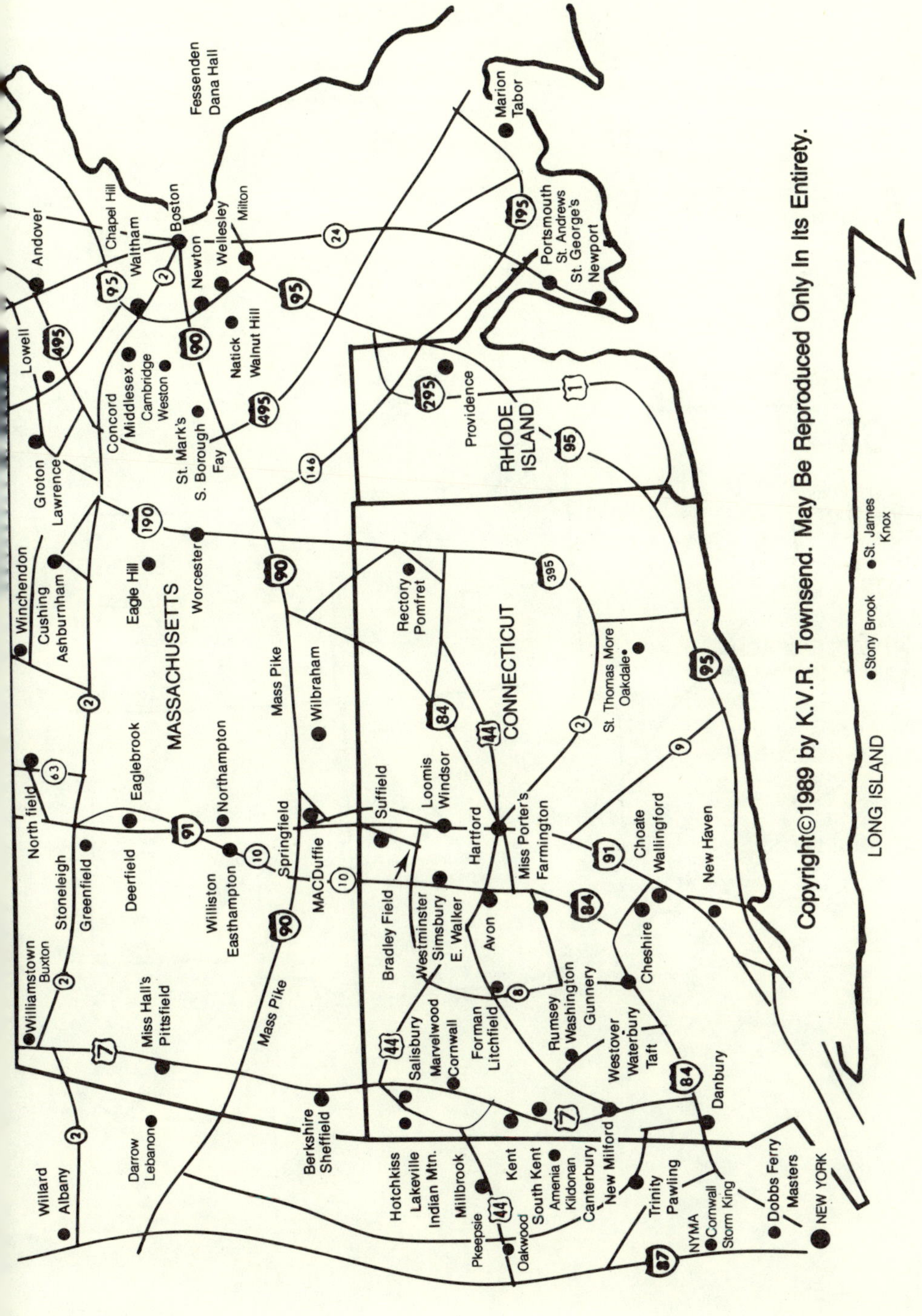
MASSACHUSETTS
CONNECTICUT
RHODE ISLAND
LONG ISLAND
NEW YORK
Boston
Chapel Hill
Waltham
Andover
Lowell
Groton
Lawrence
Concord
Middlesex
Cambridge
Weston
St. Mark's
S. Borough
Fay
Newton
Wellesley
Milton
Natick
Walnut Hill
Fessenden
Dana Hall
Winchendon
Cushing
Ashburnham
Eagle Hill
Worcester
Wilbraham
Mass Pike
Eaglebrook
Northampton
North field
Stoneleigh
Greenfield
Deerfield
Williston
Easthampton
Springfield
MACDuffie
Williamstown
Buxton
Miss Hall's
Pittsfield
Willard
Albany
Darrow
Lebanon
Berkshire
Sheffield
Providence
Portsmouth
St. Andrews
St. George's
Newport
Marion
Tabor
Rectory
Pomfret
St. Thomas More
Oakdale
Suffield
Loomis
Windsor
Hartford
Bradley Field
Westminster
Simsbury
E. Walker
Avon
Miss Porter's
Farmington
Choate
Wallingford
New Haven
Cheshire
Rumsey
Washington
Gunnery
Westover
Waterbury
Taft
Danbury
Salisbury
Marvelwood
Cornwall
Forman
Litchfield
Hotchkiss
Lakeville
Indian Mtn.
Millbrook
Kent
South Kent
Amenia
Kildonan
Canterbury
New Milford
Trinity
Pawling
NYMA
Cornwall
Storm King
Dobbs Ferry
Masters
Pkeepsie
Oakwood
Stony Brook
St. James
Knox
Copyright©1989 by K.V.R. Townsend. May Be Reproduced Only In Its Entirety.

30 WESTERN SCHOOLS
(with at least 60 boarders)

32 MIDWESTERN SCHOOLS
(with at least 60 boarders)

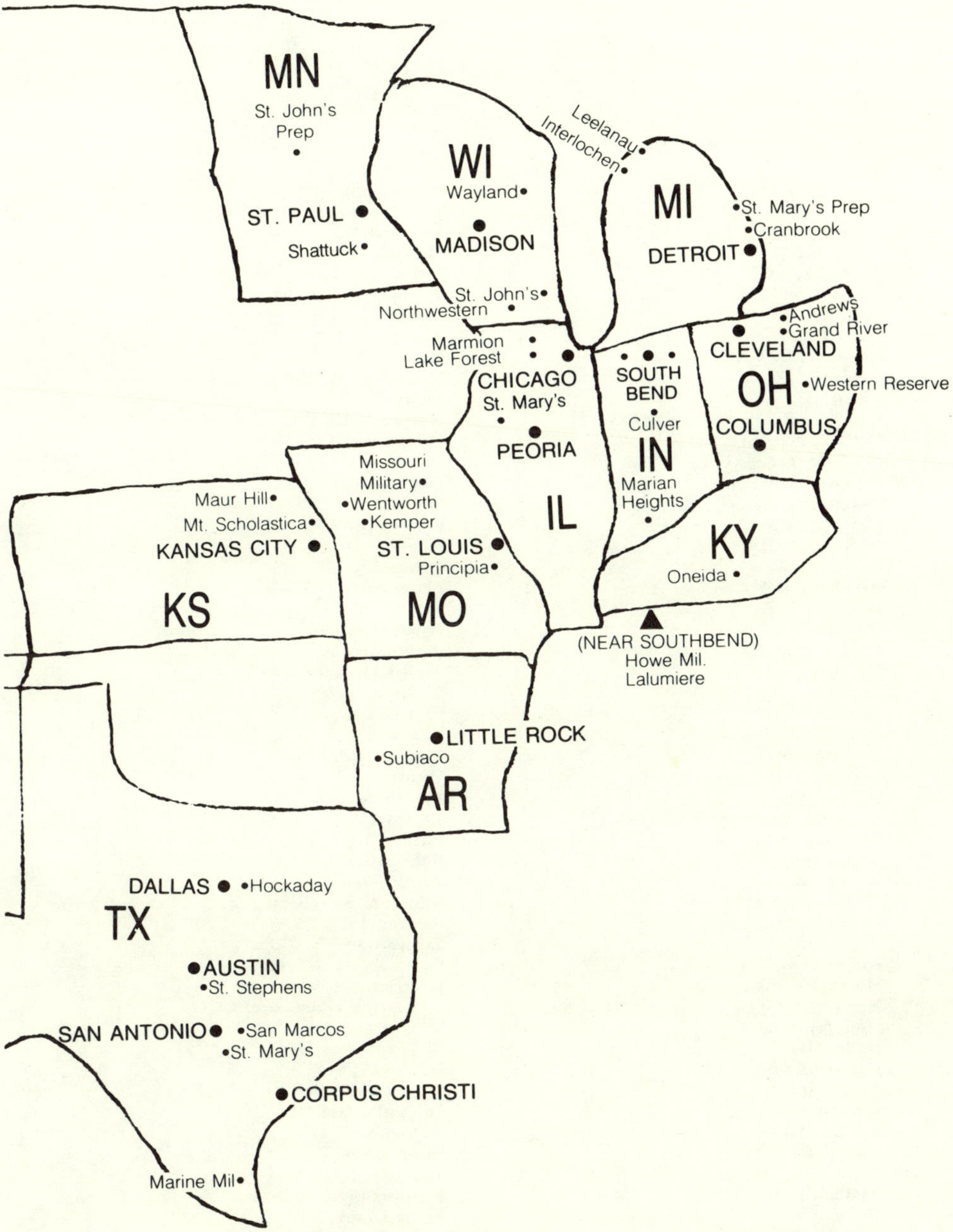

The 231 Boarding Schools

M for Military, D for Learning Differences, J for Junior Schools

Coed (144)

All Saints, MS	
Asheville, NC	
Athenian, CA	
Baylor, TN	
Berkshire, MA	
Blair, NJ	
Bolles, FL	
Brewster, NH	
Brooks, MA	
Buxton, MA	
Cambridge, MA	
Canterbury, CT	
Carson Long, PA	M
Cate, CA	
Cedu, CA	D
Chapel Hill, MA	
Cheshire, CT	
Choate, CT	
Colorado Rocky Mountain, CO	
Colorado Springs, CO	
Concord, MA	
Cranbrook, MI	
Culver, IN	
Cushing, MA	
Darlington, GA	
Darrow, NY	
Deerfield, MA	
Delphian, OR	
Dublin, NH	
Elliott-Pope, CA	
Fay, MA	J
Fenster, AZ	
Forman, CT	D
Fountain Valley, CO	
Fryeburg, ME	
George, PA	
Gould, ME	
Governor Dummer, MA	
Groton, MA	
Gunnery, CT	
Hargrave, VA	M
Hawaii Prep, HI	
Hebron, ME	
Highcroft, MA	D
Holderness, NH	
Hoosac, NY	
Hotchkiss, CT	
Hun, NJ	
Hyde, ME	D
Indian Mountain, CT	J
Indian Springs, AL	
Interlochen, MI	
Judson, AZ	
Kent, CT	
Kents Hill, ME	
Kimball Union, NH	
Knox, NY	
Lake Forest, IL	
La Lumiere, IN	
Landmark, MA	D
Lawrence, MA	
Lawrenceville, NJ	
Leelanau, MI	
Loomis, CT	
Maine Central, ME	
Marion, AL	M
Marvelwood, CT	
McDonogh, MD	
Mercersburg, PA	
Middlesex, MA	
Midland, CA	
Millbrook, NY	
Milton, MA	
Milton Hershey, PA	
Montverde, FL	
New Hampton, NH	
N Y M A, NY	M
Northfield M.H., MA	
North Country, NY	J
Northwood, NY	
Oak Creek, AZ	D
Oak Hill, VA	D
Oak Ridge Mil., NC	M
Oakwood, NY	
Ojai Valley, CA	
Oneida, KY	
Orme, AZ	
Patterson, NC	
Peddie, NJ	
Pennington, NJ	
Perkiomen, PA	
Phillips Academy, MA	
Phillips Exeter, NH	
Pine Crest, FL	
Pine Ridge, VT	D
Piney Woods, MS	
Pomfret, CT	
Principia, MO	
Proctor, NH	
Putney, VT	
Rabun, GA	
Randolph Macon, VA	M
Robert L. Stevenson, CA	
Rumsey Hall, CT	J
Saint Andrew's, FL	
St. Andrew's, DE	
St. Andrew's, RI	D
St. Andrew's-Sewanee, TN	
St. George's, RI	
St. Johnsbury, VT	
St. Mark's, MA	
St. Mary's Hall, TX	
St. Paul's, NH	
St. Stephen's, TX	
San Marcos, TX	
Shattuck, MN	
Southwestern Academy, CA	
Stony Brook, NY	
Storm King, NY	
Suffield, CT	
Tabor, MA	
Taft, CT	

Coed (144)

Thacher, CA	
Tilton, NH	
United World College, NM	
Vanguard, FL	D
Verde Valley, AZ	
Vermont Academy, VT	
Virginia Episcopal, VA	
Walnut Hill, MA	
Wasatch, UT	
Wayland, WI	
Webb, TN	
Western Reserve, OH	
Westminster, CT	
West Nottingham, MD	
Westtown, PA	
Whiteman, CO	
White Mountain, NH	
Wilbraham, MA	
Williston, MA	
Winchendon, MA	D
Worcester, MA	
Wyoming Seminary, PA	

Girls (35)

Academy of Mt. St. Scholastica, KS	
Andrews, OH	
Bartram, FL	
Brenau, GA	
Chatham Hall, VA	
Dana Hall, MA	
Emma Willard, NY	
Ethel Walker, CT	
Foxcroft, VA	
Garrison Forest, MD	
Grier, PA	
Gunston, MD	
Hockaday, TX	
Linden Hall, PA	
MacDuffie, MA	
Madeira, VA	
Marian Heights, IN	
Masters, NY	
Miss Hall's, MA	
Miss Porter's, CT	
Oldfields, MD	
Purnell, NJ	
St. Catherine's, VA	
St. Margaret's, VA	
St. Mary's Academy, IL	
St. Mary's College, NC	
St. Scholastica, CO	
St. Timothy's, MD	
Salem, NC	
San Domenico, CA	
Santa Catalina, CA	
Stoneleigh-Burnham, MA	
Stuart Hall, VA	
Vivian Webb, CA	
Westover, CT	

Boys (52)

Admiral Farragut, FL	M
Admiral Farragut, NJ	M
Army & Navy, CA	M
Avon, CT	
Blue Ridge, VA	D
Brandon Hall, GA	D
Bridgton, ME	
Camden Military, SC	M
Cardigan, NH	J
Christchurch, VA	D
Christ School, NC	
Church Farm, PA	
Dunn, CA	
Eagle Hill, MA	D
Eaglebrook, MA	J
Episcopal, VA	
Fessenden, MA	J
Florida Air, FL	M
Fork Union, VA	M
Georgetown, MD	
Gow, NY	D
Grand River, OH	D
Hill, PA	
Howe, IN	M
Kemper, MO	M
Kildonan, NY	D
Kiski, PA	
Linsly, WV	
Marine Military, TX	M
Marmion, IL	M
Maur Hill, KS	
McCallie, TN	
Missouri Military, MO	M
Northwestern, WI	M
Phelps, PA	D
Portsmouth Abbey, RI	
Rectory, CT	J
Riverside, GA	M
Saint James, MD	
Saint John's Military, WI	M
Saint John's Prep, MN	
Saint Mary's Prep, MI	
Saint Thomas More, CT	D
Salisbury, CT	
South Kent, CT	
Subiaco, AR	
Trinity-Pawling, NY	
Valley Forge, PA	M
Webb of California, CA	
Wentworth, MO	M
Woodberry Forest, VA	
Woodside Priory, CA	

The Lowest Grades That Junior Schools Take Boarders

Kindergarten		
Horizon's Edge, Canterbury, NH	C	K-8
1st Grade		
Chicago Junior, Elgin, IL	C	1-8
2nd Grade		
Bement, Deerfield, MA	C	2-9
3rd Grade		
Harker, San Jose, CA	C	3-8
Hillside, Marlboro, MA	B	3-8
4th Grade		
Aiken, Aiken, SC	B	4-9
American Boychoir, Princeton, NJ	B	4-8
Greenwood, Putney, VT	B	4-8**
Linden Hill, Northfield, MA	B	4-8**
North Country, Lake Placid, NY	C	4-8*
5th Grade		
Choir School, New York City, NY	B	5-8
Fessenden, West Newton, MA	B	5-9*
Malcolm Gordon, Garrison, NY	B	5-8
Rumsey, Washington, CT	C	5-9*
6th Grade		
Cardigan, Canaan, NH	B	6-9*
Eaglebrook, Deerfield, MA	B	6-9*
Fay, Southborough, MA	C	6-9*
Indian Mountain, Lakeville, CT	B	6-9*
Rectory, Pomfret, CT	B	6-9*

* The 8 junior boarding schools detailed in this guide (See pages 275-278)

** Specializes in learning differences.

Advantages of Boarding School

1. First, only boarding schools can offer seven days a week, 215 days a year wholesome, secure surroundings staffed around the clock by trained adults, and these adults are experienced in helping adolescents, not only intellectually but also socially, athletically and artistically.
2. All schools offer small classes — 8 to 15 — resulting in much closer attention and more teacher-student interchange, and, most important, there is no disruption or disorderly conduct tolerated.
3. The schools provide a close association with teachers, since most live on the campus and some right in the dormitory.
4. Students will have fellow students from all over the United States.
5. Some students are from other parts of the world.
6. TV and phone access is there when worthwhile or needed, but they are not aimless time consumers.
7. Each school offers a large library, exercise room, indoor and outdoor facilities within walking distance days, evenings and week-ends.
8. Also offered are additional sports and recreational activities often not otherwise available, e.g., sailing, riding, skiing, crew, squash, golf, ice hockey (see pages 36-37).
9. Students experience preparation for college, not only with academic preparation, but also with the experience of living away from home and having to function independently.
10. Last, but certainly not least, is the opportunity for a whole new set of friends to supplement those at home — and these friends are often closer and more enduring because of the experience of actually living and sharing together all the waking hours.

74 Secondary Boarding Schools with Boarders Under the 9th Grade

Coed Schools

8th Grade (13)
All Saints', MS
Elliott Pope, CA
Groton, MA
Hoosac, NY
Hyde, ME
Indian Springs, AL
Lawrenceville, NJ
Leelanau, MI
Peddie, NJ
Rabun Gap, GA
Saint Mary's, TX (Girls)
Walnut Hill, MA
Webb, TN (Girls)

7th Grade (14)
Bolles, FL
Fenster, AZ
Knox, NY
Montverde, FL
Patterson, NC
Perkiomen, PA
Pine Crest, FL
Piney Woods, MS
Shattuck, MN
Stony Brook, NY
Vanguard, FL
Webb, TN (Boys)
Wilbraham, MA
Worcester, MA

6th Grade (5)
Harvey, NY
Hawaii Prep, HI
Oneida, KY
Saint Andrew's, FL
St. Andrew's, RI (Boys)

3rd, 4th or 5th Grade (4)
Delphian, OR
Judson, AZ
Linsly, WV
Ojai Valley, CA

Kindergarten and Up (1)
Milton Hershey, PA

Boys' Schools

8th Grade (3)
Christ School, NC
Hill, PA
Saint James, MD

7th Grade (5)
Cedu, CA
Church Farm, PA
Gow, NY
Grand River, OH
Phelps, PA

5th Grade (3)
Eagle Hill, MA
Highcroft, MA
Kildonan, NY

Girls' Schools

8th Grade (4)
Hockaday, TX
Oldfields, MD
St. Margaret's, VA
Stuart Hall, VA

7th Grade (5)
Andrews, OH
Bartram, FL
Grier, PA
MacDuffie, MA
St. Scholastica, CO

Military Schools

7th Grade (10)
Admiral Farragut, NJ
Camden, NC
Florida Air, FL
Kemper, MO
Northwestern, WI
NYMA, NY (Girls)
Oak Ridge, NC
St. John's Military, WI
Valley Forge, PA
Wentworth, MO

6th Grade (3)
Carson, PA
Fort Union, VA
Hargrave, VA

5th Grade (3)
Admiral Farragut, FL
Howe, IN
NYMA, NY (Boys)

4th Grade (1)
Missouri Military, MO

Post Graduate (PG) Grade Offered (107 Schools)

Coed (78)

Asheville, NC
Berkshire, MA
Blair, NJ
Bolles, FL
Brandon Hall, GA
Brewster, NH
Bridgton, ME
Cambridge, MA
Chapel Hill, MA
Cheshire, CT
Choate, CT
Christchurch, VA
Colorado Rocky Mountain, CO
Culver, IN
Cushing, MA
Darlington, GA
Darrow, NY
Deerfield, MA
Delphian, OR
Dublin, NH
Fryeburg, ME
Gould, ME
Gow, NY
Grand River, OH
Gunnery, CT
Hawaii Prep, HI
Hebron, ME
Highcroft, MA
Hotchkiss, CT
Hun, NJ
Hyde, ME
Indian Springs, AL
Interlocken, MI
Judson, AZ
Kent, CT
Kents Hill, ME
Kimball, NH
Knox, NY
La Lumiere, IN
Lawrenceville, NJ
Loomis, CT
Maine Central, ME
Mercersburg, PA
Montverde, FL
New Hampton, NH
Northfield, M.H., MA
Northwood, NY
Oak Creek, AZ
Oak Hill, VA
Oakwood, NY
Oneida, KY
Orme, AZ
Patterson, NC
Peddie, NJ
Perkiomen, PA
Phillips Academy, MA
Phillips Exeter, NH
Robert L. Stevenson, CA
St. Johnsbury, VT
Southwestern Academy, CA
Storm King, NY
Suffield, CT
Taft, CT
Tilton, NH
United World, NM
Valley Forge, PA
Verde Valley, AZ
Vermont Academy, VT
Webb, TN
Western Reserve, OH
Westminster, CT
West Nottingham, MD
White Mtn., NH
Wilbraham, MA
Williston, MA
Winchendon, MA
Worcester, MA
Wyoming Seminary, PA

Boys (PG)(10)

Avon, CT
Bridgton, ME
Christchurch, VA
Gow, NY
Grand River, OH
Hill, PA
Kildonan, NY
Kiski, PA
Phelps, PA
St. Thomas More, CT

Girls (PG)(7)

Emma Willard, NY
Foxcroft, VA
Grier, PA
Linden Hall, PA
Masters, NY
Saint Mary's, NC
Stoneleigh-Burnham, MA

Military (PG)(12)

Admiral Farragut, NJ
Camden, NC
Florida Air, FL
Fort Union, VA
Hargrave, VA
Marine Military, TX
Missouri Military, MO
NYMA, NY
Oak Ridge, NC
Randolph Macon, VA
Riverside, GA
Valley Forge, PA

Index of Statistical Tables and Categories

I. As to the 110 larger boarding schools (listed on the next page), there are comparative statistics in 27 categories (pages 27 through 47).

The individual pages on each of these 110 larger schools are arranged alphabetically on pages 52-227.

II. As to the 66 schools with a smaller number of boarders (listed on page 50), these have less than 150 and less than 100 if all girls. The pages devoted to each of those 66 schools are interspersed alphabetically with the 110 larger schools on pages 52-227.

III. As to the 55 "special purpose" boarding schools (listed on page 51):
There are individual pages on 5 very low cost schools found on pages 228-232.
There are individual pages on 22 military schools found on pages 233-254.
There are individual pages on 20 schools for underachievers on pages 255-274.
There are individual pages on 8 junior boarding schools on pages 275-278.
Eleven others with less than 60 boarders are listed on pages 20 and 51.

IV. As to 40 other schools with relatively few boarders, they are listed on page 50.

The 110 Larger Boarding Schools
Those With At Least 150 Boarders (100 If All Girl School)

Student Requirements

	Church Attendance	Community Service
Asheville	X	X
Avon	X	X
Baylor	X	
Berkshire		X
Blair	X	
Brewster		X
Bridgton*		
Brooks	X	X
Canterbury	X	
Cate		X
Chatham Hall	X	X
Choate		X
Concord*		
Cranbrook		X
Culver	X	
Cushing		X
Dana Hall*		
Darlington	X	
Deerfield		
Emma Willard*	X	
Episcopal	X	
Ethel Walker		
Fountain Valley		X
Foxcroft		X
Garrison Forest		
George	X	X
Gould		X
Governor Dummer		X
Grier		X
Groton	X	
Gunnery		X
Hawaii Prep		
Hebron		
Hill	X	X
Holderness	X	X
Hotchkiss	X	X
Hun		
Interlochen		X
Judson		
Kent	X	X
Kents Hill		
Kimball Union		X
Kiski	X	
Knox	X	X
Lake Forest		X
Lawrence		X
Lawrenceville	X	X
Loomis Chaffee		X
Madeira		X
Marian Heights		X
Masters		X
McCallie	X	
Mercersburg		
Middlexex		
Millbrook		X
Milton	X	

	Church Attendance	Community Service
Miss Hall's		
Miss Porter's	X	
Montverde	X	
New Hampton		X
Northfield M.H.*		X
Oldfields		
Peddie	X	X
Pennington	X	
Perkiomen		
Phillips Academy*		X
Phillips Exeter		
Pomfret	X	
Portsmouth Abbey	X	
Principia		
Proctor		X
Purnell		X
Rabun Gap	X	
Robt. L. Stevenson		
St. Andrew's	X	X
St. Catherine's	X	
St. George's	X	
St. Margaret's	X	
St. Mark's	X	
St. Mary's Acad.	X	X
St. Mary's Coll.*	X	X
St. Paul's	X	X
St. Stephen's	X	X
St. Timothy's	X	X
Salem	X	
Salisbury	X	X
San Marcos	X	
Santa Catalina	X	
South Kent	X	X
Stoneleigh-Burnham		X
Stony Brook	X	
Suffield		X
Tabor		
Taft		
Thacher		
Tilton		X
Trinity-Pawling	X	X
United World Coll.		X
Vermont Academy		X
Virginia Episcopal	X	
Walnut Hill*		X
Wayland Academy	X	
Webb		
Western Reserve		X
Westminster	X	
Westover	X	
Westtown	X	
Wilbraham		
Williston		
Woodberry Forest	X	X

*No dress code

Size of Student Body (Upper School Only)

C = Coed B = Boys G = Girls

Over 800 (4)

Choate	C	1000
Northfield M.H.	C	1135
Phillips Academy	C	1215
Phillips Exeter	C	980

between 600 and 800 (5)

Cranbrook	C	700
Culver	C	675
Lawrenceville	C	720
Loomis	C	700
Milton	C	630

between 500 and 600 (10)

Darlington	C	500
Deerfield	C	550
George	C	520
Hotchkiss	C	520
Kent	C	590
McCallie	B	520
Robert L. Stevenson	C	500
St. Paul's	C	500
Tabor	C	510
Taft	C	540

between 400 and 500 (8)

Baylor	C	485
Berkshire	C	415
Hawaii Prep.	C	455
Hill	B	485
Hun	C	400
Interlochen	C	420
Peddie	C	495
Williston	C	450

between 350 and 400 (9)

Avon	B	375
Blair	C	365
Cushing	C	390
Mercersburg	C	360
Principia	C	355
Suffield	C	355
Western Reserve	C	365
Westtown	C	380
Woodberry Forest	B	360

between 300 and 350 (16)

Brooks	C	315
Concord	C	315
Dana Hall	G	320
Governor Dummer	C	330
Groton	C	320
Lawrence	C	340
Madeira	G	335
Pennington	C	300
Pomfret	C	305
St. Catherine's	G	305
St. George's	C	320
St. Mark's	C	320
St. Stephen's	C	300
Stony Brook	C	345
Westminster	C	340
Wilbraham	C	310

between 250 and 300 (22)

Brewster	C	275
Canterbury	C	290
Emma Willard	G	260
Episcopal	B	285
Gunnery	C	250
Hebron	C	250
Holderness	C	200
Kimball Union	C	275
Kiski	B	250
Lake Forest	C	255
Masters	G	270
Middlesex	C	290
Miss Porter's	G	280
New Hampton	C	290
Portsmouth Abbey	B	265
Proctor	C	285
San Marcos	C	270
Santa Catalina	G	255
Trinity-Pawling	B	295
Vermont Academy	C	250
Virginia Episcopal	C	260
Wayland Academy	C	255

between 200 and 250 (17)

Asheville	C	215
Cate	C	245
Ethel Walker	G	205
Fountain Valley	C	220
Garrison Forest	G	240
Gould	C	200
Judson	C	245
Miss Hall's	G	200
Perkiomen	C	200
Rabun Gap	C	205
St. Andrew's (DE)	C	245
Salisbury	B	230
Stoneleigh-Burnham	G	205
Thacher	C	230
Tilton	C	230
Walnut Hill	C	220
Webb of Calif.	B	230

between 150 and 200 (12)

Bridgton	B	190
Kents Hill	C	175
Knox	C	175
Marian Heights	G	180
Millbrook	C	180
Montverde	C	185
Oldfields	G	180
St. Mary's	G	170
Salem	G	170
South Kent	B	160
United World	C	200
Westover	G	160

between 100 and 150 (7)

Chatham Hall	G	120
Foxcroft	G	130
Grier	G	120
Purnell	G	130
St. Margaret's	G	130
St. Mary's Academy	G	130
St. Timothy's	G	125

Day Students and Percent of Student Body

None (8)

Bridgton		
Episcopal		
Grier		
Purnell		
St. Andrew's		
St. Paul's		
South Kent		
United World		

Less than 5% (8)

Chatham Hall	5	3%
Culver	30	4%
Interlochen	20	4%
Kent	17	3%
Marian Heights	3	2%
Montverde	3	1%
St. Mary's Academy	5	4%
Woodberry Forest	2	1%

5% to 10% (11)

Cushing	30	7%
Gunnery	24	10%
Hotchkiss	40	8%
Kents Hill	20	9%
Kiski	25	10%
Northfield M.H.	120	10%
Principia	18	5%
St. Mary's Coll.	40	10%
Salisbury	20	9%
San Marcos	25	8%
Trinity-Pawling	25	8%

10% to 15% (17)

Berkshire	50	12%
Brewster	40	14%
Cate	35	15%
Deerfield	60	11%
Foxcroft	20	14%
Gould	30	15%
Groton	35	10%
Miss Hall's	30	15%
Holderness	35	14%
Knox	25	14%
Mercersburg	45	15%
Millbrook	20	11%
Phillips Exeter	117	12%
St. George's	40	12%
St. Mark's	40	12%
Stoneleigh-Burnham	14	15%
Thacher	25	11%

15% to 20% (17)

Asheville	40	19%
Avon	60	16%
Blair	70	18%
Choate	200	20%
Ethel Walker	40	18%
Hill	80	16%
Kimball Union	50	19%
New Hampton	50	16%
Oldfields	30	16%
Pomfret	60	19%
Proctor	45	16%
Rabun Gap	34	16%
St. Timothy's	20	17%
Taft	110	20%
Wayland	40	17%
Westover	30	18%
Westtown	77	19%

20% to 30% (16)

Brooks	85	26%
Canterbury	90	30%
Emma Willard	80	30%
Fountain Valley	60	28%
Lawrenceville	190	28%
Middlesex	75	25%
Miss Porter's	65	23%
Perkiomen	60	27%
Phillips Academy	27	22%
Portsmouth Abbey	60	21%
St. Margaret's	30	21%
Suffield	100	30%
Tilton	50	21%
Vermont A.	55	22%
Virginia Episcopal	75	28%
Walnut Hill	50	23%

30% to 40% (11)

Gov. Dummer	110	33%
Hebron	85	31%
Madeira	130	39%
R. L. Stevenson	175	35%
Salem	60	32%
Santa Catalina	80	32%
Tabor	170	34%
Webb	80	34%
Western Reserve	125	35%
Westminster	100	33%
Williston	165	38%

40% to 50% (10)

Concord	155	49%
Dana Hall	130	43%
George	240	46%
Hawaii Prep.	225	50%
Lake Forest	125	48%
Masters	125	40%
Peddie	207	41%
St. Stephen's	150	49%
Stony Brook	145	45%
Wilbraham	160	50%

Over 50% (12)

Baylor	340	68%
Cranbrook	500	65%
Darlington	300	58%
Garrison Forest	130	54%
Hun	230	60%
Judson	130	52%
Lawrence	165	50%
Loomis	360	51%
McCallie	440	65%
Milton	350	56%
Pennington	170	52%
St. Catherine's	185	60%

Number of States Represented

40 States or More (10)

Choate
Culver
Hotchkiss
Interlochen
Kent
Northfield M.H.
Phillips Academy
Phillips Exeter
Principia
St. Mary's College
St. Paul's

30 to 40 States (39)

Avon
Berkshire
Brewster
Brooks
Concord
Dana Hall
Deerfield
Emma Willard
George
Groton
Gunnery
Hill
Lawrenceville
Loomis
Madeira
Masters
Milton
Miss Porter's
New Hampton
Peddie
Pomfret
Proctor
Purnell
St. George's
St. Mark's
Salisbury
South Kent
Stoneleigh-Burnham
Tabor
Taft
Tilton
Trinity-Pawling
Vermont Academy
Wayland
Western Reserve
Westminster
Westtown
Woodberry Forest

20 to 30 States (46)

Asheville
Baylor
Blair
Canterbury
Cate
Chatham Hall
Cranbrook
Cushing
Darlington
Episcopal
Ethel Walker
Foxcroft
Fountain Valley
Garrison Forest
Gould
Governor Dummer
Grier
Hebron
Holderness
Hun
Judson
Kents Hill
Kimball Union
Kiski
Knox
Lawrence
Marion Heights
McCallie
Mercersburg
Middlesex
Miss Hall's
Perkiomen
Portsmouth Abbey
R. L. Stevenson
St. Andrew's (DE)
St. Catherine's
St. Margaret's
St. Timothy's
Santa Catalina
Stony Brook
Thacher
United World
Walnut Hill
Westover
Williston
Wilbraham

Under 20 States (15)

Bridgton
Hawaii Prep
Millbrook
Montverde
Lake Forest
Oldfields
Pennington
Rabun Gap
St. Mary's Academy
St. Stephen's
Salem
San Marcos
Suffield
Virginia Episcopal
Webb (CA)

Number and Percent of Foreign Students

50 or more foreign students (13)

School	Number	%
Choate	100	10
Culver	100	15
Cushing	75	20
Deerfield	70	13
Mercersburg	60	15
Northfield M.H.	220	20
Phillips Academy	100	8
Phillips Exeter	70	7
San Marcos	80	25
Suffield	70	20
United World	140	70
Wayland Academy	50	20
Westtown	50	14

30 to 50 (23)

School	Number	%
Avon	35	8
Blair	45	12
Dana Hall	30	10
Emma Willard	35	12
Hawaii Prep	40	9
Hill	40	8
Hotchkiss	40	8
Hun	48	12
Interlochen	35	8
Judson	40	14
Kent	30	6
Milton	32	5
Lawrenceville	30	4
Loomis Chaffee	35	5
Madeira	35	10
Marian Heights	40	25
Masters	35	12
Montverde	45	25
Pennington	30	9
St. Stephen's	40	12
Stony Brook	35	11
Tabor	35	7
Walnut Hill	32	15

20 to 30 (23)

School	Number	%
Berkshire	25	6
Brooks	21	7
Concord	25	8
Darlington	25	3
Ethel Walker	21	10
Foxcroft	20	15
George	20	4
Grier	23	16
Knox	24	17
Lake Forest	22	8
Lawrence	27	8
Miss Hall's	20	10
Miss Porter's	20	7
Peddie	20	4
Portsmouth Abbey	27	10
Robert L. Stevenson	25	5
St. Andrew's		
St. Mark's	21	7
St. Paul's	25	5
Salisbury	23	10
Taft	32	6
Thacher	28	13
Webb	28	12

10 to 20 (27)

School	Number	%
Asheville	18	8
Baylor	19	3
Cranbrook	15	2
Garrison Forest	12	5
Governor Dummer	14	4
Groton	16	5
Gunnery	15	6
Kimball Union	15	6
Middlesex	18	6
Oldfields	12	6
New Hampton	18	6
Pomfret	12	4
Principia	17	5
Proctor	18	6
Purnell	12	9
Rabun Gap	19	9
St. George's	18	6
St. Mary's Academy	18	5
St. Timothy's	11	9
Salem	11	6
Santa Catalina	12	4
Stoneleigh-Burnham	14	7
Vermont Academy	15	6
Western Reserve	18	5
Westover	15	9
Wilbraham	13	4
Williston	17	4

6 to 10 (16)

School	Number	%
Brewster	8	3
Canterbury	6	2
Cate	9	4
Chatham Hall	7	5
Fountain Valley	7	3
Gould	8	4
Hebron	8	3
Holderness	7	3
Kents Hill	9	9
Millbrook	9	5
St. Mary's College	9	3
South Kent	8	2
Tilton	8	3
Virginia Episcopal	6	2
Westminster	9	2
Woodberry Forest	9	2

5 or less (8)

School	Number	%
Bridgton	4	1
Episcopal	3	1
Kiski	5	2
McCallie	5	1
Perkiomen	4	1
St. Catherine's	3	3
St. Margaret's	4	1
Trinity-Pawling	3	1

Average Mean Percentile of 9th or 10th Grade Entering Class

85% and over (6)
Groton, MA
Hotchkiss, CT
Milton, MA
Phillips Academy, MA
Phillips Exeter, NH
St. Paul's, NH

75% to 85% (13)
Brooks, MA
Cate, CA
Choate, CT
Concord, MA
Deerfield, MA
Lawrenceville, NJ
Middlesex, MA
St. Andrew's, DE
St. George's, RI
St. Mark's, MA
Taft, CT
Thacher, CA
United World, NM

70% to 75% (6)
Episcopal, VA
Loomis Chaffee, CT
Northfield MH, MA
Pomfret, CT
Santa Catalina, CA
Western Reserve, OH

65% to 70% (7)
Culver, IN
Cranbrook, MI
Governor Dummer, MA
Hill, PA
Miss Porter's, CT
Salisbury, CT
Webb, CA

60% to 65% (18)
Baylor, TN
Chatham Hall, VA
Emma Willard, NY
Ethel Walker, CT
Fountain Valley, CO
Hawaii Prep, HI
Holderness, NH
Hun, NJ
Kent, CT
Madeira, VA
Mercersburg, PA
Millbrook, NY
Portsmouth Abbey, RI
St. Stephen's, TX
Tabor, MA
Westtown, PA
Westminster, CT
Woodberry Forest, VA

55% to 60% (13)
Berkshire, MA
Blair, NJ
Dana Hall, MA
Darlington, GA
Garrison Forest, MD
Interlochen, MI
Kimball Union, NH
McCallie, TN
Peddie, NJ
Robert L. Stevenson, CA
St. Timothy's, MD
Suffield, CT
Williston, MA

50% to 55% (14)
Asheville, NC
Avon, CT
Canterbury, CT
George, PA
Gunnery, CT
Hebron, ME
Kiski, PA
Lake Forest, IL
Lawrence, MA
Masters, NY
St. Catherine's, VA
Salem, NC
Vermont Academy, VT
Westover, CT

45% to 50% (15)
Grier, PA
Judson, AZ
Miss Hall's, MA
New Hampton, NH
Oldfields, MD
Pennington, NJ
Perkiomen, PA
Proctor, NH
Rabun Gap, GA
St. Mary's College, NC
San Marcos, TX
South Kent, CT
Trinity-Pawling, NY
Virginia Episcopal, VA
Wayland Academy, WI

Under 45% (12)
Brewster, NH
Bridgton, ME
Cushing, MA
Foxcroft, VA
Gould, ME
Kents Hill, ME
Marian Heights, IN
St. Margaret's, VA
St. Mary's Academy, IL
Stoneleigh-Burnham, MA
Stony Brook, NY
Wilbraham, MA

Not Available (6)
Knox, NY
Montverde, FL
Principia, MO
Purnell, NJ
Tilton, NH
Walnut Hill, MA

Note: The above information has been supplied to the author by the schools or set out in catalogs or other publications.

Library

50,000 books or more (16)

Baylor	50,000
Choate	50,000
Concord	200,000*
Cranbrook	100,000
Culver	50,000
Deerfield	50,000
Foxcroft	50,000
Hotchkiss	60,000
Kent	60,000
Loomis	60,000
Marian Heights	60,000
Northfield M.H.	110,000
Phillips Acad.	105,000
Phillips Exeter	125,000
St. Paul's	60,000
Taft	50,000

*Includes village library across the street

30,000 — 50,000 (15)

Berkshire	35,000
Brooks	30,000
Emma Willard	33,000
Groton	35,000
Hill	30,000
Lawrenceville	30,000
McCallie	32,000
Mercersburg	38,000
Milton	40,000
New Hampton	36,000
Peddie	30,000
Saint Mary's Coll.	38,000
Salem	38,000
Westtown	34,000
Williston	30,000

25,000 to 30,000 (14)

Avon	29,000
Fountain Valley	26,000
George	25,000
Masters	25,000
Portsmouth Abbey	25,000
Principia	28,000
St. Andrew's	28,000
St. George's	28,000
St. Marks'	27,000
South Kent	27,000
Suffield	29,000
Thacher	29,000
Western Reserve	25,000
Wilbraham	27,000

20,000 to 25,000 (16)

Blair	23,000
Brewster	24,000
Cate	23,000
Cushing	24,000
Episcopal	22,000
Ethel Walker	23,000
Gov. Dummer	22,000
Hun	20,000
Lawrence	20,000
Madeira	20,000
Miss Porter's	20,000
St. Timothy's	20,000
Santa Catalina	23,000
Tabor	20,000
Wayland	20,000
Westminster	21,000

15,000 to 20,000 (27)

Asheville	15,000
Canterbury	15,000
Chatham Hall	15,000
Dana Hall	16,000
Hebron	17,000
Holderness	15,000
Kent's Hill	16,000
Kiski	16,000
Knox	15,000
Lake Forest	18,000
Middlesex	16,000
Millbrook	16,000
Pennington	15,000
Perkiomen	18,000
Pomfret	19,000
Proctor	15,000
Purnell	15,000
Robert L. Stevenson	17,000
St. Catherine's	19,000
St. Stephen's	16,000
Salisbury	17,000
San Marcos	16,000
Stony Brook	18,000
Trinity-Pawling	16,000
Virginia Episcopal	16,000
Webb	16,000
Westover	16,000

10,000 to 15,000 (14)

Darlington	10,000
Garrison Forest	12,000
Gould	13,000
Grier	10,000
Gunnery	14,000
Hawaii Prep	13,000
Interlochen	14,000
Judson	12,000
Kimball Union	10,000
Miss Hall's	12,000
Purnell	14,000
Tilton	14,000
United World	11,000
Vermont Academy	13,000

Less than 10,000 (8)

Bridgton	7,000
Montverde	8,000
Oldfields	8,000
Rabun Gap	9,000
St. Margaret's	8,000
St. Mary's Academy	8,500
Stoneleigh-Burnham	9,500
Walnut Hill	7,500

Financial Aid

Percentage of Students Aided, Total and Average Per Student

35% or More of Students (11)

	%	*Total*	*Avg*
Emma Willard, NY	40	750,000	7000
Interlochen, MI	55	1.3Mil	5000
Kimball Union, NH	40	800,000	6000
Northfield M.H., MA	42	2.3Mil	5500
Phillips Academy, MA	37	3.9Mil	9000
Principia, MO	65	1Mil	4000
St. Andrew's, DE	42	950,000	9000
St. Mary's College, NC	40	250,000	3000
United World, NM	50	500,000	5500
Vermont Academy, VT	35	350,000	4000
Wayland Academy, WI	35	480,000	5000

30% to 35% of Students (20)

	%	*Total*	*Avg*
Bridgton, ME	30	250,000	4500
Deerfield, MA	30	1.2Mil	7000
George, PA	30	900,000	5500
Gould, ME	32	320,000	5000
Gunnery, CT	30	400,000	5500
Hill, PA	30	880,000	6000
Kiski, PA	30	500,000	6000
Marian Heights, IN	30	150,000	3000
Milton, MA	30	2.3Mil	8500
Phillips Exeter, NH	30	2.6Mil	9000
Rabun Gap, GA	30	385,000	5500
St. Mary's Acad., IL	33	90,000	2000
St. Paul's, NH	30	1.3Mil	9000
Stony Brook, NY	31	600,000	5500
Walnut Hill, MA	30	340,000	5500
Western Reserve, IN	33	750,000	6500
Westover, CT	34	430,000	9000
Westtown, CT	30	1.1Mil	4000
Wilbraham, CT	33	450,000	4000
Williston, MA	30	650,000	4500

25% to 30% of Students (21)

	%	*Total*	*Avg*
Berkshire, MA	28	930,000	6000
Canterbury, CT	25	500,000	8500
Choate, CT	27	2.1Mil	8000
Culver, IN	29	1.5Mil	8000
Fountain Valley, CO	29	450,000	7000
Foxcroft, VA	25	270,000	9500
Groton, MA	25	770,000	10,000
Hebron, ME	28	420,000	8000
Hotchkiss, CT	27	1.2Mil	8500
Lawrence, MA	25	500,000	6000
Masters, NY	25	350,000	5500
Mercersburg, PA	29	700,000	7000
Millbrook, NY	26	360,000	8600
Miss Hall's, MA	29	380,000	6500
Miss Porter's, CT	25	600,000	8000
Pomfret, CT	26	550,000	7000
Portsmouth Abbey, RI	25	440,000	6000
St. George's, RI	25	640,000	8600
St. Timothy's, MD	25	180,000	6500
Tabor, MA	25	800,000	8000
Taft, CT	25	1 Mil	7500

20% to 25% of Students (30)

	%	Total	Avg
Avon, CT	21	530,000	7000
Brewster, NH	20	320,000	6000
Brooks, MA	21	670,000	10,000
Cate, CA	20	400,000	8500
Chatham Hall, VA	20	210,000	7500
Cranbrook, MI	24	1.2Mil	6000
Episcopal, VA	24	500,000	7000
Ethel Walker, CT	22	425,000	9500
Governor Dummer, MA	23	600,000	7000
Holderness, NH	21	315,000	6000
Hun, NJ	20	310,000	5500
Kents Hill, ME	24	210,000	5000
Lawrenceville, NJ	21	1.15Mil	8000
Loomis, CT	24	1Mil	7000
New Hampton, NH	24	325,000	5000
Peddie, NJ	20	700,000	7500
Pennington, NJ	23	325,000	3500
Perkiomen, PA	24	230,000	3000
Salem, NC	20	100,000	3000
St. Margaret's, VA	24	120,000	4000
St. Mark's, MA	23	600,000	8000
Salisbury, CT	22	400,000	8000
Santa Catalina, CA	20	240,000	5500
South Kent, CT	24	260,000	7000
Stoneleigh-Burnham, MA	22	240,000	4500
Suffield, CT	23	570,000	7000
Thacher, CA	20	365,000	8500
Tilton, NH	24	350,000	6500
Westminster, CT	20	500,000	8000
Woodberry Forest, VA	22	575,000	7000

15% to 20% of Students (21)

	%	Total	Avg
Baylor, TN	19	550,000	5500
Blair, NJ	19	450,000	6000
Concord, MA	16	550,000	8000
Cushing, MA	18	510,000	7000
Dana Hall, MA	17	500,000	9500
Darlington, GA	17	500,000	7000
Garrison Forest, MD	17	310,000	10,000
Grier, PA	19	110,000	5000
Hawaii Prep, HI	19	220,000	2500
Kent, CT	16	800,000	8500
Lake Forest, IL	16	330,000	8000
Madeira, VA	16	250,000	6500
McCallie, TN	19	520,000	7000
Middlesex, MA	18	530,000	9900
Proctor, NH	16	350,000	6000
R. L. Stevenson, CA	17	500,000	5000
St. Catherine's, VA	15	110,000	7500
St. Stephen's, TX	17	300,000	6000
Trinity-Pawling, NY	17	280,000	5500
Virginia Episcopal, VA	18	240,000	4500
Webb, CA	15	450,000	7500

Up to 15% of Students (7)

	%	Total	Avg
Asheville, NC	12	165,000	7000
Judson, AZ	7	125,000	5000
Knox, NY	8	100,000	5000
Montverde, FL	6	10,000	1000
Oldfields, MD	10	180,000	9500
Purnell, NJ	10	110,000	9000
San Marcos, TX	11	90,000	3000
Webb, CA	10	195,000	7000

Additional Sports Offered Other Than The Traditional

Interscholastic Teams								
Crew (21)	Ice Hockey (52)	Golf (62)(10)*	Skiing (40)		Riding (57)(15) R	Squash Courts (40) Fives (2)	Swim Team (55)	Sailing (25) Schooner (2)
		X		Asheville		X	X	
	X	X	X	Avon		X	X	
		X		Baylor			X	
X	X	X	X	Berkshire	X	X		
		X	X	Blair			X	
X	X	X	X	Brewster	X			X
	X	X	X	Bridgton				
X	X	X		Brooks		X		
	X	X		Canterbury		X	X	
		X		Cate		X	X	X
				Chatham Hall	XR		X	
X	X	X	X	Choate	X	X	X	
	X		X	Concord				
	X	X	X	Cranbrook			X	
	X	X*		Culver	XP	X	X	
	X		X	Cushing	X			
				Dana Hall	XR			
		X		Darlington			X	
X	X	X	X	Deerfield		X	X	
				Emma Willard	X			
		X		Episcopal		X		
	X			Ethel Walker	XR	X		
	X		X	Fountain Valley	XRo	X	X	
				Foxcroft	XR		X	
				Garrison Forest	XRP			
		X		George	XR		X	
		X*	X	Gould		X		
	X	X*	XC	Governor Dummer	X			
			X	Grier	XR		X	
X	X		XC	Groton		XF		X
X	X	X	X	Gunnery				
				Hawaii Prep	XP		X	
	X		X	Hebron			X	
	X	X*		Hill		X	X	X
	X	X	X	Holderness				
	X	X*	X	Hotchkiss	X	X	X	X
X		X		Hun	X		X	
		X		Interlochen				X
		X		Judson	XRo			
X				Kent	XR	X	X	X
	X	X	X	Kents Hill				
	X	X	X	Kimball Union	X		X	
		X*		Kiski	X		X	
		X		Knox	X			
	X	X		Lake Forest			X	X
	X	X	XC	Lawrence		X		
X	X	X*	X	Lawrenceville		X	X	X
	X	X		Loomis Chaffee			X	
				Madeira	XR	X	X	
				Marian Heights	XR			
				Masters	X			
		X		McCallie			X	
		X		Mercersburg		X	X	
X	X	X	XC	Middlesex		X		
	X			Millbrook	X	X		
	X	X		Milton		X	X	X

* — On or next to campus	R — Riding Ring(s) on Campus
C — Cross country team only	F — Fives; only at these two schools
P — Polo	L — Large boat; sea cruises with classes
O — Rodeo	

Interscholastic Teams

Crew (21)	Ice Hockey (52)	Golf (62)(11)*	Skiing (40)		Riding (57)(15) R	Squash Courts (40) Fives (2)	Swim Team (55)	Sailing (25) Schooner (2)
			X	**Miss Hall's**	X			
				Miss Porter's	X			
				Montverde				
	X	X	X	**New Hampton**	X			
X	X	X	X	**Northfield M.H.**			X	
				Oldfields	XR			
	X	X*		**Peddie**			X	
		X		**Pennington**	X		X	
				Perkiomen	X		X	
X	X	X	X	**Phillips Academy**		X	X	X
X	X	X		**Phillips Exeter**		X	X	
X	X			**Pomfret**		X		
	X	X		**Portsmouth Abbey**		X	X	X
		X		**Principia**			X	
			X	**Proctor**	X			
				Purnell	XR			
				Rabun Gap	X			
		X		**Robt. L. Stevenson**			X	X
X				**St. Andrew's**		X		X
				St. Catherine's	X			
	X			**St. George's**		X	X	XL
				St. Margaret's				X
X	X	X*	X	**St. Mark's**		XF		
				St. Mary's Acad				
				St. Mary's Coll.	X		X	X
X	X		X	**St. Paul's**		X		
		X		**St. Stephen's**	X		X	
				St. Timothy's	XR			
				Salem	X		X	
X	X		X	**Salisbury**	X	X		X
		X		**San Marcos**	X		X	
				Santa Catalina	X		X	X
X	X			**South Kent**				
			X	**Stoneleigh-Burnham**	XR			
				Stony Brook	X		X	X
	X	X	X	**Suffield**	X		X	
X	X	X		**Tabor**	X	X		XL
	X	X*	X	**Taft**	X	X		
				Thacher	XR		X	
	X	X	X	**Tilton**				
	X	X	X	**Trinity-Pawling**		X		
				United World Coll	X			
	X		X	**Vermont Academy**	X			X
		X		**Virginia Episcopal**	X			
				Walnut Hill	X			
	X	X	X	**Wayland Academy**			X	
		X		**Webb**				
		X		**Western Reserve**		X	X	X
	X	X		**Westminster**		X	X	
			X	**Westover**	X			
				Westtown	X		X	X
	X	X		**Wilbraham**			X	
	X	X	X	**Williston**	X	X	X	
		X*		**Woodberry Forest**		X	X	

Mean Average SAT Scores (Total)

1200 and Over (16)
Cate, CA
Choate, CT
Concord, MA
Deerfield, MA
Groton, MA
Hotchkiss, CT
Lawrenceville, NJ
Middlesex, MA
Milton, MA
Phillips Academy, MA
Phillips Exeter, NH
St. Andrew's, DE
St. Mark's, MA
St. Paul's, NH
Taft, CT
Thacher, CA

1150 to 1200 (7)
Episcopal, VA
Hill, PA
Madeira, VA
St. George's, RI
Webb, CA
Western Reserve, OH
Woodberry Forest, VA

1100 to 1150 (15)
Asheville, NC
Brooks, MA
Fountain Valley, CO
Kent, CT
Loomis, CT
McCallie, TN
Miss Porter's, CT
Northfield M.H., MA
Portsmouth Abbey, RI
Robert L. Stevenson, CA
St. Catherine's, VA
St. Stephen's, TX
United World, NM
Westminster, CT
Westtown, PA

1050 to 1100 (15)
Baylor, TN
Berkshire, MA
Cranbrook, MI
Dana Hall, MA
Governor Dummer, MA
Kimball Union, NH
Kiski, PA
Mercersburg, PA
Millbrook, NY
Peddie, NJ
Pomfret, CT
St. Timothy's, MD
Salem, NC
Salisbury, CT
Tabor, MA

1000 to 1050 (22)
Avon, CT
Blair, NJ
Canterbury, CT
Chatham Hall, VA
Culver, IN
Darlington, GA
Emma Willard, NY
Ethel Walker, CT
George, PA
Gunnery, CT
Hawaii Prep, HI
Holderness, NH
Hun, NJ
Interlochen, MI
Lake Forest, IL
Masters, NY
Principia, MO
South Kent, CT
Stony Brook, NY
Virginia Episcopal, VA
Westover, CT
Williston, MA

950 to 1000 (9)
Foxcroft, VA
Hebron, ME
Lawrence, MA
New Hampton, NH
Pennington, NJ
Perkiomen, PA
Tilton, NH
Vermont Academy, VT
Wayland Academy, WI

900 to 950 (11)
Brewster, NH
Cushing, MA
Gould, ME
Judson, AZ
Kents Hill, ME
Miss Hall's, MA
Proctor, NH
St. Margaret's, VA
St. Mary's College, NC
Stoneleigh-Burnham, MA
Wilbraham, MA

Under 900 (6)
Bridgton, ME
Grier, PA
Marian Heights, IN
Rabun Gap, GA
St. Mary's Academy, IL
San Marcos, TX

Not available (9)
Garrison Forest, MD
Knox, NY
Montverde, FL
Oldfields, MD
Purnell, NJ
Santa Catalina, CA
Suffield, CT
Trinity-Pawling, NY
Walnut Hill, MA

Note: The above information has been supplied to the author by the schools or set out in catalogs or other publications.

110 Leading Colleges and Universities

Based on a consensus of prominent publications that rank the various Colleges and Universities. Most of these rankings and scores are from 1988, and they vary somewhat from year to year.

Caps: Schools with average SATS of 1200 and accepting less than 50% of applicants.

Parentheses: 20 schools with SATS averaging 1300 or higher.

*54 schools that accepted less than 50% of their applicants.

**16 schools that accepted not over 25% of their applicants.

	AVG SATs
(AMHERST)**	1320
Babson*	1100
Bard	1210
BATES*	1230
Boston College*	1160
Boston U.	1150
(BOWDOIN)**	NA
Brandeis	1240
(BROWN)**	1300
Bryn Mawr	1280
Bucknell*	1190
Cal. State-Dominguez	NA
(CAL. TECH)*	1440
(CARLETON)*	1300
Carnegie Mellon	1240
Case Western R.	1200
CHICAGO U.*	1290
CLAREMONT McKenna*	1230
Colby	1170
COLGATE*	1210
COLORADO COLLEGE*	1215
Colorado S. of Mines	1180
(Columbia)*	1320
Columbia Barnard*	1240
Connecticut College*	1160
COOPER UNION**	1270
CORNELL*	1290
(DARTMOUTH)**	1310
DAVIDSON*	1230
Dickinson	1130
(DUKE)**	1320
Earlham	1100
EMORY*	1200
Fairfield	1100
Franklin & Marshall*	1190
GEORGETOWN**	1290
Georgia Tech	1195
Gettysburg*	1135
Grinnell	1240
Hamilton*	1180
(HARVARD)**	1365
(HARVEY MUDD)*	1370
(HAVERFORD)	1300
Holy Cross*	1200
(Johns Hopkins)*	1300

	AVG SATs
Kalamazoo	1130
Kenyon	1170
LAFAYETTE*	1200
LAWRENCE	1130
Lehigh	1200
Macalester	1220
Miami (OH)	1165
Michigan U.*	1200
MIDDLEBURY*	1250
(MIT)**	1370
Mt. Holyoke	1200
New York University	1130
NORTHWESTERN*	1230
NOTRE DAME*	1240
Oberlin*	1240
Occidental	1200
PENN U.*	1290
POMONA*	1290
(PRINCETON)**	1345
Reed	1290
Rensselaer Poly	1240
Rhodes	1185
(RICE)*	1335
Richmond*	1175
Rochester	1160
Rose-Hulman	1210
Rutgers-New Brunswick*	1145
St. John's (MD)	1230
St. Olaf	1130
Sewanee	1155
Simon's Rock	1140
Skidmore*	1120
Smith	1200
(STANFORD)**	1325
Suny-Albany*	1125
Suny-Binghampton*	1150
Suny-Genesco*	1120
(SWATHMORE)*	1310
Texas-Austin	1070
TRINITY (CT)*	1180
Trinity U. (TX)	1230
TUFTS*	1260
Tulane	1150
US AIR ACADEMY**	1240
US MILITARY ACAD.**	1200
US NAVAL ACADEMY**	1245
U. of Calif.-Berkeley	1165
Union*	1170
U. of Calif.-LA*	
U. of IL.-Champaign	1125
UNC*	1205
Vanderbilt	1195
VASSAR*	1250
Villanova*	1125
VIRGINIA*	1230
Wake Forest*	1165
WASH. & LEE*	1230
Washington U.**	1200
WELLESLEY*	1250
(WESLEYAN)*	1320
WILLIAM & MARY*	1240
(WILLIAMS)**	1355
Wisconsin-Madison	1090
Worcester Poly	1230
(YALE)**	1355

Percent of Seniors Admitted to 110 Leading Colleges

above 70% (16)
Cate, CA
Choate, CT
Concord, MA
Deerfield, MA
Groton, MA
Hotchkiss, CT
Lawrenceville, NJ
Middlesex, MA
Milton, MA
Phillips Academy, MA
Phillips Exeter, NH
St. Andrew's, DE
St. George's, RI
St. Mark's, MA
St. Paul's, NH
Taft, CT

above 50% (17)
Brooks, MA
Cranbrook, MI
Dana Hall, MA
Episcopal, VA
Hill, PA
Kent, CT
Loomis Chaffee, CT
Madeira, VA
Miss Porter's, CT
Northfield, NH
Pomfret, CT
Saint Stephen's, TX
Santa Catalina, CA
Thacher, CA
Western Reserve, OH
Westminster, CT
Woodberry Forest, VA

30% to 50% (34)
Asheville, NC
Avon, CT
Baylor, TN
Blair, NJ
Canterbury, CT
Chatham Hall, VA
Culver, IN
Emma Willard, NY
Ethel Walker, CT
Fountain Valley, CO
Garrison Forest, MD
George, PA
Governor Dummer, MA
Holderness, NH
Hun, NJ
Kimball Union, NH
Lake Forest, IL
Masters, NY
McCallie, TN
Mercersburg, PA
Millbrook, NY
Miss Hall's, MA
Peddie, NJ
Portsmouth Abbey, RI
St. Catherine's, VA
St. Timothy's, MD
Salem, NC
Salisbury, CT
Suffield, CT
Tabor, MA
Wayland Academy, WI
Webb, CA
Westtown, PA
Williston, MA

10% to 30% (25)
Berkshire, MA
Cushing, MA
Darlington, GA
Foxcroft, VA
Gould, ME
Gunnery, CT
Hawaii, HI
Hebron, ME
Kents Hill, ME
Kiski, PA
Knox, NY
Lawrence, MA
New Hampton, NH
Oldfields, MD
Pennington, NJ
Proctor, NH
Robert L. Stevenson, CA
South Kent, CT
Stoneleigh-Burnham, MA
Stony Brook, NY
Tilton, NH
Trinity-Pawling, NY
Vermont Academy, VT
Virginia Episcopal, VA
Westover, CT

5% to 10% (13)
Brewster, NH
Bridgton, ME
Grier, PA
Judson, AZ
Marian Heights, IN
Montverde, FL
Perkiomen, PA
Rabun Gap, GA
St. Margaret's, VA
St. Mary's Academy, IL
Saint Mary's College, NC
San Marcos, TX
Wilbraham, MA

Not Available (5)
Interlochen, MI
Principia, MO
Purnell, NJ
United World, NM
Walnut Hill, MA

Note: These figures can vary considerably in any one year. The above statistics are based on the matriculation lists for the last several years published by the schools.

Number of Alumni and Annual Giving

9000 or more Alumni (9)

	Alumni	*Millions*
Choate, Ct	10,000	1.60
Culver, IN	18,000	1.50
Deerfield, MA	10,400	1.80
Lawrenceville, NJ	10,000	1.80
Mercersburg, PA	10,000	.80
Northfield M.H., MA	23,000	1.40
Phillips Academy, MA	21,000	2.30
Phillips Exeter, NH	17,500	2.80
Principia, MO	13,000	

6000 to 9000 Alumni (18)

	Alumni	*Millions*
Cranbrook, MI	7,600	2.70
Dana Hall, MA	6,800	.45
Darlington, GA	6,000	.60
George, PA	7,000	.50
Hill, PA	7,000	1.30
Hotchkiss, CT	6,500	1.50
Loomis Chaffee, CT	8,000	.80
Kent, Ct	6,000	.80
McCallie, TN	6,500	.90
Milton, MA	6,500	.80
Peddie, NJ	6,000	.40
St. Mary's College, NC	8,500	.25
St. Paul's, NH	6,700	1.00
Tabor, MA	6,500	.40
Taft, CT	6,000	1.30
Westtown, PA	6,300	.30
Wilbraham, MA	7,000	.10
Williston, MA	7,400	.50

4500 to 6000 Alumni (15)

	Alumni	*Million*
Asheville, NC	4,700	.27
Baylor, TN	4,800	.60
Blair, NJ	4,500	.40
Cushing, MA	4,500	.15
Emma Willard, NY	5,000	.70
Judson, AZ	5,000	.01
Kent, CT	5,000	.90
Lake Forest, IN	4,500	.60
Masters, NY	4,500	.65
Miss Porter's, CT	5,000	.53
New Hampton, NH	4,000	.10
St. Catherine's, VA	4,000	.20
Suffield, CT	4,500	.20
Western Reserve, OH	5,500	.35
Woodberry Forest, VA	5,400	1.10

3000 to 4500 Alumni (31)

	Alumni	*Millions*
Berkshire, MA	3,000	.60
Brewster, NH	3,000	.30
Bridgton, ME	4,000	
Canterbury, CT	3,000	.50
Chatham Hall, VA	3,000	.33
Episcopal, VA	4,000	.60
Ethel Walker, CT	3,000	.40
Garrison Forest, MD	3,000	.30
Gould, ME	3,000	.10
Governor Dummer, MA	3,500	.60
Hebron, ME	4,000	.13
Hun, NJ	3,000	.10
Interlochen, MI	3,500	1.20

Kents Hill, ME	3,200	.06
Kimball Union, NH	3,500	.50
Kiski, PA	3,500	.20
Madeira, VA	3,800	.50
Middlesex, MA	4,000	.85
Pennington, NJ	3,000	.20
Perkiomen, PA	3,400	.13
Pomfret, CT	3,100	.45
Rabun Gap, GA	3,000	.50
St. Mark's, MA	3,000	.70
St. Timothy's, MD	3,000	.33
San Marcos, TX	4,200	
Stoneleigh-Burnham, MA	3,000	.05
Tilton, NH	4,000	.20
Vermont Academy, VT	3,300	.20
Walnut Hill, MA	4,000	
Wayland Academy, WI	3,200	
Westover, CT	3,000	.40

2000 to 3000 Alumni (26)

	Alumni	*Millions*
Avon, CT	2,700	.35
Brooks, MA	2,500	.33
Cate, CA	2,000	.54
Concord, MA	2,500	.40
Fountain Valley, CO	2,000	.50
Foxcroft, VA	2,000	.45
Grier, PA	2,000	.70
Groton, MA	2,200	.85
Gunnery, CT	2,100	.30
Holderness, NH	2,000	.70
Knox, NY	2,000	.25
Lawrence, MA	2,700	.25
Miss Hall's, MA	2,500	.40
Portsmouth Abbey, RI	2,000	.40
Proctor, NH	2,400	.35
Robert L. Stevenson, CA	2,100	1.10
St. George's, RI	2,400	.70
St. Margaret's, VA	2,000	.25
Salem, NC	2,200	.10
Salisbury, CT	2,200	.40
Santa Catalina, CA	2,000	
Stony Brook, NY	2,700	.70
Thacher, CA	2,200	.50
Trinity-Pawling, NY	2,500	.25
Virginia Episcopal, VA	2,800	.37
Westminster, CT	2,600	.60

Under 2000 Alumni (12)

	Alumni	*Millions*
Hawaii Prep, HI	1,500	.15
Marian Heights, IN	1,500	.20
Millbrook, NY	1,800	.40
Oldfields, MD	1,600	.25
Purnell, NJ	700	.10
Montverde, FL	1,900	
St. Andrew's, DE	1,900	.33
St. Mary's Acad., IL	1,500	.08
St. Stephen's, TX	1,800	
South Kent, CT	1,500	.35
United World, NM	1,500	
Webb, CA	1,900	.25

Total Endowment and Amount per Student

Over $100,000 Per Student (10)

	Millions	*Per Student*
Deerfield, MA	70.0	130,000
Groton, MA	60.0	185,000
Hotchkiss, CT	75.0	145,000
Lawrenceville, NJ	80.0	110,000
Phillips Academy, MA	150.0	125,000
Phillips Exeter, NH	120.0	125,000
Principia, MO	60.0	170,000
Rabun Gap, GA	36.0	160,000
St. Andrew's, DE	50.0	200,000
St. Paul's, NH	135.0	270,000

$60,000 to $100,000 Per Student (15)

	Millions	*Per Student*
Brooks, MA	20.0	65,000
Choate, CT	62.0	60,000
Cranbrook, MI	98.0	70,000
Culver, IN	50.0	70,000
Emma Willard, NY	25.0	75,000
Foxcroft, VA	10.0	80,000
Hill, PA	40.0	80,000
Miss Porter's, CT	24.0	85,000
Middlesex, MA	22.0	75,000
St. George's, RI	21.0	65,000
St. Mark's, MA	24.0	75,000
Taft, CT	35.0	65,000
United World, NM	15.0	75,000
Western Reserve, OH	30.0	80,000
Woodberry Forest, VA	37.0	95,000

$40,000 to $60,000 Per Student (13)

	Millions	*Per Student*
Asheville, NC	9.0	40,000
Baylor, TN	30.0	40,000
Chatham Hall, VA	6.0	50,000
Dana Hall, MA	12.0	40,000
Episcopal, VA	15.0	50,000
Ethel Walker, CT	10.0	50,000
Mercersburg, PA	18.0	50,000
Milton, MA	53.0	55,000
Northfield M.H., MA	48.0	45,000
St. Timothy's, MD	6.5	50,000
Thacher, CA	12.0	50,000
Westover, CT	9.6	55,000
Westtown, PA	20.0	55,000

$20,000 to $40,000 Per Student (21)

	Millions	*Per Student*
Berkshire, MA	9.0	20,000
Blair, NJ	14.0	38,000
Cate, CA	7.5	30,000
Fountain Valley, CO	6.0	30,000
George, PA	13.0	28,000
Governor Dummer, MA	12.0	38,000
Kent, CT	13.0	21,000
Kimball Union, NH	8.0	30,000
Kiski, PA	8.0	32,000
Loomis Chaffee, CT	20.0	28,000
Madeira, VA	13.0	39,000
Masters, NY	10.0	38,000
Millbrook, NY	6.0	33,000
Peddie, NJ	15.0	30,000
Pomfret, CT	11.0	35,000

Portsmouth Abbey, RI	9.0	34,000
Purnell, NJ	3.0	24,000
St. Catherine's, VA	6.8	24,000
Stony Brook, NY	6.0	20,000
Suffield, CT	9.0	26,000
Westminster, CT	12.0	36,000

$10,000 to $20,000 Per Student (22)

	Millions	*Per Student*
Avon, Ct	6.0	16,000
Brewster, NH	3.0	12,000
Concord, MA	4.0	12,000
Gould, ME	3.0	15,000
Gunnery, CT	3.0	12,000
Hawaii Prep, HI	5.0	11,000
Holderness, NH	3.5	16,000
Interlochen, MI	6.0	14,000
McCallie, TN	10.0	15,000
Miss Hall's, MA	2.1	10,000
Oldfields, MD	1.9	11,000
Proctor, NH	5.0	18,000
St. Margaret's, VA	1.8	14,000
Salisbury, CT	4.5	19,000
South Kent, CT	2.0	13,000
Tabor, MA	8.0	16,000
Tilton, NH	3.7	17,000
Trinity-Pawling, NY	4.0	14,000
Vir. Episcopal, VA	4.0	13,000
Walnut Hill, MA	2.0	10,000
Wayland Academy, WI	4.0	16,000
Williston, MA	6.6	14,000

$5,000 to $10,000 Per Students (15)

	Millions	*Per Student*
Cushing, MA	2.1	5,000
Darlington, GA	3.0	6,000
Garrison Forest, MD	2.1	5,000
Hebron, ME	1.5	6,000
Kents Hill, NH	1.5	8,500
Lake Forest, IL	1.6	6,500
Lawrence, MA	3.0	9,000
Pennington, NJ	3.0	9,000
Perkiomen, PA	1.7	8,000
Salem, NC	1.5	9,000
St. Mary's Coll., NC	3.5	9,000
St. Stephen's, TX	2.0	7,000
San Marcos, TX	1.8	6,500
Vermont Academy, VT	1.2	5,000
Webb, CA	1.2	5,000

Up to $5,000 Per Student (12)

	Millions	*Per Student*
Bridgton, ME	.5	2,000
Canterbury, CT	1.3	4,300
Grier, PA	.3	4,000
Hun, NJ	1.0	2,500
Knox, NY	.5	3,000
Marian Heights, IN	.2	1,000
New Hampton, NH	1.2	4,000
R. L. Stevenson, CA	1.5	3,000
St. Mary's Acad., IL	.5	4,500
Santa Catalina, CA	1.0	4,000
Stoneleigh-Burnham, MA	1.0	5,000
Wilbraham, MA	2.0	5,000

Endowments of $10,000,000 or More (52) Boarding Schools

Above $100,000,000 (3)
Phillips Academy, MA
Phillips Exeter, NH
St. Paul's, NH

50,000,000 to $100,000,000 (10)
Choate, CT
Cranbrook, MI
Culver, IN
Deerfield, MA
Groton, MA
Hotchkiss, CT
Lawrenceville, NJ
Milton, MA
Principia, MO
St. Andrew's, DE

$30,000,000 to $50,000,000 (8)
Baylor, TN
Hill, PA
Northfield M.H., MA
Rabun Gap, GA
Riverside Academy, GA
Taft, CT
Western Reserve, OH
Woodberry Forest, VA

$15,000,000 to $30,000,000 (13)
Brooks, MA
Emma Willard, NY
Episcopal, VA
Hockaday, TX
Loomis Chaffee, CT
McDonogh, MD
Mercersburg, PA
Middlesex, MA
Miss Porter's, CT
Piney Woods, MS
St. George's, RI
St. Mark's, MA
Westtown, PA

$10,000,000 to $15,000,000 (18)
Andrews, OH
Blair, NJ
Dana Hall, MA
Ethel Walker, CT
Foxcroft, VA
George, PA
Governor Dummer, MA
Kent, CT
Madeira, VA
Marine Military, TX
Masters, NY
McCallie, TN
Peddie, NJ
Pomfret, CT
Shattuck, MN
Thacher, CA
United World, NH
Westminster, CT

The "Hidden Dollar Value" of Boarding School

There is a "hidden dollar value" in the cost of boarding schools that is difficult to determine accurately, but it undeniably exists — and in an amount that should not be ignored.

First, there is a tremendous "dollar value" in providing the student with a class of only 8 to 15 as contrasted with the 20 to 25 in most private day schools and with even larger numbers in public schools.

And then, there is an actual dollar savings of $1500 or more that would be spent in feeding a growing teenager for those 210 days.

Miscellaneous expenditures also will run hundreds of dollars less, for he or she will not be as accessible to fast food stores, shopping malls, movies, and concerts.

Moreover, unlike the public schools and most private day schools, every boarding school offers financial aid for 10% to 50% of the entire student body (see pages 34-35) and these average from $2000 to as high as $10,000 per student, with some receiving free tuition.

These funds, available even to middle income families, if there are several children, often make the net cost no more and often less than private day schools and not very much more than public schools.

Last, but certainly of considerable intangible value, the boarding school student will not be driving a car or riding with his teenage friends for over 210 days, or almost 60% of the year. This obviously saves car operating expenses and can very well eliminate the need at 16 for a separate car and the $4000 minimum yearly cost. There are other "dollars" related not only to relative safety but also to the parents' peace of mind.

Finally, with the student living in a structured environment that cannot be duplicated at home, with the evenings and week-ends taken up with designated study hours, days with scheduled athletics and other school events, the chances of improvement in both his or her scholastic and social achievements have to be excellent. Moreover, the lack of a telephone and TV, except at limited, designated times, has to do something for the highly motivated student, as well as for the average or below average student.

When all of the above "dollar values" are added together, boarding school does not "cost," it "pays."

121 Additional Boarding Schools

66 smaller boarding schools with more than 60 but less than 150 boarders or less than 100 if all girls school (found alphabetically on pages 52-227).

Academy of Mt. Scholastica, KS	G
All Saints, MS	C
Andrews, OH	G
Athenian, CA	C
Bartram, FL	G
Bolles, FL	C
Brenau, GA	G
Buxton, MA	C
Cambridge, MA	C
Chapel Hill, MA	C
Cheshire, CT	C
Christ School, NC	B
Colorado Rocky Mountain, CO	C
Colorado Springs, CO	C
Darrow, NY	C
Delphian, OR	C
Dublin, NH	C
Dunn, CA	B
Elliott-Pope, CA	C
Fenster, AZ	C
Fryeburg, ME	C
Georgetown Prep, MD	B
Gunston, MD	G
Hockaday, TX	G
Hoosac, NY	C
Indian Springs, AL	C
La Lumiere, IN	C
Leelanau, MI	C
Linden Hall, PA	G
Linsly, WV	C
MacDuffie, MA	G
Maine Central, ME	C
Marvelwood, CT	C
Maur Hill, KS	B
McDonogh, MD	C
Midland, CA	C
Northwood, NY	C
Oakwood, NY	C
Ojai Valley, CA	C
Orme, AZ	C
Patterson, NC	C
Pine Crest, FL	C
Putney, VT	C
St. Andrew's, FL	C
Saint Andrew's-Sewanee, TN	C
Saint James, MD	B
St. Johnsbury, VT	C
Saint John's Prep, MN	B
Saint Mary's Hall, TX	C
Saint Mary's Prep, MI	B
St. Scholastica, CO	G
San Domenico, CA	G
Shattuck, MN	C
Southwestern Academy, CA	C
Storm King, NY	C
Stuart Hall, VA	G
Verde Valley, AZ	C
Vivian Webb, CA	G
Wasatch, UT	C
Webb, TN	C
West Nottingham, MD	C
Whiteman, CO	C
White Mountain, NH	C
Woodside Priory, CA	B
Worcester, MA	C
Wyoming Seminary, PA	C

Set out below are some 40 additional schools not included in this guide simply because they have a relatively small number of boarders or just 5 day boarders or students from only a few states.

Annie Wright, Tacoma, WA	G
Aspen, Aspen, CO	C
Burke Mtn., East Burke, VT	C
Castilleja, Palo Alto, CA	G
Clarkson, Potsdam, NY	C
Doane Stuart, Albany, NY	G
Fishburne, Waynesboro, VA	B
Gilmour, Gates Mill, OH	C
Green Mtn, Waitsfield, VT	C
Happy Valley, Ojai, CA	C
Harvey, Katonah, NY	C
High Mowing, Wilton, NH	C
John Woolman, Nevada City, CA	C
La Salle, Oakdale, NY	B
Lausanne, Memphis, TN	C
Lyman Ward, Camp Hill, AL	B
Massanutten, Woodstock, VA	C
Menaul, Albuquerque, NM	C
Milford, Milford, CT	B
Miller, Charlottesville, VA	B
Mtn House, Lake Placid, NY	C
Moravian, Bethlehem, PA	C
Olney Friends, Barnesville, OH	C
Oregon Episcopal, Portland, OR	C
Oxford, Westbrook, CT	B
Rosarian, W. Palm Beach, FL	G
St. Alban's, Washington, DC	B
St. Anne's, Charlottesville, VA	C
St. John's, Salina, KS	B
Sandy Springs, Sandy Springs, MD	C
Seabury Hall, Maui, HI	C
Selwyn, Denton, TX	C
Solebury, New Hope, PA	C
Stratton Mtn, Stratton Mtn, VT	C
Tahoe Acad., Stateline, NV	C
Thomas Jefferson, St. Louis, MO	C
Woodhall, Bethlehem, CT	C
Woodlands, Lake Forest, IL	G
Woodward, Atlanta, GA	C
Wooster, Danbury, CT	C

5 Very Low Cost Boarding Schools

(Pages 228-232)

		Boarders			Boarders
Church Farm	B	170	**Piney Woods**	C	306
Milton Hershey	C	500	**Subiaco**	B	160
Oneida	C	250			

22 Military Boarding Schools

(Pages 233-254)

Admiral Farragut, NJ	B	200	**Marion**	C	130
Admiral Farragut, FL	B	170	**Marmion**	B	175
Army & Navy	B	240	**Missouri**	B	320
Camden	B	250	**NYMA**	C	320
Carson Long	C	200	**Northwestern**	B	125
Florida Air	B	180	**Oak Ridge**	C	150
Fork Union	B	650	**Randolph-Macon**	C	240
Hargrave	B	250	**Riverside**	B	480
Howe	B	200	**St. John's**	B	200
Kemper	B	115	**Valley Forge**	B	750
Marine	B	380	**Wentworth**	B	200

20 Boarding Schools For Students With Learning Differences

(Pages 255-274)

Blue Ridge	B	230	**Kildonan**	B	95
Brandon Hall	B	60	**Landmark**	C	230
Cedu	C	100	**Oak Creek**	C	100
Christchurch	B	230	**Oak Hill**	C	195
Eagle Hill	B	80	**Phelps**	B	150
Forman	C	205	**Pine Ridge**	C	85
Gow	B	155	**St. Andrews, RI**	C	75
Grand River	B	95	**St. Thomas More**	B	200
Highcroft	C	80	**Vanguard**	C	120
Hyde	C	145	**Winchendon**	C	140

19 Junior Boarding Schools

(Pages 275-278)

		Boarders	Day
Aiken, SC	B	25	25
American Boychoir, NJ	B	45	25
Bement, MA	C	30	100
Cardigan, NH*	B	175	10
Chicago Junior, IL	C	40	80
Choir School, NY	B	40	0
Eaglebrook, MA*	B	180	65
Fay, MA*	C	120	125
Fessenden, MA*	B	90	175
Greenwood, VT**	B	40	0
Harker, CA	C	45	550
Hillside, MA	B	50	0
Horizon's Edge, NH	C	14	45
Indian Mountain, CT*	C	70	80
Linden Hill, MA**	B	30	0
Malcolm Gordon, NY	B	30	5
North Country, NY*	C	70	10
Rectory, CT*	B	134	40
Rumsey Hall, CT*	C	102	70

*Only These 8 With More Than 60 Boarders Are Included
**Specialize In Students With Learning Differences

Academy of Mt. St. Scholastica (Girls)

Founded 1863

1034 Green Street, Atchison, KS 66002
(913) 367-0629
Airport: Kansas City, 50 miles

Students

Total: 150 Boys: 0 Girls: 150 Grades: 9-12
Boarding: 75 Day: 75 Local Students: 50%
Number of States: 8 Countries: 5 Foreign Students: 24%

Costs and Aid

Tuition: $6100 School Extras: $
Student Aid Money Awarded: $25,000
Number Granted: 25% Avg. Per Student: $600

Additional Support

Endowment: none Per Student: $
Alumni: 2500 Annual Gifts: $ Giving: %

Admission

Largest Grade Entry: 9th Applied: 36
Accepted: 32 Entered: 31
Median Percentile Entering Grade: %
Application Deadline: rolling Remedial Program: No

Academics

Advanced Placement Preparation in Test Areas
Class Size: 15 Student-Teacher Ratio: 8-1
Number of Seniors: 30 Combined SATS:

Facilities

Rooms: Singles 0% Doubles: 100% Larger: %
Library Volumes: 5000 Acres: 150 Plant:

Other Facts

Affiliated with Roman Catholic Church; operated by Benedictine Sisters; All buildings were constructed after 1970 and are air conditioned.

Locale

Adjacent to Maur Hill Prep School, a boy's boarding school operated by Benedictine monks. Town Pop. 12,000.

All Saints Episcopal School (Coed)

Founded 1908

2725 Confederate Avenue, Vicksburg, MS 39180
(601) 636-5266
Airport: Jackson, 45 miles

Students

Total: 180 Boys: 90 Girls: 90 Grades: 8-12
Boarding: 148 Day: 13 Local Students: 10%
Number of States: 15 Countries: 3 Foreign Students: 2%

Costs and Aid

Tuition: $10,500 School Extras: $500
Student Aid Money Awarded: $100,000
Number Granted: 17% Avg. Per Student: $3500

Additional Support

Endowment: $500,000 Per Student: $2800
Alumni: 2000 Annual Gifts: $120,000 Giving: %

Admission

Largest Grade Entry: 10th Applied: 24
Accepted: 17 Entered: 17
Median Percentile Entering Grade: %
Application Deadline: rolling Remedial Program: Yes

Academics

Advanced Placement Preparation in Test Areas
Class Size: 12-16 Student-Teacher Ratio: 6-1
Number of Seniors: 40 Combined SATS: NA

Facilities

Rooms: Singles 0% Doubles: 100% Larger: %
Library Volumes: 9000 Acres: 40 Plant: 6 Mil

Other Facts

Owned by Episcopal Dioceses. Church attendance required. 50% Episcopalian. Boys admitted after 1970. 15 additional boys in 8th grade.

Locale

In historic Vicksburg. Pop. 35,000. Less than one mile from city center and overlooks Mississippi River.

Andrews School (Girls)

Founded 1910

38588 Mentor Avenue, Willoughby, OH 44094
(216) 942-3600
Airport: Cleveland Hopkins, 35 miles

Students

Total: 154 Boys: 0 Girls: 154 Grades: 7-12
Boarding: 71 Day: 83 Local Students: 54%
Number of States: 13 Countries: 7 Foreign Students: 10%

Costs and Aid

Tuition: $10,600 School Extras: $300
Student Aid Money Awarded: $254,620
Number Granted: 45% Avg. Per Student: $3,637

Additional Support

Endowment: $12,000,000 Per Student: $75,000
Alumni: 2,800 Annual Gifts: $97,292 Giving: 14%

Admission

Largest Grade Entry: 9 Applied: 28
Accepted: 18 Entered: 15
Median Percentile Entering 9 Grade: 54%
Application Deadline: Rolling Remedial Program: No

Academics

Advanced Placement Preparation in 3 Test Areas
Class Size: 10 Student-Teacher Ratio: 6-1
Number of Seniors: 39 Combined SATS: 897

Facilities

Rooms: Singles 7% Doubles: 73% Larger: 20%
Library Volumes: 12,000 Acres: 300 Plant: 16 Mil.

Other Facts

100% college acceptance; 7 sports; on-campus equestrian facility with indoor arena; 4 musical performing groups; 7+ plays produced on Main Stage and Shadowbox Theatre.

Locale

½ mile from town center (pop. 20,000); 9 motels; 20 miles from Cleveland (pop. 500,000); museums, orchestra, ballet, professional theatre, collegiate and professional sports

Asheville School (Coed)

Founded 1900

Asheville, NC 28806
(704) 254-6345
Airport: Asheville, 12 miles

Students

Total: 213 Boys: 158 Girls: 55 Grades: 9-PG
Boarding: 158 Day: 55 Local Students: 25%
Number of States: 18 Countries: 15 Foreign Students: 9.7%

Costs and Aid

Tuition: $12,200 School Extras: $300
Student Aid Money Awarded: $166,000
Number Granted: 11.54% Avg. Per Student: $6900

Additional Support

Endowment: $9 million Per Student: $41,000
Alumni: 4700 Annual Gifts: $265,484 Giving: 31%

Admission

Largest Grade Entry: 10th Applied: 176
Accepted: 147 Entered: 89
Median Percentile Entering 9th Grade: 51%
Application Deadline: Rolling Remedial Program: No

Academics

Advanced Placement Preparation in 4 Test Areas
Class Size: 12 Student-Teacher Ratio: 5-1
Number of Seniors: 53 Combined SATS: 1120

Facilities

Rooms: Singles 94% Doubles: 6% Larger: 0%
Library Volumes: 15,000 Acres: 300 Plant: 11 Mil.

Other Facts

Mountaineering program; English speaking union; ski lifts 40 minutes away; study projects program; additional girls' dormitory planned.

Locale

Located in the Blue Ridge Mountains of NC 5 miles from town center; pop. 60,000

Athenian School (Coed)

Founded 1961

2100 Mt. Diablo Scenic Blvd., Danville, CA 94526
(415) 837-5375
Airport: San Francisco, 40 miles

Students

Total: 250 Boys: 125 Girls: 125 Grades: 6-12
Boarding: 120 Day: 130 Local Students: 66%
Number of States: 8 Countries: 6 Foreign Students: 11%

Costs and Aid

Tuition: $14,800 School Extras: $500
Student Aid Money Awarded: $280,000
Number Granted: 15% Avg. Per Student: $4000

Additional Support

Endowment: $250,000 Per Student: $920
Alumni: 1077 Annual Gifts: $147,287 Giving: 13%

Admission

Largest Grade Entry: 6-9 Applied: 179
Accepted: 100 Entered: 60
Median Percentile Entering Grade: %
Application Deadline: Feb. 1 Remedial Program: No

Academics

Advanced Placement Preparation in 5 Test Areas
Class Size: 12-15 Student-Teacher Ratio: 8-1
Number of Seniors: 55 Combined SATS: 1250

Facilities

Rooms: Singles 66% Doubles: 33% Larger: %
Library Volumes: 16,000 Acres: 120 Plant: 3 mil

Other Facts

New science building; wilderness program required; community service; foreign exchange; 120 acre campus with pool, gym, soccer and baseball fields.

Locale

Pop. 7,000; 35 miles east of San Francisco at the edge of Mt. Diablo State Park.

Avon Old Farms School (Boys)

Founded 1927

Avon, CT 06001
(203) 673-3244
Airport: Hartford, 25 miles

Students

Total: 374 Boys: 374 Girls: 0 Grades: 9-12
Boarding: 298 Day: 74 Local Students: 35%
Number of States: 33 Countries: 16 Foreign Students: 6%

Costs and Aid

Tuition: $14,900 School Extras: $500
Student Aid Money Awarded: $530,000
Number Granted: 21% Avg. Per Student: $6900

Additional Support

Endowment: $6,000,000 Per Student: $16,000
Alumni: 2800 Annual Gifts: $350,000 Giving: 32%

Admission

Largest Grade Entry: 10th Applied: 167
Accepted: 95 Entered: 58
Median Percentile Entering 10th Grade: 50%
Application Deadline: 2/15 Remedial Program: No

Academics

Advanced Placement Preparation in 8 Test Areas
Class Size: 12 Student-Teacher Ratio: 8-1
Number of Seniors: 112 Combined SATS: 1000

Facilities

Rooms: Singles 55% Doubles: 39% Larger: 6%
Library Volumes: 29,000 Acres: 900 Plant: 100 Mil.

Other Facts

Study skills program required grades 9 and 10. Athletics or drama required. Strong programs in art, music and drama. Weekend activities program with 7 girls' schools.

Locale

Wooded rural pocket in suburb of Hartford situated between Ethel Walker School and Miss Porter's School. Shopping malls accessible by school transportation on weekends.

Bartram School (Girls)

Founded 1934

2264 Bartram Road, Jacksonville, FL
(904) 724-8850
Airport: Jacksonville, 30 miles

Students

Total: 155 Boys: Girls: 156 Grades: 7-12
Boarding: 60 Day: 90 Local Students: 65%
Number of States: 10 Countries: 5 Foreign Students: 6%

Costs and Aid

Tuition: $11,500 School Extras: $
Student Aid Money Awarded: $100,000
Number Granted: 20% Avg. Per Student: $2500

Additional Support

Endowment: $None Per Student: $
Alumni: 1800 Annual Gifts: $ Giving: %

Admission

Largest Grade Entry: 9th Applied: 17
Accepted: 11 Entered: 8
Median Percentile Entering Grade: %
Application Deadline: rolling Remedial Program: Yes

Academics

Advanced Placement Preparation in 8 Test Areas
Class Size: 12 Student-Teacher Ratio: 9-1
Number of Seniors: 28 Combined SATS: 915

Facilities

Rooms: Singles 0% Doubles: 100% Larger: %
Library Volumes: 8000 Acres: 25 Plant: 1.5 Mil.

Other Facts

65 in lower grades (5-8); new science building (1981); marine science program; limnology course.

Locale

South of downtown; pop. 600,000; along Little Pottsburg Creek; suburban location.

Baylor School (Coed)

Founded 1893

P.O. Box 1337, Chattanooga, TN 37401
(615) 267-8505
Airport: Chattanooga, 15 miles

Students

Total: 712 Boys: 500 Girls: 212 Grades: 7-12
Boarding: 200 Day: 512 Local Students: 71%
Number of States: 20 Countries: 5 Foreign Students: 5%

Costs and Aid

Tuition: $12,700 School Extras: $500
Student Aid Money Awarded: $575,000
Number Granted: 20% Avg. Per Student: $5400

Additional Support

Endowment: $30,000,000 Per Student: $40,000
Alumni: 4800 Annual Gifts: $600,000 Giving: NA%

Admission

Largest Grade Entry: 10th Applied: 100
Accepted: 40 Entered: 30
Median Percentile Entering 10 Grade: 60%
Application Deadline: None Remedial Program: No

Academics

Advanced Placement Preparation in 13 Test Areas
Class Size: 15 Student-Teacher Ratio: 9-1
Number of Seniors: 138 Combined SATS: 1090

Facilities

Rooms: Singles 0% Doubles: 100% Larger: 0%
Library Volumes: 50,000 Acres: 600 Plant:$25,000,000

Other Facts

Several outstanding extracurricular opportunities; state and nationally ranked athletics; walkabout — extensive outdoors program.

Locale

Located on the banks of the Tennessee River between Signal and Elder Mountains; 4 miles north of Chattanooga; pop. 170,000.

Berkshire School (Coed)

Founded 1907

Sheffield, MA 01257
(413) 229-8511
Airport: Hartford, 45 miles

Students

Total: 415 Boys: 259 Girls: 156 Grades: 9-PG
Boarding: 358 Day: 57 Local Students: 15%
Number of States: 32 Countries: 15 Foreign Students: 7%

Costs and Aid

Tuition: $15,100 School Extras: $500
Student Aid Money Awarded: $930,000
Number Granted: 28% Avg. Per Student: $6200

Additional Support

Endowment: $9 million Per Student: $19,000
Alumni: 3200 Annual Gifts: $601,000 Giving: 60%

Admission

Largest Grade Entry: 10 Applied: 167
Accepted: 106 Entered: 70
Median Percentile Entering 10 Grade: 55%
Application Deadline: 2/15 Remedial Program: No

Academics

Advanced Placement Preparation in 6 Test Areas
Class Size: 10-14 Student-Teacher Ratio: 6-1
Number of Seniors: 120 Combined SATS: 1080 (avg.)

Facilities

Rooms: Singles 10% Doubles: 90% Larger: 0%
Library Volumes: 35,000 Acres: 500 Plant: 18 Mil.

Other Facts

FM public radio (student operated); outdoor education program; "Writing Across the Curriculum" Program; two theaters. Tanglewood nearby.

Locale

Berkshire County; 4 miles from Sheffield Village; pop. 3000; 10 miles from Great Barrington; 2½ hours from New York or Boston.

Blair Academy (Coed)

Founded 1841

Blairstown, NJ 07825
(201) 362-8921
Airport: Newark, 55 miles

Students

Total: 371 Boys: 233 Girls: 138 Grades: 9-PG
Boarding: 280 Day: 91 Local Students: 68%
Number of States: 24 Countries: 14 Foreign Students: 8%

Costs and Aid

Tuition: $13,700 School Extras: $650
Student Aid Money Awarded: $450,000
Number Granted: 21% Avg. Per Student: $6,300

Additional Support

Endowment: $14,000,000 Per Student: $38,000
Alumni: 4500 Annual Gifts: $400,000 Giving: 86,000%

Admission

Largest Grade Entry: 9 Applied: 160
Accepted: 90 Entered: 55
Median Percentile Entering 9 Grade: 55%
Application Deadline: None Remedial Program: No

Academics

Advanced Placement Preparation in 14 Test Areas
Class Size: 12 Student-Teacher Ratio: 9-1
Number of Seniors: 120 Combined SATS: 1040

Facilities

Rooms: Singles 33% Doubles: 67% Larger: 0%
Library Volumes: 23,000 Acres: 315 Plant: 33 Mil.

Other Facts

New 3.2 million-dollar science/math/computer building completed Fall 1989. Aeronautical program; outdoor skills program; year abroad program.

Locale

Adjacent to the village of Blairstown, pop. 5000. 10 minutes away from the Appalachian Trail and the Delaware Water Gap, and 1½ hours from New York City and 2 hours from Philadelphia.

The Bolles School (Coed)

Founded 1933

7400 San Jose Blvd., Jacksonville, FL 32217
(904) 733-9292
Airport: Jacksonville, 20 miles

Students

Total: 550 Boys: 350 Girls: 200 Grades: K-PG
Boarding: 75 Day: 475 Local Students: 85%
Number of States: 13 Countries: 12 Foreign Students: 5%

Costs and Aid

Tuition: $10,550 School Extras: $None
Student Aid Money Awarded: $220,000
Number Granted: 15% Avg. Per Student: $2500

Additional Support

Endowment: $2 mil Per Student: $4000
Alumni: 6300 Annual Gifts: $500,000 Giving: %

Admission

Largest Grade Entry: 9th Applied: 50
Accepted: 35 Entered: 25
Median Percentile Entering Grade: %
Application Deadline: rolling Remedial Program: No

Academics

Advanced Placement Preparation in 13 Test Areas
Class Size: 17 Student-Teacher Ratio: 10-1
Number of Seniors: 135 Combined SATS: 1090

Facilities

Rooms: Singles 0% Doubles: 100% Larger: %
Library Volumes: 17,000 Acres: 50 Plant: 15 M

Other Facts

No girl boarders; 1100 in school; boating facilities; state award for best athletic program the last 8 years.

Locale

On St. John's River; built originally as a hotel property; in suburbs; sailing club; golf course next to campus.

Brenau Academy (Girls)

Founded 1928

Academy St., Gainesville, GA 30501
(404) 534-6140
Airport: Hartsfield (Atlanta), 75 miles

Students

Total: 80 Boys: 0 Girls: 80 Grades: 9-12
Boarding: 73 Day: 7 Local Students: %
Number of States: 7 Countries: 3 Foreign Students: 5%

Costs and Aid

Tuition: $10,300 School Extras: $300/books
Student Aid Money Awarded: $None
Number Granted: % Avg. Per Student: $

Additional Support

Endowment: $ Per Student: $
Alumni: 2000 Annual Gifts: $5000 Giving: 8%

Admission

Largest Grade Entry: 11 Applied: 48
Accepted: 34 Entered: 29
Median Percentile Entering Grade: 90%
Application Deadline: None Remedial Program: None

Academics

Advanced Placement Preparation in Test Areas (College courses offered)
Class Size: 14 Student-Teacher Ratio: 10-1
Number of Seniors: 30 Combined SATS: N/A

Facilities

Rooms: Singles 10% Doubles: 90% Larger: 0%
Library Volumes: 65,000 Acres: 52 Plant: 8,750,000

Other Facts

Shares campus with Brenau College; students seniors can take college courses; sister school with Riverside Military Academy.

Locale

50 miles north of Atlanta; near North Georgia mountains; located 2 blocks from downtown Gainesville; Pop. 15,000.

Brewster Academy (Coed)

Founded 1820

52 South Main St., Wolfeboro, NH 03894
(603) 569-1604
Airport: Boston, 120 miles

Students

Total: 275 Boys: 181 Girls: 94 Grades: 9-PG
Boarding: 225 Day: 50 Local Students: 18%
Number of States: 29 Countries: 11 Foreign Students: 9%

Costs and Aid

Tuition: $15,000 School Extras: $
Student Aid Money Awarded: $320,000
Number Granted: 20% Avg. Per Student: $6,300

Additional Support

Endowment: $3,000,000 Per Student: $11,000
Alumni: 3200 Annual Gifts: $300,000 Giving: 40%

Admission

Largest Grade Entry: 9 Applied: 98
Accepted: 54 Entered: 45
Median Percentile Entering 9 Grade: 35%
Application Deadline: Feb. 10 Remedial Program: Yes

Academics

Advanced Placement Preparation in 4 Test Areas
Class Size: 11-14 Student-Teacher Ratio: 6-1
Number of Seniors: 68 Combined SATS: 900

Facilities

Rooms: Singles 0% Doubles: 100% Larger: 0%
Library Volumes: 25,000 Acres: 75 Plant: 7.5 M

Other Facts

New boat house, student lounge and cafeteria. Learning skills development center; Across the Curriculum Writing Program; study skills program.

Locale

½ mile of shore front on Lake Winnepausakee; America's oldest summer resort — pop. 4000; heart of White Mountains ski country.

Bridgton Academy (Boys)

Founded 1808

P.O. Box 292, North Bridgton, Maine 04057
(207) 647-3322
Airport: Portland, 45 miles

Students

Total: 192 Boys: 192 Girls: 0 Grades: 12-PG
Boarding: 191 Day: 1 Local Students: 1%
Number of States: 21 Countries: 3 Foreign Students: 3%

Costs and Aid

Tuition: $14,900 School Extras: $500
Student Aid Money Awarded: $250,000
Number Granted: 30% Avg. Per Student: $4400

Additional Support

Endowment: $400,000 Per Student: $2000
Alumni: 4000 Annual Gifts: $ Giving: %

Admission

Largest Grade Entry: 13 Applied: 329
Accepted: 257 Entered: 192
Median Percentile Entering Grade: %
Application Deadline: rolling Remedial Program: Yes

Academics

Advanced Placement Preparation in Test Areas
Class Size: 12-15 Student-Teacher Ratio: 10-1
Number of Seniors: 187 Combined SATS: 850

Facilities

Rooms: Singles 6 Doubles: 82 Larger: 12
Library Volumes: 7000 Acres: 50 Plant: 2.5 M

Other Facts

Bridgton Academy is the nation's only one-year prep school for the college-bound young man. Eight courses carry college credit.

Locale

Rural Maine village, pop. 3500. Located on Long Lake, in the foothills of the White Mountains; one hour to ocean; three hours to Boston; ski area within 5 miles.

Brooks School (Coed)

Founded 1926

1160 Great Pond Rd., N. Andover, MA 01845
(508) 686-6101
Airport: Boston, 30 miles

Students

Total: 312 Boys: 184 Girls: 128 Grades: 9-12
Boarding: 231 Day: 81 Local Students: 26%
Number of States: 27 Countries: 16 Foreign Students: 6%

Costs and Aid

Tuition: $14,900 School Extras: $1,380
Student Aid Money Awarded: $671,368
Number Granted: 21% Avg. Per Student: $10,020

Additional Support

Endowment: $20 M Per Student: $64,103
Alumni: 2500 Annual Gifts: $N/A Giving: 46%

Admission

Largest Grade Entry: 10 Applied: 201
Accepted: 135 Entered: 50
Median Percentile Entering 10th Grade: 75%
Application Deadline: Rolling Remedial Program: No

Academics

Advanced Placement Preparation in All Test Areas
Class Size: 12 Student-Teacher Ratio: 5-1
Number of Seniors: 86 Combined SATS: 1140

Facilities

Rooms: Singles 25% Doubles: 74% Larger: 1%
Library Volumes: 30,000 Acres: 251 Plant: 25 M

Other Facts

New dorms feature loft area for sleeping, downstairs for studying. New science wing; hockey arena; community service program.

Locale

On shore of large lake. Laid out as a New England Village. Town 2 miles away. Pop. 28,000.

Buxton School (Coed)

Founded 1928

P.O. Box 646, Williamstown, MA 01267
(413) 458-3919
Airport: Hartford, 90 miles

Students

Total: 90 Boys: 46 Girls: 44 Grades: 9-12
Boarding: 90 Day: Local Students: 3%
Number of States: 18 Countries: 6 Foreign Students: 5%

Costs and Aid

Tuition: $14,750 School Extras: $
Student Aid Money Awarded: $250,000
Number Granted: 32% Avg. Per Student: $4,500

Additional Support

Endowment: $700,000 Per Student: $7000
Alumni: 1200 Annual Gifts: $60,000 Giving: 60%

Admission

Largest Grade Entry: 10 Applied: 60
Accepted: 25 Entered: 28
Median Percentile Entering Grade: %
Application Deadline: March 15 Remedial Program:

Academics

Advanced Placement Preparation in 2 Test Areas
Class Size: 8 Student-Teacher Ratio: 4-1
Number of Seniors: 26 Combined SATS: N/A

Facilities

Rooms: Singles 0% Doubles: 60% Larger: 40%
Library Volumes: 6000 Acres: 150 Plant: 14 buildings

Other Facts

Work program covers all phases inside and outside in the maintenance and betterment of the school. Broad curriculum.

Locale

Pop. 9000. Williams College and Clark Museum within walking distance; ski lifts 15 minutes away.

Cambridge School of Weston (Coed)

Founded 1886

Georgian Road, Weston, MA 02193
(617) 642-8600
Airport: Boston, 20 miles

Students

Total: 205 Boys: 85 Girls: 120 Grades: 9-PG
Boarding: 65 Day: 140 Local Students: 70%
Number of States: 15 Countries: 6 Foreign Students: 6%

Costs and Aid

Tuition: $17,400 School Extras: $none
Student Aid Money Awarded: $200,000
Number Granted: 20% Avg. Per Student: $5000

Additional Support

Endowment: $none Per Student: $
Alumni: 3000 Annual Gifts: $200,000 Giving: %

Admission

Largest Grade Entry: 9th Applied: 97
Accepted: 80 Entered: 34
Median Percentile Entering Grade: %
Application Deadline: rolling Remedial Program: Yes

Academics

Advanced Placement Preparation in 6 Test Areas
Class Size: 12 Student-Teacher Ratio: 7-1
Number of Seniors: 71 Combined SATS: 1065

Facilities

Rooms: Singles 20% Doubles: 70% Larger: 5%
Library Volumes: 15,000 Acres: 140 Plant: 1.7 Mil

Other Facts

Modular plan (7 modules); just 2 or 3 courses at a time; 165 courses to choose from; off campus trips for 5 weeks to Holland, Grand Canyon, and Europe.

Locale

Attractive historic suburb of 11,000; 75-acre wooded area; 2 miles from downtown Weston.

Canterbury School (Coed)

Founded 1915

Aspetuck Ave., New Milford, CT 06776
(203) 355-3103
Airport: Hartford, 45 miles

Students

Total: 288 Boys: 180 Girls: 108 Grades: 9-PG
Boarding: 204 Day: 84 Local Students: 27%
Number of States: 24 Countries: 13 Foreign Students: 5%

Costs and Aid

Tuition: $15,500 School Extras: $200
Student Aid Money Awarded: $515,000
Number Granted: 25% Avg. Per Student: $8500

Additional Support

Endowment: $1.3 mil Per Student: $4200
Alumni: 3000 Annual Gifts: $500,000 Giving: %

Admission

Largest Grade Entry: 9th Applied: 76
Accepted: 65 Entered: 35
Median Percentile Entering 9th Grade: 50%
Application Deadline: March 1 Remedial Program: No

Academics

Advanced Placement Preparation in 5 Test Areas
Class Size: 12 Student-Teacher Ratio: 6-1
Number of Seniors: 105 Combined SATS: 1030

Facilities

Rooms: Singles 80% Doubles: 20% Larger: 0%
Library Volumes: 13,000 Acres: 150 Plant: 18 Mil

Other Facts

Conducted by Roman Catholic laity; 80% of students are Roman Catholic; new building in 1983 with a dining room, library, and auditorium.

Locale

New Milford — pop. 19,000; within walking distance; 35 miles from New Haven; near the Berkshires; 85 miles from New York.

Cate School (Coed)

Founded 1910

1360 Cate Mesa Road, Carpinteria, CA 93013
(805) 684-4127
Airport: Santa Barbara, 21 miles

Students

Total: 245 Boys: 133 Girls: 112 Grades: 9-12
Boarding: 205 Day: 40 Local Students: 20%
Number of States: 26 Countries: 8 Foreign Students: 3%

Costs and Aid

Tuition: $14,900 School Extras: $700
Student Aid Money Awarded: $396,000
Number Granted: 20% Avg. Per Student: $8,600

Additional Support

Endowment: $7,200,000 Per Student: $29,300
Alumni: 2000 Annual Gifts: $540,000 Giving: 50%

Admission

Largest Grade Entry: 9 Applied: 245
Accepted: 66 Entered: 55
Median Percentile Entering 9 Grade: 82%
Application Deadline: Feb. 1 Remedial Program: No

Academics

Advanced Placement Preparation in 11 Test Areas
Class Size: 12 Student-Teacher Ratio: 5-1
Number of Seniors: 67 Combined SATS: 1240

Facilities

Rooms: Singles 80% Doubles: 20% Larger: 0%
Library Volumes: 23,000 Acres: 710 Plant: 25 M

Other Facts

Designated Exemplary School by U.S. Dept. of Education 1987; won California Academic Decathalon 1988; new ceramics studio 1988; sailing as varsity sport spring 1989.

Locale

3 miles from beach community of Carpinteria; 10 miles from city of Santa Barbara; school overlooks Pacific Ocean and Santa Ynez mountains.

Chapel Hill-Chauncy Hall School (Coed)

Founded 1828

785 Beaver St., Waltham, MA 02154
(617) 894-2644
Airport: Hartford, 90 miles

Students

Total: 150 Boys: 84 Girls: 66 Grades: 9-PG
Boarding: 69 Day: 81 Local Students: 20%
Number of States: 15 Countries: 8 Foreign Students: 12%

Costs and Aid

Tuition: $15,000 School Extras: $1,700
Student Aid Money Awarded: $165,000
Number Granted: 22% Avg. Per Student: $7,500

Additional Support

Endowment: $ Per Student: $
Alumni: 2200 Annual Gifts: $98,000 Giving: %

Admission

Largest Grade Entry: 9 Applied: 35
Accepted: 24 Entered: 18
Median Percentile Entering Grade: %
Application Deadline: rolling Remedial Program: Yes

Academics

Advanced Placement Preparation in 5 Test Areas
Class Size: 6-14 Student-Teacher Ratio: 5-1
Number of Seniors: 54 Combined SATS:

Facilities

Rooms: Singles 15% Doubles: 80% Larger: 5%
Library Volumes: 9,000 Acres: 35 Plant: $2.9 M

Other Facts

Grades 9 and 10 only; individually guided studies program for small number of students with significant learning difficulties; 3 levels ESL for foreign students.

Locale

Pop. 60,000; 10 miles west of Boston; 3 motels and 2 hotels under construction; near Brandeis Univ. and Bentley College.

Chatham Hall (Girls)

Founded 1894

Chatham, VA 24531
(804) 432-2941
Airport: Greensboro, 45 miles

Students

Total: 120 Boys: 0 Girls: 120 Grades: 6-12, PG
Boarding: 147 Day: 103 Local Students: 40%
Number of States: 24 Countries: 8 Foreign Students: 6%

Costs and Aid

Tuition: $15,000 School Extras: $850 (riding, books, athletic equipment)
Student Aid Money Awarded: $206,800
Number Granted: 20% Avg. Per Student: $7700

Additional Support

Endowment: $6 million Per Student: $50,000
Alumni: 3,100 Annual Gifts: $330,050 Giving: 45%

Admission

Largest Grade Entry: 9th Applied: 85
Accepted: 58 Entered: 44
Median Percentile Entering 9th Grade: 65%
Application Deadline: April 10 Remedial Program: No

Academics

Advanced Placement Preparation in 10 Test Areas
Class Size: 1-10 Student-Teacher Ratio: 5-1
Number of Seniors: 41 Combined SATS: 1050

Facilities

Rooms: Singles 62% Doubles: 38% Larger: 0%
Library Volumes: 13,000 Acres: 360 Plant: 7 Million

Other Facts

New, fully computerized library; Fulbright exchange; study abroad programs — year in France, Woodberry Forest in England trimester; 25% faculty have Ph.D.'s; Morehead and Jefferson Scholarship programs.

Locale

½ mile from town center — population 2500; 1 motel, 2 Bed & Breakfasts; 18 miles north of Danville; 45 miles south of Lynchburg; Hargrave Military School also in Chatham.

Cheshire Academy (Coed)

Founded 1794

10 Main Street, Cheshire, CT 06410
(203) 272-5396
Airport: Hartford, 30 miles

Students

Total: 250 Boys: 157 Girls: 93 Grades: 6-12
Boarding: 147 Day: 103 Local Students: 40%
Number of States: 14 Countries: 14 Foreign Students: 21%

Costs and Aid

Tuition: $14,650 School Extras: $500
Student Aid Money Awarded: $300,000
Number Granted: 23% Avg. Per Student: $6,000

Additional Support

Endowment: $3 mil Per Student: $12,000
Alumni: 3800 Annual Gifts: $ Giving: %

Admission

Largest Grade Entry: 10 Applied: 51
Accepted: 43 Entered: 25
Median Percentile Entering 10 Grade: 58%
Application Deadline: rolling Remedial Program: No

Academics

Advanced Placement Preparation in 4 Test Areas
Class Size: 12 Student-Teacher Ratio: 8-1
Number of Seniors: 51 Combined SATS: 900

Facilities

Rooms: Singles 20% Doubles: 70% Larger: none%
Library Volumes: 14,000 Acres: 100 Plant: 15 M

Other Facts

1 credit in Fine Arts is a requirement (13 electives); a new Student Activities Center opening fall, '88; indoor 6-lane swimming pool; ESL and Reading/ Study Skills.

Locale

Cheshire — pop. 25,000. The school is located at its center, ½ hour's drive to either New Haven or Hartford; New York City and Boston are two hours drive.

Choate Rosemary Hall (Coed)

Founded 1889

Wallingford, CT 06492
(203) 269-7722
Airport: Hartford, 30 miles

Students

Total: 1002 Boys: 528 Girls: 474 Grades: 9-PG
Boarding: 792 Day: 210 Local Students: 21%
Number of States: 42 Countries: 36 Foreign Students: 18%

Costs and Aid

Tuition: $14,800 School Extras: $700
Student Aid Money Awarded: $2.1 mil.
Number Granted: 27% Avg. Per Student: $8000

Additional Support

Endowment: $62,000,000 Per Student: $57,000
Alumni: 10,000 Annual Gifts: $1.6 mil. Giving: %

Admission

Largest Grade Entry: 9th Applied: 590
Accepted: 286 Entered: 152
Median Percentile Entering 9th Grade: 76%
Application Deadline: Feb. 1 Remedial Program: No

Academics

Advanced Placement Preparation in 25 Test Areas
Class Size: 12-15 Student-Teacher Ratio: 7-1
Number of Seniors: 331 Combined SATS: 1205

Facilities

Rooms: Singles 33% Doubles: 64% Larger: 2%
Library Volumes: 50,000 Acres: 300 Plant: 100,000,000

Other Facts

I M Pei Art Center; new 15 million dollar I M Pei Science Center; term abroad programs in France, Spain, Germany, Russia.

Locale

Pop. 37,000; within walking distance of town and RR station with train to New York City; 14 miles north of New Haven.

Christ School (Boys)

Founded 1900

Christ School Road, Arden, NC 28704
(704) 684-6232
Airport: Asheville, 4 miles

Students

Total: 124 Boys: 124 Girls: 0 Grades: 8-12
Boarding: 123 Day: 1 Local Students: 2%
Number of States: 12 Countries: 4 Foreign Students: 2%

Costs and Aid

Tuition: $11,800 School Extras: $1000
Student Aid Money Awarded: $98,250
Number Granted: 6% Avg. Per Student: $4,678.57

Additional Support

Endowment: $2.5 million Per Student: $20,000
Alumni: 1891 Annual Gifts: $161,000 Giving: 32%

Admission

Largest Grade Entry: 10th Applied: 28
Accepted: 26 Entered: 18
Median Percentile Entering Grade: %
Application Deadline: No deadline Remedial Program: No

Academics

Advanced Placement Preparation in 6 Test Areas
Class Size: 10-12 Student-Teacher Ratio: 6-1
Number of Seniors: 27 Combined SATS: 950 to 1000 average

Facilities

Rooms: Singles 8% Doubles: 90% Larger: 2%
Library Volumes: 8500 Acres: 500 Plant:

Other Facts

Affiliated with Episcopal Church with daily chapel; students work on campus 2 hours on Saturday; offers Outward Bound wilderness trips.

Locale

Small community — population 800; 10 miles south of Asheville — population 53,000; altitude 2200 ft.; near Great Smoky Mountains and ski lifts.

Colorado Rocky Mountain School (Coed)

Founded 1953

1493 County Road 106, Carbondale, CO 81623
(303) 963-2562
Airport: Aspen, 30 miles

Students

Total: 139 Boys: 74 Girls: 65 Grades: 9-12
Boarding: 104 Day: 35 Local Students: 25%
Number of States: 22 Countries: 10 Foreign Students: 7%

Costs and Aid

Tuition: $14,850 School Extras: $400
Student Aid Money Awarded: $324,125
Number Granted: 42% Avg. Per Student: $7,717

Additional Support

Endowment: $250,000 Per Student: $1800
Alumni: 1526 Annual Gifts: $256,700 Giving: 34%

Admission

Largest Grade Entry: 11 Applied: 35
Accepted: 28 Entered: 23
Median Percentile Entering Grade: %
Application Deadline: Rolling Remedial Program: No

Academics

Advanced Placement Preparation in 2 Test Areas
Class Size: 12-15 Student-Teacher Ratio: 6-1
Number of Seniors: 41 Combined SATS: 928

Facilities

Rooms: Singles 15% Doubles: 85% Larger: 0%
Library Volumes: 18,000 Acres: 350 Plant: 6 M

Other Facts

Strong arts, outdoor program, work program; competitive alpine and nordic ski teams; horses available; a ceramic studio.

Locale

Located on ranch in western Colorado, 1 mile from Carbondale, population 2,200; 180 miles west of Denver. Elevation 6200 feet; 30 miles from Aspen.

Colorado Springs School (Coed)

Founded 1962

21 Broadmoor Avenue, Colorado Springs, CO 80906
(719) 475-9747
Airport: Colorado Springs, 7 miles

Students

Total: 158 Boys: 75 Girls: 75 Grades: 9-12
Boarding: 90 Day: 60 Local Students: 40%
Number of States: 25 Countries: 6 Foreign Students: 6%

Costs and Aid

Tuition: $14,350 School Extras: $
Student Aid Money Awarded: $200,000
Number Granted: 28% Avg. Per Student: $6000

Additional Support

Endowment: $1,000,000 Per Student: $6500
Alumni: 2000 Annual Gifts: $250,000 Giving: 25%

Admission

Largest Grade Entry: 10th Applied: 94
Accepted: 64 Entered: 44
Median Percentile Entering 10th Grade: 63%
Application Deadline: Rolling Remedial Program: No

Academics

Advanced Placement Preparation in 0 Test Areas
Class Size: 12 Student-Teacher Ratio: 12-1
Number of Seniors: 40 Combined SATS: 1100

Facilities

Rooms: Singles 20% Doubles: 70% Larger: 10%
Library Volumes: 20,000 Acres: 35 Plant: 10 M

Other Facts

Long recognized as a leader in innovative education, The Colorado Springs School utilizes block scheduling and affords opportunities for study overseas and throughout the U.S. Hockey rink nearby.

Locale

Located in suburban area of Colorado Springs, population 300,000. Three blocks from world-famous Broadmoor Hotel and ten minutes from downtown; home of Colorado College and U.S. Air Force Academy.

Concord Academy (Coed)

Founded 1922

166 Main St., Concord, MA 01742
(508) 369-6080
Airport: Boston, 20 miles

Students

Total: 320 Boys: 140 Girls: 180 Grades: 9-12
Boarding: 160 Day: 160 Local Students: 60%
Number of States: 29 Countries: 14 Foreign Students: 7%

Costs and Aid

Tuition: $15,600 School Extras: $200
Student Aid Money Awarded: $510,000
Number Granted: 17% Avg. Per Student: $9500

Additional Support

Endowment: $4 mil Per Student: $17,000
Alumni: 2500 Annual Gifts: $480,000 Giving: 48%

Admission

Largest Grade Entry: 11th Applied: 514
Accepted: 201 Entered:
Median Percentile Entering 9th Grade: 82%
Application Deadline: Jan. 31 Remedial Program: No

Academics

Advanced Placement Preparation in all Test Areas
Class Size: 15 Student-Teacher Ratio: 8-1
Number of Seniors: 90 Combined SATS: 1220

Facilities

Rooms: Singles 25% Doubles: 40% Larger: 35%
Library Volumes: 20,000 Acres: 37 Plant: 11 M

Other Facts

Optional year abroad in France or Spain; juniors can attend mountain school for a semester; 408 seat theatre.

Locale

On Main Street of historic village. Pop. 18,000; dorms are 7 houses; 200,000 volume public library across street.

Cranbrook Kingswood School (Coed)

Founded 1922

885 Cranbrook Road, Bloomfield Hills, MI 48013
(313) 645-3610
Airport: Detroit, 30 miles

Students

Total: 700 Boys: 385 Girls: 315 Grades: 9-12
Boarding: 260 Day: 440 Local Students: 65%
Number of States: 25 Countries: 12 Foreign Students: 2%

Costs and Aid

Tuition: $13,600 School Extras: $700
Student Aid Money Awarded: $1.2 M
Number Granted: 24% Avg. Per Student: $6,200

Additional Support

Endowment: $98 million Per Student: $70,000
Alumni: 7600 Annual Gifts: $2.7 million Giving: 62%

Admission

Largest Grade Entry: 9 Applied: 120
Accepted: 83 Entered: 67
Median Percentile Entering 9 Grade: 65%
Application Deadline: Rolling Remedial Program: No

Academics

Advanced Placement Preparation in 8 Test Areas
Class Size: 15 Student-Teacher Ratio: 8-1
Number of Seniors: 190 Combined SATS: 1070

Facilities

Rooms: Singles 65% Doubles: 35% Larger: %
Library Volumes: 100,000 Acres: 325 Plant: 32 million

Other Facts

A graduate school of art with public museum; and Cranbrook Institute of Science; a natural history museum and research center with observatory, planetarium, and laserium.

Locale

In the Birmingham, Troy, Pontiac area of Michigan close to major professional sports events and several cultural centers; only 45 minutes from Univ. of Michigan at Ann Arbor.

Culver Academies (Coed)

Founded 1894

Culver, IN 46511
(219) 842-8202
Airport: South Bend, 40 miles

Students

Total: 675 Boys: 415 Girls: 225 Grades: 9-12 PG
Boarding: 645 Day: 30 Local Students: 5%
Number of States: 36 Countries: 26 Foreign Students: 14%

Costs and Aid

Tuition: $13,550 School Extras: $none
Student Aid Money Awarded: $1.5 mil.
Number Granted: 29% Avg. Per Student: $8000

Additional Support

Endowment: $50 mil Per Student: $70,000
Alumni: 18,000 Annual Gifts: $1.5 M Giving: 28%

Admission

Largest Grade Entry: 10th Applied: 150
Accepted: 110 Entered: 94
Median Percentile Entering 10th Grade: N/A%
Application Deadline: rolling Remedial Program: No

Academics

Advanced Placement Preparation in 13 Test Areas
Class Size: 15 Student-Teacher Ratio: 8-1
Number of Seniors: 215 Combined SATS: 1000

Facilities

Rooms: Singles 3% Doubles: 95% Larger: 2%
Library Volumes: 50,000 Acres: 1500 Plant: 80 M

Other Facts

Polo; airport on campus; indoor Equestrian Center, largest in the country; auditorium seats 1500; rough riding; diving pool; new library in 1990.

Locale

One hour from South Bend; 2 hours from Chicago and Indianapolis; campus on a lake. Population 1600; walking distance to town.

Cushing Academy (Coed)

Founded 1865

Ashburnham, MA 01430
(508) 827-5911
Airport: Boston, 55 miles

Students

Total: 390 Boys: 243 Girls: 147 Grades: 9-13
Boarding: 360 Day: 30 Local Students: 5.2%
Number of States: 24 Countries: 23 Foreign Students: 22%

Costs and Aid

Tuition: $15,600 School Extras: $1500
Student Aid Money Awarded: $510,000
Number Granted: 18% Avg. Per Student: $7264.96

Additional Support

Endowment: $2,100,000 Per Student: $5000
Alumni: 4500 Annual Gifts: $142,252 Giving: %

Admission

Largest Grade Entry: 10 Applied: 257
Accepted: 130 Entered: 56
Median Percentile Entering 9th Grade: 44%
Application Deadline: Feb. 1 Remedial Program: Yes

Academics

Advanced Placement Preparation in 6 Test Areas
Class Size: 10 Student-Teacher Ratio: 7-1
Number of Seniors: 126 Combined SATS: 900

Facilities

Rooms: Singles 7% Doubles: 90% Larger: 3%
Library Volumes: 25,000 Acres: 70 Plant: 17,500,000

Other Facts

Completed Fisher-Watkins Library in 1984, and student center and dining room in 1987; a term abroad program that sends students to Asia and Europe.

Locale

North Central Massachusetts between Worcester and Boston; town pop. 4000; nearby mountains provide skiing and mountain climbing.

Dana Hall School (Girls)

Founded 1881

45 Dana Road, Wellesley, MA 02181
(617) 235-3010
Airport: Boston, 12 miles

Students

Total: 319 Boys: 0 Girls: 319 Grades: 6-12
Boarding: 150 Day: 167 Local Students: 40%
Number of States: 21 Countries: 22 Foreign Students: 8%

Costs and Aid

Tuition: $15,475 School Extras: $460-775
Student Aid Money Awarded: $500,000
Number Granted: 17% Avg. Per Student: $9500

Additional Support

Endowment: $12,000,000 Per Student: $40,000
Alumni: 6800 Annual Gifts: $440,000 Giving: %

Admission

Largest Grade Entry: 10th Applied: 80
Accepted: 57 Entered: 24
Median Percentile Entering 10th Grade: 55%
Application Deadline: 3/10 Remedial Program: none

Academics

Advanced Placement Preparation in 6 Test Areas
Class Size: 12 Student-Teacher Ratio: 7-1
Number of Seniors: 78 Combined SATS: 1065

Facilities

Rooms: Singles 25% Doubles: 75% Larger: 0%
Library Volumes: 16,000 Acres: 50 Plant: 27 M

Other Facts

Optional conference period every day; extensive riding program with indoor and outdoor rings; a Writing Center where students can take their rough drafts of papers to have them critiqued.

Locale

½ mile from center of town — population 30,000; 12 miles from Boston; Wellesley and Babson College also in Wellesley.

Darlington School (Coed)

Founded 1905

Rome, GA 30161
(404) 235-6051
Airport: Atlanta, 75 miles

Students

Total: 498 Boys: 251 Girls: 247 Grades: 9-12
Boarding: 245 Day: 253 Local Students: 50%
Number of States: 23 Countries: 19 Foreign Students: 6%

Costs and Aid

Tuition: $11,700 School Extras: $none
Student Aid Money Awarded: $500,000
Number Granted: 17% Avg. Per Student: $7000

Additional Support

Endowment: $3,000,000 Per Student: $6000
Alumni: 6000 Annual Gifts: $625,000 Giving: %

Admission

Largest Grade Entry: 11 Applied: 265
Accepted: 182 Entered: 141
Median Percentile Entering 9th Grade: 57%
Application Deadline: Rolling Remedial Program: None

Academics

Advanced Placement Preparation in 14 Test Areas
Class Size: 12 Student-Teacher Ratio: 11-1
Number of Seniors: 130 Combined SATS: 1018

Facilities

Rooms: Singles 0% Doubles: 100% Larger: 0%
Library Volumes: 10,000 Acres: 400 Plant: 11.5 million

Other Facts

New Science Center; new weight room; new girls dorm; 12 new tennis courts; annual ski trip to Austrian Alps and cultural trip to France, England, or Mexico.

Locale

Northwest Georgia Medical and business center of northwest Georgia — pop. 30,000; 55 miles from Atlanta.

Darrow School (Coed)

Founded 1932

New Lebanon, NY 12125
(518) 794-7700
Airport: Albany, 35 miles

Students

Total: 120 Boys: 85 Girls: 35 Grades: 9-PG
Boarding: 115 Day: 5 Local Students: 10%
Number of States: 20 Countries: 3 Foreign Students: %

Costs and Aid

Tuition: $14,000 School Extras: $1,600
Student Aid Money Awarded: $130,000
Number Granted: 20% Avg. Per Student: $5,900

Additional Support

Endowment: $170,000 Per Student: $6550
Alumni: 1600 Annual Gifts: $170,000 Giving: 20%

Admission

Largest Grade Entry: 11 Applied: 60
Accepted: 50 Entered: 40
Median Percentile Entering Grade: %
Application Deadline: Rolling Remedial Program: LD program

Academics

Advanced Placement Preparation in 1 Test Areas
Class Size: 10 Student-Teacher Ratio: 5-1
Number of Seniors: 46 Combined SATS: 1000

Facilities

Rooms: Singles 20% Doubles: 50% Larger: 30%
Library Volumes: 20,000 Acres: 385 Plant: 21 buildings

Other Facts

Campus occupies of first permanent Shaker village; hands-on history program takes advantage of site and village museum.

Locale

Located in the Berkshires; noted for cultural and tourist attractions; 10 miles west of Pittsfield

Deerfield Academy (Coed)

Founded 1797

Old Deerfield, MA 01342
(413) 772-0241
Airport: Hartford, 55 miles

Students

Total: 550 Boys: 440 Girls: 110 Grades: 9-PG
Boarding: 500 Day: 50 Local Students: 10%
Number of States: 36 Countries: 22 Foreign Students: 13%

Costs and Aid

Tuition: $13,600 School Extras: $470
Student Aid Money Awarded: $1,210,000
Number Granted: 30% Avg. Per Student: $7200

Additional Support

Endowment: $70,000,000 Per Student: $127,000
Alumni: 10,400 Annual Gifts: $1,775,000 Giving: 54%

Admission

Largest Grade Entry: 10 Applied: 400
Accepted: 130 Entered: 70
Median Percentile Entering 10th Grade: 80%
Application Deadline: Feb. 1 Remedial Program: No

Academics

Advanced Placement Preparation in 14 Test Areas
Class Size: 12-14 Student-Teacher Ratio: 7.5-1
Number of Seniors: 176 Combined SATS: 1200

Facilities

Rooms: Singles 80% Doubles: 19% Larger: 1%
Library Volumes: 50,000 Acres: 500 Plant: 60 M

Other Facts

First coed boarding class in Sept. 1989 (120 girls). New Fine Arts Center; three new dormitories; recently completed 36.2 million capital campaign.

Locale

In historic restored Deerfield Village — population 4500. Three miles from Greenfield — population 19,000. 25 minutes from ski lifts; 2 hours from Boston; historic Deerfield Inn next door to campus.

Delphian School (Coed)

Founded 1973

20950 Southwest Rock Creek Rd., Sheridan, OR 97378
(503) 843-3521
Airport: Portland, 50 miles

Students

Total: 75 Boys: 40 Girls: 35 Grades: K-12
Boarding: 75 Day: 0 Local Students: %
Number of States: 19 Countries: 10 Foreign Students: 20%

Costs and Aid

Tuition: $15,200 School Extras: $800
Student Aid Money Awarded: $Limited
Number Granted: % Avg. Per Student: $

Additional Support

Endowment: $ Per Student: $
Alumni: 100 Annual Gifts: $ Giving: %

Admission

Largest Grade Entry: 8th Applied: 100
Accepted: 35 Entered:
Median Percentile Entering Grade: %
Application Deadline: rolling Remedial Program: No

Academics

Advanced Placement Preparation in Test Areas
Class Size: 15 Student-Teacher Ratio:
Number of Seniors: 13 Combined SATS: N/A

Facilities

Rooms: Singles 10% Doubles: 50% Larger: 40%
Library Volumes: 8000 Acres: 800 Plant: 8 M

Other Facts

Individualized programs provide challenge for each student; unique study methods leading to mastery of subject.

Locale

Population 2000 — very much rural setting.

Dublin School (Coed)

Founded 1935

New Harrisville Rd., Dublin, NH 03444
(603) 563-8584
Airport: Boston, 85 miles

Students

Total: 105 Boys: 66 Girls: 39 Grades: 9-12
Boarding: 80 Day: 25 Local Students: 30%
Number of States: 25 Countries: 5 Foreign Students: 6%

Costs and Aid

Tuition: $15,100 School Extras: $800
Student Aid Money Awarded: $120,000
Number Granted: 30% Avg. Per Student: $3750

Additional Support

Endowment: $300,000 Per Student: $3,000
Alumni: 1000 Annual Gifts: $120,000 Giving: 33%

Admission

Largest Grade Entry: 9 Applied: 25
Accepted: 20 Entered: 13
Median Percentile Entering 10 Grade: 45%
Application Deadline: March 1; then rolling Remedial Program: Yes

Academics

Advanced Placement Preparation in 4 Test Areas
Class Size: 11 Student-Teacher Ratio: 5-1
Number of Seniors: 30 Combined SATS: 950

Facilities

Rooms: Singles 10% Doubles: 80% Larger: 10%
Library Volumes: 8,000 Acres: 400 Plant: 3 M

Other Facts

New science building (1987); new recital hall (1987); own ski area and program in alpine/cross-country skiing.

Locale

Located in town of 1600; 5 miles from Petersburg, town of 6000; adjacent to Mount Monadnock; 1½ hours to Boston.

Dunn School (Boys)

Founded 1957

2621 W. Highway 154, Los Olivos, CA 93441
(805) 688-6471
Airport: Santa Barbara, 28 miles

Students

Total: 150 Boys: 120 Girls: 30 Grades: 6-12
Boarding: 105 Day: 45 Local Students: 30%
Number of States: 8 Countries: 5 Foreign Students: 4%

Costs and Aid

Tuition: $12,300 School Extras: $500
Student Aid Money Awarded: $160,000
Number Granted: 20% Avg. Per Student: $5000

Additional Support

Endowment: $700,000 Per Student: $5000
Alumni: 800 Annual Gifts: $100,000 Giving: %

Admission

Largest Grade Entry: 9th Applied: 155
Accepted: 32 Entered:
Median Percentile Entering 9th Grade: 50%
Application Deadline: rolling Remedial Program: No

Academics

Advanced Placement Preparation in Test Areas
Class Size: 11 Student-Teacher Ratio: 6-1
Number of Seniors: 35 Combined SATS: 1075

Facilities

Rooms: Singles 40% Doubles: 60% Larger: %
Library Volumes: 14,000 Acres: 65 Plant: 3.5 M

Other Facts

30 girls, day only; 80% of students from California; 35 in elementary school; new library, computer center, new science building, learning skills program; fulltime outdoor education program.

Locale

Population 1000. Walking distance of downtown; 30 minutes to Santa Barbara.

Elliott-Pope Preparatory School (Coed)

Founded 1930

P.O. Box 338, Idyllwild, CA 92349
(714) 659-2191
Airport: Ontario, 70 miles

Students

Total: 133 Boys: 70 Girls: 63 Grades: 7-12
Boarding: 109 Day: 24 Local Students: 16%
Number of States: 10 Countries: 12 Foreign Students: 20%

Costs and Aid

Tuition: $15,200 School Extras: $500+
Student Aid Money Awarded: $250,000
Number Granted: 34% Avg. Per Student: $5000

Additional Support

Endowment: $350,000 Per Student: $2,600
Alumni: 1500 Annual Gifts: $ Giving: %

Admission

Largest Grade Entry: 11th Applied: 67
Accepted: 64 Entered: 46
Median Percentile Entering 11th Grade: 34%
Application Deadline: Rolling Remedial Program: No

Academics

Advanced Placement Preparation in 6 Test Areas
Class Size: 15 Student-Teacher Ratio: 7-1
Number of Seniors: 35 Combined SATS: 887

Facilities

Rooms: Singles 10% Doubles: 85% Larger: 5%
Library Volumes: 15,000 Acres: 100 Plant: 3 M

Other Facts

English as a Second Language Program; wilderness program; summer school — 2 five-week sessions; pool, horseback riding, Chrysalis program, tennis courts.

Locale

One mile from mountain village of Idyllwild; 110 miles from Los Angeles and San Diego; 50 miles from Palm Springs; 5,600' altitude, San Jacinto Mountains, pine forest.

Emma Willard School (Girls)

Founded 1814

285 Pawling Ave., Troy, NY 12180
(518) 274-4440
Airport: Albany, 8 miles

Students

Total: 258 Boys: 0 Girls: 258 Grades: 9-12 & PG
Boarding: 167 Day: 91 Local Students: 35%
Number of States: 28 Countries: 15 Foreign Students: 12%

Costs and Aid

Tuition: $15,000 School Extras: $550
Student Aid Money Awarded: $740,000
Number Granted: 40% Avg. Per Student: $7000

Additional Support

Endowment: $25,000,000 Per Student: $85,000
Alumni: 5000 Annual Gifts: $725,000 Giving: 40%

Admission

Largest Grade Entry: 9 Applied: 83
Accepted: 67 Entered: 35
Median Percentile Entering 9 Grade: 60%
Application Deadline: 2/15 Remedial Program: No

Academics

Advanced Placement Preparation in 9 Test Areas
Class Size: 10 Student-Teacher Ratio: 8-1
Number of Seniors: 98 Combined SATS: 1040

Facilities

Rooms: Singles 70% Doubles: 23% Larger: 7%
Library Volumes: 33,500 Acres: 92 Plant: 50,000,000

Other Facts

Challenging curriculum; strong arts program; strong dance program; competitive athletics program; 9 interscholastic sports offered.

Locale

8 miles north of Albany, capital of New York. Pop. 300,000. 150 miles north of NYC; walking distance of Troy, pop. 56,000 and of Russell Sage College.

Episcopal High School (Boys)
Founded 1839

1200 N. Quaker Lane, Alexandria, VA 22302
(703) 379-6530
Airport: Washington, 10 miles

Students
Total: 287 Boys: 287 Girls: 0 Grades: 9-12
Boarding: 287 Day: 0 Local Students: %
Number of States: 24 Countries: 5 Foreign Students: 5%

Costs and Aid
Tuition: $13,200 School Extras: $350
Student Aid Money Awarded: $508,550
Number Granted: 24% Avg. Per Student: $7265

Additional Support
Endowment: $15.5 mil. Per Student: $54,000
Alumni: 2000 Annual Gifts: $541,490 Giving: 57%

Admission
Largest Grade Entry: 10 Applied: 70
Accepted: 65 Entered: 44
Median Percentile Entering 10 Grade: 70%
Application Deadline: Jan. 30 Remedial Program: No

Academics
Advanced Placement Preparation in 13 Test Areas
Class Size: 12-15 Student-Teacher Ratio: 8-1
Number of Seniors: 72 Combined SATS: 1180

Facilities
Rooms: Singles 13% Doubles: 85% Larger: 2%
Library Volumes: 22,000 Acres: 130 Plant: 30 Mil

Other Facts
Strong, century-old Honor Code; 2000 seat football stadium; Washington studies program; foreign studies program; indoor field house for field & track events.

Locale
Located on a 130 acre campus, ten miles from the Nation's Capital and 20 minutes from National Airport.

Ethel Walker School (Girls)

Founded 1911

Bushy Hill Rd., Simsbury, CT 06070
(203) 658-4467
Airport: Hartford, 15 miles

Students

Total: 205 Boys: none Girls: 205 Grades: 9-12/PG
Boarding: 80% Day: 20% Local Students: %
Number of States: 18 Countries: 15 Foreign Students: 11%

Costs and Aid

Tuition: $15,500 School Extras: $
Student Aid Money Awarded: $425,000
Number Granted: 22% Avg. Per Student: $9680

Additional Support

Endowment: $10,000,000 Per Student: $50,000
Alumni: 3000 Annual Gifts: $350,000 Giving: 36%

Admission

Largest Grade Entry: 9 Applied: 215
Accepted: Entered: 50
Median Percentile Entering 10 Grade: 60%
Application Deadline: 2/15 Remedial Program: No

Academics

Advanced Placement Preparation in 7 Test Areas
Class Size: 10-12 Student-Teacher Ratio: 8-1
Number of Seniors: 64 Combined SATS: 1030

Facilities

Rooms: Singles 25% Doubles: 65% Larger: 10%
Library Volumes: 23,000 Acres: 620 Plant: 4.6 M

Other Facts

Writing Across the Curriculum programs; dance workshop; riding program; one of largest indoor riding rings; new 2 million dollar library in 1987.

Locale

Suburb of Hartford; 20 minutes from city center; 2 hours from Boston; 2½ hours from NYC; major arts and sports programs nearby. Simsbury pop. 21,000.

Fenster School (Coed)

Founded 1944

8500 E. Octillo Dr., Tucson, AZ 85715
(602) 749-3340
Airport: Tucson, 20 miles

Students

Total: 84 Boys: 41 Girls: 43 Grades: 7-12
Boarding: 68 Day: 16 Local Students: 20%
Number of States: 13 Countries: 8 Foreign Students: 20%

Costs and Aid

Tuition: $13,850 School Extras: $None
Student Aid Money Awarded: $203,000
Number Granted: 16% Avg. Per Student: $5000

Additional Support

Endowment: $none Per Student: $
Alumni: 3000 Annual Gifts: $150,000 Giving: %

Admission

Largest Grade Entry: 11 Applied: 45
Accepted: 38 Entered: 30
Median Percentile Entering Grade: %
Application Deadline: rolling Remedial Program: No

Academics

Advanced Placement Preparation in Test Areas
Class Size: 10-12 Student-Teacher Ratio: 7-1
Number of Seniors: 14 Combined SATS: 800

Facilities

Rooms: Singles % Doubles: 100% Larger: %
Library Volumes: 13,000 Acres: 160 Plant: 3 M

Other Facts

Western and English riding; riding arena. Archaeology program; desert dwellers enrichment program.

Locale

Population 600,000. 15 miles from downtown in suburban area. Located on ruins of an Indian village.

Fountain Valley School (Coed)

Founded 1930

Colorado Springs, CO 80911
(719) 390-7035
Airport: Colorado Springs, 6 miles

Students

Total: 220 Boys: 120 Girls: 100 Grades: 9-12
Boarding: 160 Day: 60 Local Students: 37%
Number of States: 29 Countries: 3 Foreign Students: 2%

Costs and Aid

Tuition: $14,000 School Extras: $600
Student Aid Money Awarded: $450,000
Number Granted: 29% Avg. Per Student: $7000

Additional Support

Endowment: $6.5 mil. Per Student: $30,000
Alumni: 2100 Annual Gifts: $450,000 Giving: %

Admission

Largest Grade Entry: 9th Applied: 70
Accepted: 45 Entered: 35
Median Percentile Entering 9th Grade: 65%
Application Deadline: Feb. 1st Remedial Program: No

Academics

Advanced Placement Preparation in 11 Test Areas
Class Size: 7-15 Student-Teacher Ratio: 7-1
Number of Seniors: 58 Combined SATS: 1120

Facilities

Rooms: Singles 10% Doubles: 90% Larger: 0%
Library Volumes: 25,000 Acres: 1100 Plant: 15 M

Other Facts

New 1.2 million dollar Community Center; new Visual Arts Center; extensive riding program, covered ring; also mountain campus in the Rockies used on week-ends.

Locale

Nine miles south of Colorado Springs; 65 miles south of Denver; ski lifts nearby; near Colorado College, Broadmoor Hotel and zoo.

Foxcroft School (Girls)

Founded 1914

Middleburg, VA 22117
(703) 687-5555
Airport: Dulles (Washington), 25 miles

Students

Total: 127 Boys: 0 Girls: 127 Grades: 9-PG
Boarding: 117 Day: 10 Local Students: 9%
Number of States: 28 Countries: 14 Foreign Students: 18%

Costs and Aid

Tuition: $15,000 School Extras: $500
Student Aid Money Awarded: $276,352
Number Granted: 23% Avg. Per Student: $9,500

Additional Support

Endowment: $10,000,000 Per Student: $79,000
Alumni: 2600 Annual Gifts: $445,845 Giving: 50%

Admission

Largest Grade Entry: 9th Applied: 104
Accepted: 79 Entered: 52
Median Percentile Entering 9th Grade: 45%
Application Deadline: rolling Remedial Program: No

Academics

Advanced Placement Preparation in 10 Test Areas
Class Size: 8-10 Student-Teacher Ratio: 4-1
Number of Seniors: 50 Combined SATS: 970

Facilities

Rooms: Singles 10% Doubles: 70% Larger: 20%
Library Volumes: 50,000 Acres: 510 Plant: 15,000,000

Other Facts

Term in England; extensive horseback riding program with 110 x 220 indoor arena; pool; interim session to promote global awareness; all full-time faculty live on campus.

Locale

3.5 miles from downtown Middleburg: Population 800; 45 miles from Washington, D.C. in northern Virginia's "hunt country."

Fryeburg Academy (Coed)

Founded 1792

152 Main Street, Fryeburg, ME 04037
(207) 935-2001
Airport: Portland, 50 miles

Students

Total: 512 Boys: 292 Girls: 220 Grades: 9-PG
Boarding: 135 Day: 365 Local Students: 60%
Number of States: 15 Countries: 8 Foreign Students: 20%

Costs and Aid

Tuition: $10,600 School Extras: $600
Student Aid Money Awarded: $125,000
Number Granted: 30% Avg. Per Student: $3000

Additional Support

Endowment: $3.2 M Per Student: $
Alumni: 5,583 Annual Gifts: $193,600 Giving: 10%

Admission

Largest Grade Entry: 11 Applied: 39
Accepted: 32 Entered: 26
Median Percentile Entering Grade: %
Application Deadline: Rolling Remedial Program: Yes

Academics

Advanced Placement Preparation in 4 Test Areas
Class Size: 15-18 Student-Teacher Ratio: 10-1
Number of Seniors: 132 Combined SATS: 980

Facilities

Rooms: Singles 5% Doubles: 95% Larger: 0%
Library Volumes: 10,000 Acres: 25 Plant: 6 M

Other Facts

Industrial Arts, Business Ed & Home Ec.; special Ski & School program — Mt. Washington Valley minutes away; ESL & LD Training; new wing includes Dining Hall & Student Union.

Locale

3000 pop.; 2 motels; 4 restaurants; 4 season resort area with 3 major ski areas, malls, hotels, and theatres; 3 hrs. from Boston; hiking, canoeing, skiing; 1 hr. from Portland, ME.

Garrison Forest School (Girls)

Founded 1910

Garrison, Maryland 21055
(301) 363-1500
Airport: Baltimore, 15 miles

Students

Total: 240 Boys: 0 Girls: 240 Grades: 9-12
Boarding: 100 Day: 130 Local Students: 50%
Number of States: 29 Countries: 12 Foreign Students: 4%

Costs and Aid

Tuition: $15,200 School Extras: $300
Student Aid Money Awarded: $310,000
Number Granted: 17% Avg. Per Student: $9,800

Additional Support

Endowment: $2,100,000 Per Student: $5,000
Alumni: 2,600 Annual Gifts: $325,000 Giving: 43%

Admission

Largest Grade Entry: 10 Applied: 32
Accepted: 23 Entered: 12
Median Percentile Entering Grade: %
Application Deadline: rolling Remedial Program: No

Academics

Advanced Placement Preparation in 13 Test Areas
Class Size: 12-14 Student-Teacher Ratio: 8-1
Number of Seniors: 57 Combined SATS: NA

Facilities

Rooms: Singles 6% Doubles: 82% Larger: 12%
Library Volumes: 12,000 Acres: 100 Plant: 5 M

Other Facts

New library and computer center; 450-seat theater; indoor riding arena; 25 extracurricular clubs; service league; 9 interscholastic sports, including riding and polo.

Locale

12 miles northwest of Baltimore; 40 miles from Washington, D.C.; rural setting in suburban part of Baltimore with easy access to cultural, social, and recreational opportunities.

George School (Coed)

Founded 1893

Newtown, PA 18940
(215) 968-3811
Airport: Philadelphia, 35 miles

Students

Total: 520 Boys: 260 Girls: 260 Grades: 9-12
Boarding: 286 Day: 234 Local Students: 40%
Number of States: 24 Countries: 18 Foreign Students: 4.4%

Costs and Aid

Tuition: $13,500 School Extras: $200
Student Aid Money Awarded: $921,650
Number Granted: 31% Avg. Per Student: $5,500

Additional Support

Endowment: $13 mil Per Student: $28,000
Alumni: 7000 Annual Gifts: $514,040 Giving: 47%

Admission

Largest Grade Entry: 9 Applied: 370
Accepted: 190 Entered: 99
Median Percentile Entering 9 Grade: 53%
Application Deadline: Feb. 1 Remedial Program: No

Academics

Advanced Placement Preparation in 6 Test Areas
Class Size: 12-15 Student-Teacher Ratio: 8-1
Number of Seniors: 130 Combined SATS: 1010

Facilities

Rooms: Singles 0% Doubles: 95% Larger: 5%
Library Volumes: 25,000 Acres: 265 Plant: 50 Mil

Other Facts

New student union (1985); 8-lane 25 meter pool; 18-hole golf course 2 miles from campus; excellent soccer & lacrosse programs.

Locale

1 mile from Newtown — pop. 2519; 4 motels; 25 miles northeast of Phila.; 11 miles to Trenton.

Georgetown Preparatory School (Boys)

Founded 1789

10900 Rockville Pike, Rockville, MD 20852
(301) 493-5000
Airport: National, 20 miles

Students

Total: 400 Boys: 400 Girls: 0 Grades: 9-12
Boarding: 102 Day: 298 Local Students: 70%
Number of States: 24 Countries: 28 Foreign Students: 14%

Costs and Aid

Tuition: $14,450 School Extras: $200
Student Aid Money Awarded: $340,000
Number Granted: 16% Avg. Per Student: $5000

Additional Support

Endowment: $4,300,000 Per Student: $10,808
Alumni: 3,500 Annual Gifts: $520,000 Giving: 37%

Admission

Largest Grade Entry: 9 Applied: 275
Accepted: 110 Entered: 85
Median Percentile Entering 9th Grade: 70%
Application Deadline: Feb. 1 Remedial Program: No

Academics

Advanced Placement Preparation in 11 Test Areas
Class Size: 17 Student-Teacher Ratio: 8-1
Number of Seniors: 104 Combined SATS: 1170

Facilities

Rooms: Singles 45% Doubles: 55% Larger: 0%
Library Volumes: 14,000 Acres: 92 Plant: 21 M

Other Facts

Oldest Catholic secondary school in nation; 100% graduating to four year colleges; pool and 9-hole golf course; nationally recognized art and athletic programs.

Locale

Across the street from subway stop; pop. 45,000; 17 miles from nation's capital; museums, monuments, etc.; affords opportunity for internships in government agencies.

Gould Academy (Coed)

Founded 1836

P.O. Box 860, Bethel, ME 04217
(207) 824-2196
Airport: Portland, ME, 70 miles

Students

Total: 201 Boys: 130 Girls: 71 Grades: 9-12
Boarding: 180 Day: 21 Local Students: 12%
Number of States: 27 Countries: 7 Foreign Students: 7%

Costs and Aid

Tuition: $14,750 School Extras: $300
Student Aid Money Awarded: $316,800
Number Granted: 32% Avg. Per Student: $5000

Additional Support

Endowment: $3,000,000 Per Student: $15,000
Alumni: 3,000 Annual Gifts: $82,260 Giving: 36%

Admission

Largest Grade Entry: 11 Applied: 51
Accepted: 43 Entered: 27
Median Percentile Entering Grade: %
Application Deadline: Rolling Remedial Program: No

Academics

Advanced Placement Preparation in 3 Test Areas
Class Size: 10-13 Student-Teacher Ratio: 8-1
Number of Seniors: 72 Combined SATS: 930

Facilities

Rooms: Singles 30% Doubles: 30% Larger: 16%
Library Volumes: 13,000 Acres: 425 Plant: 12 M

Other Facts

Cooperative programs with Hurricane Island outward bound school; nationally known alpine and nordic skiers and coaches; exceptional opportunities in Fine Arts.

Locale

¼ mile from town center — population 2300; ski touring center; golf course adjacent to campus; six miles from Maine's largest ski area.

Governor Dummer Academy (Coed)

Founded 1763

1 Elm St., Byfield, MA 01922
(508) 465-1763
Airport: Logan, 30 miles

Students

Total: 330 Boys: 200 Girls: 130 Grades: 9-12
Boarding: 220 Day: 110 Local Students: 30%
Number of States: 25 Countries: 12 Foreign Students: 3%

Costs and Aid

Tuition: $14,600 School Extras: $700
Student Aid Money Awarded: $665,000
Number Granted: 23% Avg. Per Student: $7000

Additional Support

Endowment: $12,000,000 Per Student: $38,000
Alumni: 3500 Annual Gifts: $600,000 Giving: 50%

Admission

Largest Grade Entry: 9 Applied: 250
Accepted: 110 Entered: 60
Median Percentile Entering 9th Grade: 65%
Application Deadline: Feb. 1 Remedial Program: No

Academics

Advanced Placement Preparation in Test Areas
Class Size: 12 Student-Teacher Ratio: 7-1
Number of Seniors: 85 Combined SATS: 1100

Facilities

Rooms: Singles 65% Doubles: 35% Larger: %
Library Volumes: 22,000 Acres: 600 Plant: 30 buildings

Other Facts

Regular trips to cultural events in Boston; required community service; 9-hole golf course; 350-seat auditorium.

Locale

Pop. 2000; rural; 35 miles to Boston; 4 miles to Newburyport, pop. 16,000; 3 miles from the ocean.

Grier School (Girls)

Founded 1853

Tyrone, PA 16686
(814) 684-3000
Airport: Altoona, 20 miles

Students

Total: 118 Boys: 0 Girls: 118 Grades: 7-12
Boarding: 118 Day: 0 Local Students: 0%
Number of States: 22 Countries: 9 Foreign Students: 17%

Costs and Aid

Tuition: $13,500 School Extras: $800
Student Aid Money Awarded: $105,000
Number Granted: 19% Avg. Per Student: $5000

Additional Support

Endowment: $500,000 Per Student: $4100
Alumni: 2000 Annual Gifts: $60,000 Giving: 20%

Admission

Largest Grade Entry: 10 Applied: 35
Accepted: 30 Entered: 24
Median Percentile Entering 10th Grade: 50%
Application Deadline: Rolling Remedial Program: Yes

Academics

Advanced Placement Preparation in 3 Test Areas
Class Size: 5-13 Student-Teacher Ratio: 6-1
Number of Seniors: 24 Combined SATS: 875

Facilities

Rooms: Singles 20% Doubles: 80% Larger: 0%
Library Volumes: 8000 Acres: 150 Plant: 6 million

Other Facts

New gym (1983); new performing arts center (1987); 25% underachievers (take learning skills); excellent horseback riding program.

Locale

2 m. from Tyrone, pop. 8000; 20 miles from Altoona (100,000); ski lift, 20 miles; 2 hrs. to Pittsburgh; 3 hours to Washington, D.C.

Groton School (Coed)

Founded 1884

Box 991, Groton, MA 01450
(508) 448-3367
Airport: Boston, 35 miles

Students

Total: 320 Boys: 180 Girls: 140 Grades: 8-12
Boarding: 285 Day: 35 Local Students: 5%
Number of States: 34 Countries: 14 Foreign Students: 5%

Costs and Aid

Tuition: $13,900 School Extras: $700
Student Aid Money Awarded: $770,000
Number Granted: 24% Avg. Per Student: $10,250

Additional Support

Endowment: $60 mil Per Student: $185,000
Alumni: 2200 Annual Gifts: $848,200 Giving: 68%

Admission

Largest Grade Entry: 9 Applied: 320
Accepted: 70 Entered: 32
Median Percentile Entering 9th Grade: 85%
Application Deadline: Feb. 1 Remedial Program: No

Academics

Advanced Placement Preparation in 12 Test Areas
Class Size: 10-15 Student-Teacher Ratio: 6-1
Number of Seniors: 82 Combined SATS: 1250

Facilities

Rooms: Singles 30% Doubles: 55% Larger: 15%
Library Volumes: 35,000 Acres: 280 Plant: 47 M

Other Facts

Extensive woodworking program. Completed in last 10 years: science center, an art center, and a new school center with snack bar and student lounge.

Locale

One mile from town center — population 6000. Adjoins Nashua River with school boathouse.

The Gunnery (Coed)

Founded 1850

Washington, CT 06793
(203) 868-7334
Airport: Hartford, 60 miles

Students

Total: 250 Boys: 163 Girls: 87 Grades: 9-PG
Boarding: 226 Day: 24 Local Students: 11%
Number of States: 28 Countries: 8 Foreign Students: 7%

Costs and Aid

Tuition: $15,500 School Extras: $600
Student Aid Money Awarded: $400,000
Number Granted: 30% Avg. Per Student: $5300

Additional Support

Endowment: $3 million Per Student: $12,000
Alumni: 2100 Annual Gifts: $320,00 Giving: 36%

Admission

Largest Grade Entry: 9th Applied: 98
Accepted: 81 Entered: 34
Median Percentile Entering 9th Grade: 50%
Application Deadline: rolling Remedial Program: No

Academics

Advanced Placement Preparation in 5 Test Areas
Class Size: 13 Student-Teacher Ratio: 7-1
Number of Seniors: 82 Combined SATS: 1000

Facilities

Rooms: Singles 59% Doubles: 40% Larger: 1%
Library Volumes: 14,000+ Acres: 220+ Plant: 10 mil

Other Facts

School cabin for outing club within 1.5 miles of school; extensive hiking trails also surrounding campus; American Indian Museum 2 miles from campus.

Locale

1 mile from town center. Pop. 3700; 9 inns within 10-15 miles of school; 2 hours to New York and Boston; in foothills of the Berkshire Mountains.

Gunston School (Girls)
Founded 1911

Box 200, Centreville, MD 21617
(301) 758-0620
Airport: Washington, 55 miles

Students
Total: 85 Boys: none Girls: 85 Grades: 9-12
Boarding: 78 Day: 7 Local Students: 9%
Number of States: 20 Countries: 0 Foreign Students: 1%

Costs and Aid
Tuition: $12,500 School Extras: $350
Student Aid Money Awarded: $30,000
Number Granted: 14% Avg. Per Student: $2500

Additional Support
Endowment: $400,000 Per Student: $4500
Alumni: 650 Annual Gifts: $55,000 Giving: 19%

Admission
Largest Grade Entry: 10 Applied: 15
Accepted: 13 Entered: 13
Median Percentile Entering Grade: %
Application Deadline: rolling Remedial Program: Yes

Academics
Advanced Placement Preparation in Test Areas
Class Size: 10 Student-Teacher Ratio: 6-1
Number of Seniors: 22 Combined SATS: 800

Facilities
Rooms: Singles 3% Doubles: 90% Larger: 7%
Library Volumes: 5000 Acres: 40 Plant: 2.5 M

Other Facts
New Field House with dance room; library; auditorium addition in 1980. Week-long off campus program in winter.

Locale
Population 2000; Annapolis is across Chesapeake Bay; school on Corsica River; sailing in fall and spring; 25 stall stables and riding ring on campus.

Hawaii Preparatory Academy (Coed)

Founded 1949

P.O. Box 428, Kamuela, HI 96743
(808) 885-7321
Airport: Kona, 35 miles

Students

Total: 456 Boys: 251 Girls: 205 Grades: 6-12
Boarding: 207 Day: 249 Local Students: 65%
Number of States: 11 Countries: 19 Foreign Students: 10%

Costs and Aid

Tuition: $11,600 School Extras: $300
Student Aid Money Awarded: $218,000
Number Granted: 19% Avg. Per Student: $2,600

Additional Support

Endowment: $5,100,000 Per Student: $11,000
Alumni: 1500 Annual Gifts: $147,000 Giving: 28%

Admission

Largest Grade Entry: 9 Applied: 104
Accepted: 87 Entered: 68
Median Percentile Entering 9th Grade: 65%
Application Deadline: 3/3/89 Remedial Program: Yes

Academics

Advanced Placement Preparation in 13 Test Areas
Class Size: 6-20 Student-Teacher Ratio: 14-1
Number of Seniors: 80 Combined SATS: 1067

Facilities

Rooms: Singles 15% Doubles: 85% Larger: 0%
Library Volumes: 13,000 Acres: 88 Plant: 20 M

Other Facts

Separate campuses for Middle and Upper schools; new swimming pool (1987), arts complex (1989); courses in SCUBA, Marine Biology, Astronomy, Japanese, Horse Program.

Locale

Rural setting in Kamuela (Waimea), pop. 2600; 40 minutes from Kona; 1 hour from Hilo.

Hebron Academy (Coed)

Founded 1804

Hebron, ME 04238
(207) 966-2100
Airport: Portland, 43 miles

Students

Total: 250 Boys: 175 Girls: 75 Grades: 9-PG
Boarding: 180 Day: 70 Local Students: 28%
Number of States: 22 Countries: 7 Foreign Students: 5%

Costs and Aid

Tuition: $15,900 School Extras: $650
Student Aid Money Awarded: $420,000
Number Granted: 29% Avg. Per Student: $8000

Additional Support

Endowment: $1.5 mil. Per Student: $6000
Alumni: 3700 Annual Gifts: $210,000 Giving: 60%

Admission

Largest Grade Entry: 9th Applied: 200
Accepted: 160 Entered: 120
Median Percentile Entering 9th Grade: 50%
Application Deadline: rolling Remedial Program: No

Academics

Advanced Placement Preparation in 11 Test Areas
Class Size: 10-12 Student-Teacher Ratio: 7-1
Number of Seniors: 110 Combined SATS: 1000

Facilities

Rooms: Singles 8% Doubles: 92% Larger: 0%
Library Volumes: 17,000 Acres: 1500 Plant: 7 M

Other Facts

New athletic facility and fine arts building in progress; strong music program.

Locale

Population 600; 15 minutes from Auburn and Bates College; rural community. In center of ski country; Sugar Loaf Mountain 1½ hours.

Hill School (Boys)

Founded 1851

Pottstown, PA 19464
(215) 326-1000
Airport: Philadelphia, 40 miles

Students

Total: 485 Boys: 485 Girls: Grades: 8-PG
Boarding: 397 Day: 88 Local Students: 20%
Number of States: 26 Countries: 17 Foreign Students: 9.3%

Costs and Aid

Tuition: $14,000 School Extras: $550
Student Aid Money Awarded: $880,000
Number Granted: 31% Avg. Per Student: $5,870

Additional Support

Endowment: $40,000,000 Per Student: $80,000
Alumni: 7,245 Annual Gifts: $1,300,000 Giving: 38.5%

Admission

Largest Grade Entry: 9 Applied: 235
Accepted: 82 Entered: 56
Median Percentile Entering 9th Grade: 65%
Application Deadline: March 1 Remedial Program: No

Academics

Advanced Placement Preparation in 15 Test Areas
Class Size: 12 Student-Teacher Ratio: 7.5-1
Number of Seniors: 148 Combined SATS: 1175

Facilities

Rooms: Singles 1% Doubles: 90% Larger: 9%
Library Volumes: 29,000 Acres: 220 Plant: 32 M

Other Facts

New Performing Arts Building ('89); study abroad; computer center; community service program; pool; golf (18 holes); 6 squash and 15 tennis courts; skeet and trap; ice hockey rink; ski team (30 minutes to slopes).

Locale

On a hill overlooking Pottstown (Pop. 23,000); 3 hotels; 32 miles from Philadelphia; 15 miles from Valley Forge Park; 2 hours to New York; 3 hours to Washington, D.C.

The Hockaday School (Girls)

Founded 1913

11600 Welch Road, Dallas, TX 75229
(214) 363-6311
Airport: D/FW and Love Field, 10 miles

Students

Total: 847 Boys: 0 Girls: 847 Grades: PS-12
Boarding: 79 Day: 768 Local Students: 90%
Number of States: 8 Countries: 6 Foreign Students: 3%

Costs and Aid

Tuition: $16,000 School Extras: $400
Student Aid Money Awarded: $294,500
Number Granted: 65% Avg. Per Student: $4530

Additional Support

Endowment: $16 mil Per Student: $20,000
Alumni: 6200 Annual Gifts: $605,000 Giving: %

Admission

Largest Grade Entry: 9-11 Applied: N/A
Accepted: 50% Entered: 86%
Median Percentile Entering 9-11 Grade: 86%%
Application Deadline: Rolling Remedial Program: No

Academics

Advanced Placement Preparation in 13 Test Areas
Class Size: 12-15 Student-Teacher Ratio: 9-1
Number of Seniors: 96 Combined SATS: 1150

Facilities

Rooms: Singles 8% Doubles: 92% Larger: 0%
Library Volumes: 46,000 Acres: 100 Plant: 31 M

Other Facts

Semester Abroad Programs; swimming pool; 35 student clubs; 2 theatres, 100+ computers; largest independent girls school in nation.

Locale

Dallas, TX; 6th largest city in US; urban residential; close airports; 3 hours to LA or NY by air; very temperate climate, lots of arts, shopping, restaurants.

Holderness School (Coed)

Founded 1879

Plymouth, New Hampshire 03264
(603) 536-1747
Airport: Boston, 120 miles

Students

Total: 260 Boys: 169 Girls: 91 Grades: 9-12
Boarding: 216 Day: 44 Local Students: 3%
Number of States: 27 Countries: 2 Foreign Students: 3%

Costs and Aid

Tuition: $14,750 School Extras: $400
Student Aid Money Awarded: $315,480
Number Granted: 21% Avg. Per Student: $5800

Additional Support

Endowment: $3,500,000 Per Student: $14,000
Alumni: 2000 Annual Gifts: $713,822 Giving: 46%

Admission

Largest Grade Entry: 9 Applied: 115
Accepted: 70 Entered: 43
Median Percentile Entering ninth Grade: 60%
Application Deadline: Feb. 1st Remedial Program: No

Academics

Advanced Placement Preparation in 7 Test Areas
Class Size: 13 Student-Teacher Ratio: 8-1
Number of Seniors: 78 Combined SATS: 1045

Facilities

Rooms: Singles 21% Doubles: 75% Larger: 4%
Library Volumes: 15,000 Acres: 620± Plant: 7,000,000

Other Facts

Academic excellence combined with nationally recognized outdoor and ski program; 18-hole PGA course, 2 mi.; Waterville Valley, 25 min.; 10-day Outback.

Locale

Located at base of White Mtns. in Lakes Region of NH; 1 mi. from center of Plymouth (college town of 5000+); 2 hrs. north of Boston, directly off I-93.

Hoosac School (Coed)

Founded 1889

Hoosick, New York, 12089
(518) 686-7331
Airport: Albany, 30 miles

Students

Total: 104 Boys: 64 Girls: 40 Grades: 8-12
Boarding: 100 Day: 4 Local Students: 1%
Number of States: 23 Countries: 4 Foreign Students: 8%

Costs and Aid

Tuition: $12,900 School Extras: $2,000
Student Aid Money Awarded: $120,000
Number Granted: 22% Avg. Per Student: $6,000

Additional Support

Endowment: $1.5 million Per Student: $14,000
Alumni: 3,400 Annual Gifts: $200,000 Giving: %

Admission

Largest Grade Entry: 9/10 Applied: 300 (over 2 year period)
Accepted: 110 Entered: 98
Median Percentile Entering 9/10 Grade: %
Application Deadline: Open Remedial Program: Yes

Academics

Advanced Placement Preparation in Test Areas
Class Size: 8 Student-Teacher Ratio: 6-1
Number of Seniors: 14 Combined SATS: 820

Facilities

Rooms: Singles 40% Doubles: 50% Larger: 10%
Library Volumes: 11,000 Acres: 400 ± Plant:

Other Facts

New gymnasium; new dorm; affiliated with Episcopal Church; 1828 Freestone Gothic Castle remodeled for classrooms, dormitory, etc.

Locale

Pop. 600; 10 miles west of Bennington — pop. 3500; 15 miles from Williams College and Clark Museum.

The Hotchkiss School (Coed)

Founded 1891

Lakeville, CT 06039
(203) 435-2591
Airport: Hartford, 45 miles

Students

Total: 525 Boys: 315 Girls: 210 Grades: 9-PG
Boarding: Day: 30 Local Students: %
Number of States: 42 Countries: 17 Foreign Students: 7%

Costs and Aid

Tuition: $14,100 School Extras: $none
Student Aid Money Awarded: $1.2 million
Number Granted: 27% Avg. Per Student: $8500

Additional Support

Endowment: $75 M Per Student: $145,000
Alumni: 6500 Annual Gifts: $2.2 M Giving: %

Admission

Largest Grade Entry: 10 Applied: 450
Accepted: 130 Entered: 77
Median Percentile Entering 10 Grade: 87%
Application Deadline: Jan. 31 Remedial Program: No

Academics

Advanced Placement Preparation in 11 Test Areas
Class Size: 12 Student-Teacher Ratio: 6-1
Number of Seniors: 160 Combined SATS: 1250

Facilities

Rooms: Singles 70% Doubles: 30% Larger:
Library Volumes: 60,000 Acres: 490 Plant: 50 M

Other Facts

New dormitory and all other buildings being upgraded under 5 year long range plan; 100M capital campaign.

Locale

1 mile from Lakeville — pop. 1500; 2½ hours from NYC; numerous lakes nearby and school golf course on campus.

The Hun School of Princeton (Coed)

Founded 1914

Box 271, Edgerstoune Road, Princeton, NJ 08542
(609) 921-7600
Airport: Newark, 40 miles

Students

Total: 400 Boys: 255 Girls: 145 Grades: 9-PG
Boarding: 170 Day: 230 Local Students: 60%
Number of States: 20 Countries: 15 Foreign Students: 13%

Costs and Aid

Tuition: $13,975 School Extras: $300
Student Aid Money Awarded: $311,700
Number Granted: 18% Avg. Per Student: $5500

Additional Support

Endowment: $1,000,000 Per Student: $2500
Alumni: 3000 Annual Gifts: $60,000 Giving: 10%

Admission

Largest Grade Entry: 9th Applied: 100
Accepted: 80 Entered: 55
Median Percentile Entering 9th Grade: 60%
Application Deadline: March 10 Remedial Program: No

Academics

Advanced Placement Preparation in 6 Test Areas
Class Size: 15 Student-Teacher Ratio: 8-1
Number of Seniors: 121 Combined SATS: 1000

Facilities

Rooms: Singles 10% Doubles: 88% Larger: 2%
Library Volumes: 20,000 Acres: 50 Plant: 17 M

Other Facts

100 day students in grades 6-8; small learning program and international student/ESL program; recently completed math/science/computer wing in academic center.

Locale

The university town of Princeton, NJ, (within walking distance) is located midway between New York City and Philadelphia, providing both cosmopolitan and rural exposure.

Indian Springs School (Coed)

Founded 1952

6000 Cahaba Valley Rd., Helena, AL 35080
(205) 988-3350
Airport: Birmingham, 20 miles

Students

Total: 243 Boys: 123 Girls: 120 Grades: 8-PG
Boarding: 69 Day: 174 Local Students: %
Number of States: 10 Countries: 6 Foreign Students: 5%

Costs and Aid

Tuition: $11,000 School Extras: $300
Student Aid Money Awarded: $244,200
Number Granted: 23% Avg. Per Student: $4360

Additional Support

Endowment: $5,000,000 Per Student: $20,000
Alumni: 1300 Annual Gifts: $65,000 Giving: 24%

Admission

Largest Grade Entry: 8th Applied: 38
Accepted: 32 Entered: 30
Median Percentile Entering 8th Grade: 75%
Application Deadline: Rolling Remedial Program: No

Academics

Advanced Placement Preparation in 14 Test Areas
Class Size: 15 Student-Teacher Ratio: 10-1
Number of Seniors: 52 Combined SATS: 1226

Facilities

Rooms: Singles 50% Doubles: 50% Larger: 0%
Library Volumes: 13,000 Acres: 350 Plant: 15 Million

Other Facts

Lake (swimming, canoeing, fishing), 350 wooded acres; all classroom teachers hold master's or doctorate degrees; computer center opened in 1983.

Locale

Pop. 2100; 15 miles south of Birmingham — pop. 300,000 — with its art museum, symphony orchestra, zoo, botanical gardens. Next to a state park, with acres of woods, trails, lakes, and rock climbing.

Interlochen Arts Academy (Coed)

Founded 1962

Interlochen, MI 49643
(616) 276-9221
Airport: Traverse City, 10 miles

Students

Total: 430 Boys: 155 Girls: 275 Grades: 9-PG
Boarding: 405 Day: 20 Local Students: 5%
Number of States: 45 Countries: 24 Foreign Students: 9%

Costs and Aid

Tuition: $11,900 School Extras: $
Student Aid Money Awarded: $1.3 M
Number Granted: 55% Avg. Per Student: $5000

Additional Support

Endowment: $7 million Per Student: $15,000
Alumni: 3400 Annual Gifts: $1.2 M Giving: %

Admission

Largest Grade Entry: 10 Applied: 300
Accepted: Entered: 180
Median Percentile Entering Grade: NA%
Application Deadline: Rolling Remedial Program: No

Academics

Advanced Placement Preparation in 4 Test Areas
Class Size: 14 Student-Teacher Ratio: 7-1
Number of Seniors: 180 Combined SATS: 1010

Facilities

Rooms: Singles 0% Doubles: 100% Larger: 0%
Library Volumes: 14,000 Acres: 1200 Plant: 15 M

Other Facts

1000 seat performing arts center. Very large music library; 250 seat recital hall; part of the National Music Camp.

Locale

1 mile from town — pop. 100; between two lakes. Close to Lake Michigan; 15 miles SW of Traverse City.

Judson School (Coed)

Founded 1928

P.O. Box 1569, Scottsdale, AZ 85252
(602) 948-7731 Fax (602) 483-6425
Airport: Phoenix, 11 miles

Students

Total: 395 Boys: 228 Girls: 167 Grades: K-PG (boarding 3-PG)
Boarding: 255 Day: 140 Local Students: 73%
Number of States: 30 Countries: 28 Foreign Students: 27%

Costs and Aid

Tuition: $13,800 School Extras: $2000
Student Aid Money Awarded: $124,900
Number Granted: 7% Avg. Per Student: $4800

Additional Support

Endowment: $None Per Student: $
Alumni: 5000 Annual Gifts: $3000 Giving: 1%

Admission

Largest Grade Entry: 11 Applied: 55
Accepted: 48 Entered: 39
Median Percentile Entering Grade: %
Application Deadline: Rolling Remedial Program: Yes

Academics

Advanced Placement Preparation in 2 Test Areas
Class Size: 14 Student-Teacher Ratio: 8-1
Number of Seniors: 66 Combined SATS: 945

Facilities

Rooms: Singles 50% Doubles: 45% Larger: 5%
Library Volumes: 14,000 Acres: 55 Plant: 3,000,000

Other Facts

An alternative to the highly pressured preparatory school, providing a general curriculum to extend the limits of those not working to full potential and a Learning Resource Center for mild LD.

Locale

A resort city of 125,000 with a mild climate adjoining Phoenix, a city of 960,000; 20 minutes from Arizona State University and numerous cultural opportunities.

Kent School (Coed)

Founded 1906

P.O. Box 2006, Kent, CT 06757
(203) 927-3501
Airport: Hartford, 50 miles

Students

Total: 590 Boys: 350 Girls: 240 Grades: 9-12 & PG
Boarding: 573 Day: 17 Local Students: 3-5%
Number of States: 28 Countries: 28 Foreign Students: 6%

Costs and Aid

Tuition: $15,200 School Extras: $1200
Student Aid Money Awarded: $825,000
Number Granted: 16% Avg. Per Student: $8700

Additional Support

Endowment: $13 mil Per Student: $21,500
Alumni: 5996 Annual Gifts: $798,500 Giving: 43%

Admission

Largest Grade Entry: 10 Applied: 160
Accepted: 122 Entered: 47
Median Percentile Entering 10th Grade: 60%
Application Deadline: Feb. 15 Remedial Program: None

Academics

Advanced Placement Preparation in 10 Test Areas
Class Size: 14 Student-Teacher Ratio: 10-1
Number of Seniors: 200 Combined SATS: 1110

Facilities

Rooms: Singles 0% Doubles: 96% Larger: 4%
Library Volumes: 60,000 Acres: 2000 Plant: 50 million

Other Facts

International Baccalaureate program; affiliated with Episcopal Church; indoor riding rings and outdoor rings.

Locale

Small New England town of 2000 just across Housatonic River from school; 90 miles from NYC; in the Berkshire foothills.

Kents Hill School (Coed)

Founded 1862

P.O. Box 257, Kents Hill, ME 04349
(207) 685-4914
Airport: Portland, 65 miles

Students

Total: 172 Boys: 129 Girls: 43 Grades: 9-PG
Boarding: 157 Day: 15 Local Students: 9%
Number of States: 26 Countries: 9 Foreign Students: 10%

Costs and Aid

Tuition: $14,900 School Extras: $550
Student Aid Money Awarded: $210,000
Number Granted: 25% Avg. Per Student: $5000

Additional Support

Endowment: $1.5 million Per Student: $8500
Alumni: 3200 Annual Gifts: $56,546 Giving: 19%

Admission

Largest Grade Entry: 12 Applied: 140
Accepted: 116 Entered: 86
Median Percentile Entering 12 Grade: 32%
Application Deadline: Rolling Remedial Program: Yes

Academics

Advanced Placement Preparation in 5 Test Areas
Class Size: 8-12 Student-Teacher Ratio: 7-1
Number of Seniors: 55 Combined SATS: 900

Facilities

Rooms: Singles 68% Doubles: 32% Larger: 0%
Library Volumes: 10,000 Acres: 600 Plant: 5.2 M

Other Facts

News library (James Cochrane Memorial — 1988); school operates own ski area with snowmaking and night skiing.

Locale

12 miles NW of Augusta — pop. 22,000; Belgrade Lakes region of Maine; located near apple orchards; 1 hr. 15 min. to Portland.

Kimball Union Academy (Coed)

Founded 1813

Main St., Meriden, NH 03770
(603) 469-3211
Airport: Lebanon, 8 miles

Students

Total: 275 Boys: 185 Girls: 92 Grades: 9-PG
Boarding: 220 Day: 55 Local Students: 25%
Number of States: 25 Countries: 10 Foreign Students: 7%

Costs and Aid

Tuition: $14,200 School Extras: $500
Student Aid Money Awarded: $800,000
Number Granted: 40% Avg. Per Student: $6000

Additional Support

Endowment: $8,000,000 Per Student: $30,000
Alumni: 3500 Annual Gifts: $450,000 Giving: 41%

Admission

Largest Grade Entry: 10 Applied: 400
Accepted: 160 Entered: 100
Median Percentile Entering 10 Grade: 55%
Application Deadline: rolling Remedial Program: No

Academics

Advanced Placement Preparation in 11 Test Areas
Class Size: 10-12 Student-Teacher Ratio: 7-1
Number of Seniors: 85 Combined SATS: 1070

Facilities

Rooms: Singles 75% Doubles: 25% Larger: 0%
Library Volumes: 16,000 Acres: 1500 Plant: 13 mil

Other Facts

New arts center ($2.5 mil); 400-seat theater; music dept.; art dept.; new indoor ice rinks/field house ($2.5 mil); 2 indoor tennis courts; pool and team.

Locale

14 mi. south of Dartmouth College; skiing from 10 minutes away to 1½ hours away; Killington is 50 minutes from campus; 2 hrs. from Boston. Hilltop campus in the New Hampshire mountains.

Kiski School (Boys)

Founded 1888

1888 Brett Lane, Saltsburg, PA 15681
(412) 639-3586
Airport: Pittsburgh, 50 miles

Students

Total: 250 Boys: 0 Girls: 250 Grades: 9-PG
Boarding: 225 Day: 25 Local Students: 10%
Number of States: 22 Countries: 10 Foreign Students: 4%

Costs and Aid

Tuition: $12,000 School Extras: $400
Student Aid Money Awarded: $500,000
Number Granted: 30% Avg. Per Student: $6000

Additional Support

Endowment: $8,000,000 Per Student: $32,000
Alumni: 4,200 Annual Gifts: $225,000 Giving: 20%

Admission

Largest Grade Entry: 9 Applied: 87
Accepted: 47 Entered: 42
Median Percentile Entering 9th Grade: 50%
Application Deadline: Rolling Remedial Program: No

Academics

Advanced Placement Preparation in 12 Test Areas
Class Size: 10 Student-Teacher Ratio: 7-1
Number of Seniors: 70 Combined SATS: 1080

Facilities

Rooms: Singles 0% Doubles: 100% Larger: 0%
Library Volumes: 16,000 Acres: 350 Plant: 15 M

Other Facts

4- and 6-week summer academic camp 5th-8th grades; 6-week summer school 9th-12th grades; ski slope/rope tow; 9-hole golf course on campus.

Locale

Rural setting; pop. 1000; 35 miles east of Pittsburgh, "America's most livable city."

The Knox School (Coed)

Founded 1904

St. James, NY 11780
(516) 584-5500
Airport: La Guardia/Kennedy, 50 miles

Students

Total: 175 Boys: 95 Girls: 80 Grades: 7-PG
Boarding: 150 Day: 25 Local Students: 14%
Number of States: 25 Countries: 20 Foreign Students: 14%

Costs and Aid

Tuition: $13625 School Extras: $1000
Student Aid Money Awarded: $90,000
Number Granted: 8% Avg. Per Student: $5000

Additional Support

Endowment: $500,000 Per Student: $3000
Alumni: 2000 Annual Gifts: $ Giving: %

Admission

Largest Grade Entry: 10 Applied: 65
Accepted: 24 Entered: 22
Median Percentile Entering N/A Grade: N/A%
Application Deadline: Rolling Remedial Program: Yes

Academics

Advanced Placement Preparation in N/A Test Areas
Class Size: 13 Student-Teacher Ratio: 5-1
Number of Seniors: 40 Combined SATS: N/A

Facilities

Rooms: Singles 1% Doubles: 52% Larger: 47%
Library Volumes: 15,000 Acres: 70 Plant: 6 M

Other Facts

New classroom building 1989; new dorm 1987; exchan gland; stables and 25 horses; golf course 1½ miles awa Orton Gillingham program.

Locale

55 miles from NYC in rural setting; weekly trips fo events in NYC; ½ from Atlantic Ocean beaches; pop. (

Lake Forest Academy (Coed)

Founded 1857

1500 W. Kennedy Rd., Lake Forest, IL 60045
(312) 615-3267
Airport: Chicago, 20 miles

Students

Total: 253 Boys: 131 Girls: 122 Grades: 9-12
Boarding: 149 Day: 104 Local Students: 40%
Number of States: 17 Countries: 13 Foreign Students: 8%

Costs and Aid

Tuition: $13,500 School Extras: $500
Student Aid Money Awarded: $334,000
Number Granted: 16% Avg. Per Student: $8,150

Additional Support

Endowment: $1,600,000 Per Student: $6,400
Alumni: 4700 Annual Gifts: $600,000 Giving: 27%

Admission

Largest Grade Entry: 9 Applied: 83
Accepted: 61 Entered: 49
Median Percentile Entering 9 Grade: 55%
Application Deadline: Rolling Remedial Program: No

Academics

Advanced Placement Preparation in 8 Test Areas
Class Size: 10-14 Student-Teacher Ratio: 7-1
Number of Seniors: 59 Combined SATS: 1010

Facilities

Rooms: Singles 5% Doubles: 95% Larger: 0%
Library Volumes: 18,000 Acres: 200 Plant: 14,350,000

Other Facts

Ice hockey rink; ESL program; summer study skills course; # 1 state of Illinois — JETS academic competition.

Locale

2 miles from center of Lake Forest — 17,000 pop.; 30 miles north of Chicago.

La Lumiere School (Coed)

Founded 1963

P.O. Box 5005, La Porte, IN 46350
(219) 326-7450
Airport: Chicago, 65 miles

Students

Total: 90 Boys: 55 Girls: 35 Grades: 9-PG
Boarding: 65 Day: 25 Local Students: 9%
Number of States: 7 Countries: 8 Foreign Students: 12%

Costs and Aid

Tuition: $12,400 School Extras: $
Student Aid Money Awarded: $55,000
Number Granted: 14% Avg. Per Student: $4100

Additional Support

Endowment: $ Per Student: $
Alumni: 400 Annual Gifts: $ Giving: %

Admission

Largest Grade Entry: 10 Applied: 79
Accepted: 39 Entered: 31
Median Percentile Entering 9th Grade: 55%
Application Deadline: none Remedial Program: No

Academics

Advanced Placement Preparation in 4 Test Areas
Class Size: 8 Student-Teacher Ratio: 5-1
Number of Seniors: 25 Combined SATS: N/A

Facilities

Rooms: Singles 90% Doubles: 10% Larger: 0%
Library Volumes: 11,000 Acres: 150 Plant: 6 M

Other Facts

Founded by Catholic laymen; fine arts building; chapel; gym; computer room with 12 computers.

Locale

25 miles from South Bend in heart of Indiana's dune country; 5 miles from Lake Michigan; La Porte pop. 1000; rural setting.

Lawrence Academy (Coed)

Founded 1793

Box 992, Groton, MA 01450
(508) 448-6535
Airport: Boston, 35 miles

Students

Total: 330 Boys: 190 Girls: 140 Grades: 9-12
Boarding: 170 Day: 150 Local Students: 50%
Number of States: 15 Countries: 12 Foreign Students: 6%

Costs and Aid

Tuition: $15,400 School Extras: $100
Student Aid Money Awarded: $500,000
Number Granted: 25% Avg. Per Student: $

Additional Support

Endowment: $3 Mil Per Student: $9000
Alumni: 2800 Annual Gifts: $250,000 Giving: %

Admission

Largest Grade Entry: 9 Applied: 140
Accepted: 80 Entered: 50
Median Percentile Entering 9th Grade: 55%
Application Deadline: rolling Remedial Program: No

Academics

Advanced Placement Preparation in 4 Test Areas
Class Size: 14 Student-Teacher Ratio: 8-1
Number of Seniors: 85 Combined SATS: 970

Facilities

Rooms: Singles 5% Doubles: 90% Larger: 5%
Library Volumes: 20,000 Acres: 90 Plant: 13 M

Other Facts

2-weeks art and adventure program; independent on and off campus; strong connections local community and resources.

Locale

Historic New England town — pop. 6000; Groton School just 1 mile away.

The Lawrenceville School (Coed)

Founded 1810

P.O. Box 6008, Lawrenceville, NJ 08648
(609) 896-0400
Airport: Newark & Phila., 50 miles

Students

Total: 721 Boys: 476 Girls: 245 Grades: 8-PG
Boarding: 524 Day: 197 Local Students: 25%
Number of States: 35 Countries: 16 Foreign Students: 4%

Costs and Aid

Tuition: $14,500 School Extras: $
Student Aid Money Awarded: $1,153,000
Number Granted: 21% Avg. Per Student: $7,900

Additional Support

Endowment: $80,000,000 Per Student: $111,000
Alumni: 10,000 Annual Gifts: $1,844,000 Giving: 43%

Admission

Largest Grade Entry: 10 Applied: 335
Accepted: 139 Entered: 80
Median Percentile Entering 10th Grade: 77%
Application Deadline: 2/15 Remedial Program: No

Academics

Advanced Placement Preparation in 13 Test Areas
Class Size: 4-16 Student-Teacher Ratio: 6-1
Number of Seniors: 218 Combined SATS: 1210

Facilities

Rooms: Singles 60% Doubles: 40% Larger: 0%
Library Volumes: 30,000 Acres: 360 Plant: 100,000,000

Other Facts

4 new houses (1987); 1 new senior house (31 girls) (1988) (30 girls each); capital gifts of 4.3 m.

Locale

5 miles from Princeton, NJ — pop. 15,000. Lawrenceville — pop. 2000; 55 miles to NYC; 40 miles to Philadelphia.

Leelanau School (Coed)

Founded 1929

One Old Homestead Road, Glen Arbor, MI 49636
(616) 334-3072
Airport: Traverse City, 26 miles

Students

Total: 90 Boys: 54 Girls: 36 Grades: 8-12
Boarding: 78 Day: 12 Local Students: 10%
Number of States: 8 Countries: 1 Foreign Students: 2%

Costs and Aid

Tuition: $13,200 School Extras: $500
Student Aid Money Awarded: $150,000
Number Granted: 22% Avg. Per Student: $6,200

Additional Support

Endowment: $150,000 Per Student: $1,600
Alumni: 2,600 Annual Gifts: $350,000 Giving: 6%

Admission

Largest Grade Entry: 9 Applied: 52
Accepted: 42 Entered: 36
Median Percentile Entering Grade: %
Application Deadline: Rolling Remedial Program: Yes

Academics

Advanced Placement Preparation in 1 Test Areas
Class Size: 10 Student-Teacher Ratio: 7-1
Number of Seniors: 12 Combined SATS: 950

Facilities

Rooms: Singles 0% Doubles: 100% Larger: 0%
Library Volumes: 10,000 Acres: 90 Plant: 5 M

Other Facts

Skiing is a varsity sport; feature a "Mountain Term." Reading Development Program for college-bound dyslexics.

Locale

Inside Sleeping Bear Dunes National Lakeshore, on the shore of Lake Michigan, 30 minutes west of Traverse City, MI. Pop. 16,000.

Linden Hall (Girls)

Founded 1746

212 E. Main St., Lititz, PA 17543
(717) 626-8512
Airport: Lancaster, 3 miles

Students

Total: 95-100 Boys: 0 Girls: 95-100 Grades: 9-PG
Boarding: 95 Day: 3 Local Students: 3%
Number of States: 17 Countries: 7 Foreign Students: 10%

Costs and Aid

Tuition: $14,400 School Extras: $600
Student Aid Money Awarded: $8000
Number Granted: 4% Avg. Per Student: $2,000

Additional Support

Endowment: $214,600 Per Student: $2,800
Alumni: 1957 Annual Gifts: $80,000 Giving: 31%

Admission

Largest Grade Entry: 10 & 11 Applied: 65
Accepted: 11 & 18 Entered: 10 & 16
Median Percentile Entering NA Grade: NA%
Application Deadline: Rolling Remedial Program: Yes

Academics

Advanced Placement Preparation in 2 Test Areas
Class Size: 1-14 Student-Teacher Ratio: 5-1
Number of Seniors: 30 Combined SATS: 900+

Facilities

Rooms: Singles 20% Doubles: 80% Larger: 0%
Library Volumes: 12,000 Acres: 46 Plant: 8 M

Other Facts

ESL Program; LD Action program; LD student with average to gifted ability; all buildings connected by enclosed walkways.

Locale

Pop. 8000; 7 mi. N. of Lancaster; 30 mi. E. of Harrisburg; 3 hrs. from Washington, D.C.; 3 hrs. from NYC; 2½ hours from Baltimore, MD.

Linsly (Coed)

Founded 1814

Knox Lane, Wheeling, WV 26003
(304) 233-3260
Airport: Pittsburgh, 60 miles

Students

Total: 250 Boys: 200 Girls: 50 Grades: 5-12
Boarding: 100 Day: 150 Local Students: 85%
Number of States: 5 Countries: 4 Foreign Students: 2%

Costs and Aid

Tuition: $10,070 School Extras: $None
Student Aid Money Awarded: $195,000
Number Granted: 20% Avg. Per Student: $3000

Additional Support

Endowment: $3 mil Per Student: $
Alumni: 2600 Annual Gifts: $140,000 Giving: %

Admission

Largest Grade Entry: 9 Applied: 40
Accepted: 25 Entered: 20
Median Percentile Entering Grade: %
Application Deadline: rolling Remedial Program: No

Academics

Advanced Placement Preparation in 6 Test Areas
Class Size: 13 Student-Teacher Ratio: 11-1
Number of Seniors: 53 Combined SATS: 1050

Facilities

Rooms: Singles 0% Doubles: 100% Larger: %
Library Volumes: 8,000 Acres: 60 Plant: 10 M

Other Facts

Girls accepted, grades 5-11 after 1988. Operating outdoor environmental and adventure courses.

Locale

Population 28,000. In residential section, within ten minutes of Oglbay Park which has golf course, riding and hotel accommodations.

Loomis Chaffee School (Coed)

Founded 1914

Batchelder Road, Windsor, CT 06095
(203) 688-4934
Airport: Hartford, 6 miles

Students

Total: 700 Boys: 374 Girls: 326 Grades: 9-PG
Boarding: 340 Day: 360 Local Students: 6%
Number of States: 27 Countries: 14 Foreign Students: 5%

Costs and Aid

Tuition: $15,100 School Extras: $450
Student Aid Money Awarded: $1 M
Number Granted: 24% Avg. Per Student: $7000

Additional Support

Endowment: $20 M Per Student: $28,000
Alumni: 8100 Annual Gifts: $800,000 Giving: 37%

Admission

Largest Grade Entry: 9 Applied: 400
Accepted: 260 Entered:
Median Percentile Entering 9th Grade: 70%
Application Deadline: Feb. 1 Remedial Program: No

Academics

Advanced Placement Preparation in 13 Test Areas
Class Size: 14 Student-Teacher Ratio: 7-1
Number of Seniors: 210 Combined SATS: 1110

Facilities

Rooms: Singles 35% Doubles: 60% Larger: 5%
Library Volumes: 60,000 Acres: 300 Plant: 33 M

Other Facts

New girls dorm (1986); new multimillion dollar student center (1989); academic program abroad (France, Spain).

Locale

Suburb of Hartford (6 miles); within walking distance of village — pop. 25,000; campus borders Farmington River.

MacDuffie School (Girls)

Founded 1890

Ames Hill Drive, Springfield, MA 01105
(413) 734-4971
Airport: Hartford, 20 miles

Students

Total: 128 Boys: 0 Girls: 128 Grades: 7-12
Boarding: 55 Day: 73 Local Students: 57%
Number of States: 10 Countries: 12 Foreign Students: 20%

Costs and Aid

Tuition: $14,900 School Extras: $500
Student Aid Money Awarded: $261,200
Number Granted: 44% Avg. Per Student: $4,838

Additional Support

Endowment: $1,000,000 Per Student: $
Alumni: 2000 Annual Gifts: $202,188.34 Giving: 32%

Admission

Largest Grade Entry: 9 Applied: 19
Accepted: 14 Entered: 12
Median Percentile Entering 9th Grade: %
Application Deadline: Rolling Remedial Program: No

Academics

Advanced Placement Preparation in 5 Test Areas
Class Size: 10-12 Student-Teacher Ratio: 9-1
Number of Seniors: 32 Combined SATS: Median V545 M508

Facilities

Rooms: Singles 13% Doubles: 65% Larger: 22%
Library Volumes: 7,500 Acres: 12.5 Plant: 3 M

Other Facts

MacDuffie offers a supportive community, active visual and performing arts program, as well as competitive sports program.

Locale

MacDuffie boasts of a beautiful campus in historic district of Springfield. The campus is a few minutes walk to downtown which has an excellent library, museums, a symphony orchestra and professional theater.

The Madeira School (Girls)

Founded 1906

8328 Georgetown Pike, McLean, VA 22102
(703) 556-8253
Airport: Washington, 13 miles

Students

Total: 330 Boys: 0 Girls: 330 Grades: 9-12
Boarding: 205 Day: 125 Local Students: %
Number of States: 30 Countries: 15 Foreign Students: 10%

Costs and Aid

Tuition: $15,000 School Extras: $
Student Aid Money Awarded: $250,000
Number Granted: 15% Avg. Per Student: $6500

Additional Support

Endowment: $13 mil Per Student: $39,000
Alumni: 3800 Annual Gifts: $500,000 Giving: %

Admission

Largest Grade Entry: 9th Applied: 125
Accepted: 75 Entered: 55
Median Percentile Entering Grade: %
Application Deadline: July 1 Remedial Program: No

Academics

Advanced Placement Preparation in 12 Test Areas
Class Size: 15 Student-Teacher Ratio: 8-1
Number of Seniors: 90 Combined SATS: 1170

Facilities

Rooms: Singles 5% Doubles: 90% Larger: 5%
Library Volumes: 20,000 Acres: 400 Plant: 8 M

Other Facts

Unique internship program every Wednesday, utilizing nearby D.C. area and Capitol Hill; 550 seat chapel; auditorium for theatre; very large indoor riding ring.

Locale

Rural setting; overlooks Potomac River.

Maine Central Institute (Coed)

Founded 1866

Pittsfield, Maine 04967
(207) 487-3355
Airport: Bangor, 30 miles

Students

Total: 449 Boys: 258 Girls: 191 Grades: 9-PG
Boarding: 124 Day: 325 Local Students: 68%
Number of States: 20 Countries: 7 Foreign Students: 7%

Costs and Aid

Tuition: $11,200 School Extras: $700
Student Aid Money Awarded: $200,000
Number Granted: 35% Avg. Per Student: $5000

Additional Support

Endowment: $489,000 Per Student: $1000
Alumni: 6000 Annual Gifts: $60,000 Giving: 35%

Admission

Largest Grade Entry: PG Applied: 230
Accepted: 160 Entered: 100
Median Percentile Entering PG Grade: %
Application Deadline: Rolling Remedial Program: Yes

Academics

Advanced Placement Preparation in 6 Test Areas
Class Size: 13-20 Student-Teacher Ratio: 14-1
Number of Seniors: 145 Combined SATS: 1000

Facilities

Rooms: Singles 0% Doubles: 100% Larger: 0%
Library Volumes: 15,000 Acres: 200 Plant: 4 million

Other Facts

New $1 million gym; golf course; ski hill; library; tutorial program; vocational program; competitive athletics; large PG program.

Locale

Center of Maine village; movie theatre; bowling alley; restaurants; motel; 35 miles from Bangor; 3½ hours from Boston.

Marian Heights Academy (Girls)

Founded 1870

Box 1076, Ferdinand, IN 47532
(812) 367-1431
Airport: Louisville, KY, 70 miles

Students

Total: 180 Boys: 0 Girls: 180 Grades: 9-12
Boarding: 179 Day: 1 Local Students: 10%
Number of States: 22 Countries: 6 Foreign Students: 34%

Costs and Aid

Tuition: $7500 School Extras: $600
Student Aid Money Awarded: $160,000
Number Granted: 30% Avg. Per Student: $3000

Additional Support

Endowment: $165,000 Per Student: $1000
Alumni: 2500 Annual Gifts: $50,000 Giving: %

Admission

Largest Grade Entry: 10 Applied: 100
Accepted: 50 Entered: 30
Median Percentile Entering 9 Grade: 42%
Application Deadline: Rolling Remedial Program: No

Academics

Advanced Placement Preparation in Test Areas
Class Size: 10-15 Student-Teacher Ratio: 8-1
Number of Seniors: 45 Combined SATS: 890

Facilities

Rooms: Singles 5% Doubles: 95% Larger: 0%
Library Volumes: 60,000 Acres: 190 Plant: 11 M

Other Facts

80% of students are Roman Catholic; new gym in 1980; 4-year programs in music and art; monthly historical site excursions; annual trips abroad.

Locale

Pop. 2500; rural setting; one hour from Louisville; 2 blocks from downtown.

Marvelwood School (Coed)

Founded 1957

Jewell St., Cornwall, CT 06753
(203) 672-6612
Airport: Hartford, 42 miles

Students

Total: 102 Boys: 74 Girls: 28 Grades: 9-12
Boarding: 92 Day: 10 Local Students: 10%
Number of States: 20 Countries: 6 Foreign Students: 6%

Costs and Aid

Tuition: $15,900 School Extras: $1000
Student Aid Money Awarded: $80,000
Number Granted: 15% Avg. Per Student: $7000

Additional Support

Endowment: $ Per Student: $
Alumni: 575 Annual Gifts: $125,000 Giving: 14%

Admission

Largest Grade Entry: 9 Applied: 36
Accepted: 24 Entered: 18
Median Percentile Entering 9 Grade: 40%
Application Deadline: Rolling Remedial Program: Yes

Academics

Advanced Placement Preparation in 0 Test Areas
Class Size: 10 Student-Teacher Ratio: 4-1
Number of Seniors: 25 Combined SATS: 850

Facilities

Rooms: Singles 10% Doubles: 80% Larger: 10%
Library Volumes: 8,000 Acres: 30 Plant: 2.4 million

Other Facts

Optional Skills Program provides intensive transitional support in language arts and study skills; 1 mile to Mohawk Mt. Ski Area.

Locale

In the rural village of Cornwall in the Berkshire Hills of Northern Litchfield County; 2 hrs. north of NYC.

Masters School (Girls)

Founded 1877

49 Clinton Ave., Dobbs Ferry, NY 10522
(914) 693-1400
Airport: JFK or LaGuardia, 20 miles

Students

Total: 270 Boys: 0 Girls: 270 Grades: 9-12
Boarding: 147 Day: 123 Local Students: 40%
Number of States: 21 Countries: 19 Foreign Students: 15%

Costs and Aid

Tuition: $15,500 School Extras: $200
Student Aid Money Awarded: $370,000
Number Granted: 25% Avg. Per Student: $5,500

Additional Support

Endowment: $10 million Per Student: $38,000
Alumni: 4500 Annual Gifts: $644,000 Giving: 41%

Admission

Largest Grade Entry: 9th Applied: 60
Accepted: 45 Entered: 43
Median Percentile Entering NA Grade: 55%
Application Deadline: Rolling Remedial Program: No

Academics

Advanced Placement Preparation in 13 Test Areas
Class Size: 10-15 Student-Teacher Ratio: 6-1
Number of Seniors: 85 Combined SATS: 1020

Facilities

Rooms: Singles 50% Doubles: 50% Larger: 0%
Library Volumes: 25,000 Acres: 96 Plant: 23,000,000

Other Facts

New ESL Immersion program; 450 seat theatre and visual art studio; middle school 6-8, day students only.

Locale

20 miles north of New York City, in beautiful suburbs of the Hudson Valley; local train provides easy access to downtown Manhattan; surrounded by historic Hudson River estates and museums.

Maur Hill Prep School (Boys)

Founded 1919

10th & Green St., Atchison, KS 66002
(913) 367-5482
Airport: Kansas City, 35 miles

Students

Total: 260 Boys: 260 Girls: 0 Grades: 9-12
Boarding: 135 Day: 125 Local Students: 45%
Number of States: 11 Countries: 15 Foreign Students: 35%

Costs and Aid

Tuition: $6100 School Extras: $150
Student Aid Money Awarded: $50,000
Number Granted: % Avg. Per Student: $

Additional Support

Endowment: $Church Support Per Student: $
Alumni: 3000 Annual Gifts: $500,000 Giving: %

Admission

Largest Grade Entry: 10th Applied:
Accepted: Entered: 55
Median Percentile Entering Grade: %
Application Deadline: Rolling Remedial Program:

Academics

Advanced Placement Preparation in Test Areas
Class Size: 12-15 Student-Teacher Ratio: 10-1
Number of Seniors: 55 Combined SATS:

Facilities

Rooms: Singles 0% Doubles: 100% Larger: 0%
Library Volumes: 7000 Acres: 150 Plant: 10 mil

Other Facts

Relatively new campus; golf team; shares classes and staff with St. Scholastica, a girl's school adjoining campus.

Locale

Pop. 12,000; located on edge of town; 20 miles from St. Joe, MO; Benedictine College in town.

The McCallie School (Boys)

Founded 1905

2850 McCallie Ave., Chattanooga, TN 37404
(615) 622-2163
Airport: Chattanooga, 10 miles

Students

Total: 670 Boys: 670 Girls: 0 Grades: 7-12
Boarding: 230 Day: 440 Local Students: 65%
Number of States: 20 Countries: 6 Foreign Students: 1%

Costs and Aid

Tuition: $12,800 School Extras: $200
Student Aid Money Awarded: $520,000
Number Granted: 19% Avg. Per Student: $7000 Boarding

Additional Support

Endowment: $10,000,000 Per Student: $15,000
Alumni: 6,600 Annual Gifts: $925,000 Giving: 40%

Admission

Largest Grade Entry: 9th Applied: 90
Accepted: 63 Entered: 37
Median Percentile Entering 9 Grade: 55%
Application Deadline: Rolling Remedial Program: No

Academics

Advanced Placement Preparation in 17 Test Areas
Class Size: 10-15 Student-Teacher Ratio: 11-1
Number of Seniors: 122 Combined SATS: 1111

Facilities

Rooms: Singles 1% Doubles: 99% Larger: 0%
Library Volumes: 32,000 Acres: 70 Plant: 20 million

Other Facts

Coordinate academic/social program with Girls Preparatory School of Chattanooga; 15 tennis courts (2 indoor); indoor and outdoor pools; 4 gyms; extensive wilderness program.

Locale

Metropolitan Chattanooga — pop. 250,000; 2 hours drive from the major cities of Atlanta, Knoxville, Nashville; campus located on historic Missionary Ridge.

McDonogh School (Coed)

Founded 1873

McDonogh, MD 21208
(301) 363-0600
Airport: Baltimore, 18 miles

Students

Total: 515 Boys: Girls: Grades: 1-12
Boarding: 70 Day: Local Students: %
Number of States: 4 Countries: Foreign Students: %

Costs and Aid

Tuition: $ School Extras: $
Student Aid Money Awarded: $
Number Granted: % Avg. Per Student: $

Additional Support

Endowment: $18 mil Per Student: $
Alumni: Annual Gifts: $ Giving: %

Admission

Largest Grade Entry: 9 Applied:
Accepted: Entered:
Median Percentile Entering Grade: 72%
Application Deadline: Remedial Program:

Academics

Advanced Placement Preparation in Test Areas
Class Size: Student-Teacher Ratio:
Number of Seniors: 130 Combined SATS: 1120

Facilities

Rooms: Singles % Doubles: % Larger: %
Library Volumes: Acres: Plant:

Other Facts

Starting in the 1989-90 school year, only 5 day boarders will be accepted.

Locale

Mercersburg Academy (Coed)

Founded 1893

Mercersburg, PA 17236
(717) 328-2151
Airport: Hagerstown, MD, 20 miles

Students

Total: 357 Boys: 218 Girls: 139 Grades: 9-12 & PG
Boarding: 316 Day: 41 Local Students: 41%
Number of States: 29 Countries: 25 Foreign Students: 7%

Costs and Aid

Tuition: $13,500 School Extras: $500
Student Aid Money Awarded: $695,600
Number Granted: 29% Avg. Per Student: $7000

Additional Support

Endowment: $18,000,000 Per Student: $50,000
Alumni: 10,000 Annual Gifts: $800,000 Giving: 38%

Admission

Largest Grade Entry: 9th Applied: 56
Accepted: 41 Entered: 22
Median Percentile Entering 10th Grade: 62%
Application Deadline: rolling Remedial Program: No

Academics

Advanced Placement Preparation in 12 Test Areas
Class Size: 10-12 Student-Teacher Ratio: 7-1
Number of Seniors: 114 Combined SATS: 1096

Facilities

Rooms: Singles 10% Doubles: 80% Larger: no%
Library Volumes: 38,000 Acres: 300 Plant: 35 mil

Other Facts

700-seat theatre and center for performing arts; nationally recognized swimming program; orientation — school farm; outdoor education program.

Locale

Close proximity to Washington, D.C. and Baltimore, MD (both 75 miles away); town pop. 1600.

Middlesex School (Coed)

Founded 1901

1400 Lowell Road, Concord, MA 01742
(508) 369-2550
Airport: Boston, 20 miles

Students

Total: 289 Boys: 176 Girls: 113 Grades: 9-12
Boarding: 223 Day: 66 Local Students: 25%
Number of States: 26 Countries: 13 Foreign Students: 6%

Costs and Aid

Tuition: $15,200 School Extras: $600
Student Aid Money Awarded: $526,000
Number Granted: 18% Avg. Per Student: $9,846

Additional Support

Endowment: $22¼ mil Per Student: $76,000
Alumni: 3,974 Annual Gifts: $838,000 Giving: 72%

Admission

Largest Grade Entry: 9 Applied: 250
Accepted: 90 Entered: 40
Median Percentile Entering 9th Grade: 80%
Application Deadline: Jan. 31st Remedial Program: No

Academics

Advanced Placement Preparation in 12 Test Areas
Class Size: 11 Student-Teacher Ratio: 5-1
Number of Seniors: 70 Combined SATS: 1200

Facilities

Rooms: Singles 81% Doubles: 15% Larger: 4%
Library Volumes: 16,000 Acres: 350 Plant: 26 M

Other Facts

New gym 1988 ($4½ mil); student exchange program — England; 13% minority population; 75% faculty hold advanced degrees; opportunity to go beyond advanced placement level in math, science, history, English.

Locale

20 miles west of Boston; 2½ miles west of historic Concord, Massachusetts (pop. 16,000); pond adjoins school.

Midland School (Coed)

Founded 1932

Box 8 Figuerda Mtn. Rd., Los Olivos, CA 93441
(805) 688-5114
Airport: Santa Barbara, 40 miles

Students

Total: 80 Boys: 55 Girls: 25 Grades: 9-12
Boarding: 80 Day: 0 Local Students: %
Number of States: 6 Countries: 3 Foreign Students: 3%

Costs and Aid

Tuition: $9300 School Extras: $300-400
Student Aid Money Awarded: $95,000
Number Granted: 35% Avg. Per Student: $3400

Additional Support

Endowment: $ Per Student: $
Alumni: Annual Gifts: $100,000 Giving: %

Admission

Largest Grade Entry: 9 Applied: 35
Accepted: 18 Entered: 14
Median Percentile Entering 9 Grade: 70%
Application Deadline: March Remedial Program: No

Academics

Advanced Placement Preparation in 5 Test Areas
Class Size: 12 avg. Student-Teacher Ratio: 6-1
Number of Seniors: 22 Combined SATS: 1080

Facilities

Rooms: Singles 10% Doubles: 90% Larger: %
Library Volumes: 12,000 Acres: 2860 Plant: 60 Mil

Other Facts

Students and faculty build and maintain the school; philosophy emphasizes individual and community responsibility.

Locale

Rural; bordering National Forest; campus a ranch; 5 miles from village; 35 miles north of Santa Barbara; Dunn Boarding School (boys only) in same town.

Millbrook School (Coed)

Founded 1931

School Road, Millbrook, NY 12545
(914) 677-8261
Airport: Hartford, 60 miles

Students

Total: 180 Boys: 100 Girls: 80 Grades: 9-12
Boarding: 160 Day: 20 Local Students: 25%
Number of States: 22 Countries: 10 Foreign Students: 5%

Costs and Aid

Tuition: $14,900 School Extras: $250
Student Aid Money Awarded: $360,000 (89-90)
Number Granted: 26% Avg. Per Student: $8600

Additional Support

Endowment: $6,000,000 Per Student: $33,000
Alumni: 1800 Annual Gifts: $400,000 Giving: 42%

Admission

Largest Grade Entry: 9, 10 Applied: 80/80
Accepted: 50/50 Entered: 25/25
Median Percentile Entering 9/10 Grade: 60%
Application Deadline: March 10 Remedial Program: No

Academics

Advanced Placement Preparation in 8 Test Areas
Class Size: 12 Student-Teacher Ratio: 7-1
Number of Seniors: 50 Combined SATS: 1050

Facilities

Rooms: Singles 35% Doubles: 60% Larger: 5%
Library Volumes: 16,000 Acres: 600 Plant: 4.5 M

Other Facts

Trevor Teaching Zoo; observatory; wetlands; nature trail; new dorm completed Fall '88; all other dorms in process of renovation; gym; 5 playing fields; stables; ice hockey rink.

Locale

Located in the rolling hills of Dutchess County's Hunt Country, 20 miles northeast of Poughkeepsie (Vassar College) and 8 miles from the Connecticut border; 90 miles from NYC.

Milton Academy (Coed)

Founded 1798

170 Centre Street, Milton, MA 02186
(617) 698-7800
Airport: Boston, 11 miles

Students

Total: 633 Boys: 376 Girls: 257 Grades: K-12
Boarding: 273 Day: 360 Local Students: 50%
Number of States: 35 Countries: 34 Foreign Students: 5%

Costs and Aid

Tuition: $15,100 School Extras: $350
Student Aid Money Awarded: $2,300,000
Number Granted: 30% Avg. Per Student: $8,700

Additional Support

Endowment: $52,900,000 Per Student: $56,000
Alumni: 6500 Annual Gifts: $831,858 Giving: 51%

Admission

Largest Grade Entry: 9th Applied: 478
Accepted: 124 Entered: 66
Median Percentile Entering 9th Grade: 90%
Application Deadline: Feb. 1 Remedial Program: No

Academics

Advanced Placement Preparation in 12 Test Areas
Class Size: 12 Student-Teacher Ratio: 6-1
Number of Seniors: 169 Combined SATS: 1240

Facilities

Rooms: Singles 30% Doubles: 60% Larger: 10%
Library Volumes: 40,000 Acres: 125 Plant: 30 mil

Other Facts

6-week exchange program for foreign study in France and Spain; owns the mountain school in Vermont with a semester program for juniors.

Locale

Rapid rail to downtown Boston, just 10 miles; residential community — pop. 26,000; 6000-acre Blue Ridge reservation with ski lifts within walking distance.

Miss Hall's School (Girls)

Founded 1898

492 Holmes Rd., Pittsfield, MA 01201
(413) 443-6401
Airport: Hartford, 60 miles

Students

Total: 200 Boys: 0 Girls: 200 Grades: 9-12
Boarding: 170 Day: 30 Local Students: 15%
Number of States: 27 Countries: 20 Foreign Students: 10%

Costs and Aid

Tuition: $14,900 School Extras: $700
Student Aid Money Awarded: $380,000
Number Granted: 30% Avg. Per Student: $6200

Additional Support

Endowment: $2,100,000 Per Student: $10,000
Alumni: 2500 Annual Gifts: $400,000 Giving: %

Admission

Largest Grade Entry: 9th Applied: 180
Accepted: 90 Entered: 26
Median Percentile Entering 9th Grade: 45%
Application Deadline: Rolling Remedial Program: Yes

Academics

Advanced Placement Preparation in 6 Test Areas
Class Size: 13 Student-Teacher Ratio: 7-1
Number of Seniors: 60 Combined SATS: 950

Facilities

Rooms: Singles 6% Doubles: 94% Larger: %
Library Volumes: 12,500 Acres: 70+ Plant: 6,000,000

Other Facts

Junior class trip to England (15 days) paid for by the school; academic skills center for individual and group skills strengthening and support.

Locale

2 miles from town center — 50,000 pop.; museum, mall shopping, cinema centers; easy access to ski areas and Appalachian trail; 2½ hrs. to Boston; 3 hrs. to NYC.

Miss Porter's School (Girls)

Founded 1843

60 Main Street, Farmington, CT 06032
(203) 677-1321
Airport: Hartford, 25 miles

Students

Total: 280 Boys: 0 Girls: 280 Grades: 9-12
Boarding: 215 Day: 65 Local Students: 20%
Number of States: 31 Countries: 17 Foreign Students: 9%

Costs and Aid

Tuition: $15,600 School Extras: $500
Student Aid Money Awarded: $635,000
Number Granted: 25% Avg. Per Student: $8,000

Additional Support

Endowment: $24,500,000 Per Student: $85,000
Alumni: 4500 Annual Gifts: $524,063 Giving: 49%

Admission

Largest Grade Entry: 10th Applied: 125
Accepted: 75 Entered: 44
Median Percentile Entering 10 Grade: 65%
Application Deadline: Feb.15 Remedial Program: No

Academics

Advanced Placement Preparation in 13 Test Areas
Class Size: 11 Student-Teacher Ratio: 10-1
Number of Seniors: 97 Combined SATS: 1140

Facilities

Rooms: Singles 10% Doubles: 75% Larger: 15%
Library Volumes: 20,000 Acres: 30 Plant:

Other Facts

Internship program/January for juniors and seniors; winterim program for other students; excellent fine arts; dance & drama.

Locale

Small New England town; warm community; close to cultural assets of Hartford; 2 hours from New York City and Boston. Near two boy's schools.

Montverde Academy (Coed)

Founded 1912

P.O. Box 97, Montverde, FL 34756
(407) 469-2561
Airport: Orlando, 35 miles

Students

Total: 225 Boys: 120 Girls: 105 Grades: 7-PG
Boarding: 210 Day: 15 Local Students: %
Number of States: 10 Countries: 20 Foreign Students: 25%

Costs and Aid

Tuition: $8900 School Extras: $1000
Student Aid Money Awarded: $0
Number Granted: % Avg. Per Student: $

Additional Support

Endowment: $0 Per Student: $
Alumni: Annual Gifts: $25,000 Giving: %

Admission

Largest Grade Entry: 10 Applied: 73
Accepted: 65 Entered: 57
Median Percentile Entering Grade: %
Application Deadline: July 1 Remedial Program: No

Academics

Advanced Placement Preparation in 2 Test Areas
Class Size: 15-18 Student-Teacher Ratio: 8-1
Number of Seniors: 53 Combined SATS: N/A

Facilities

Rooms: Singles 5% Doubles: 88% Larger: 7%
Library Volumes: 5000 Acres: 125 Plant: 10 M

Other Facts

New library (1987); fine arts center (1981); dining hall (1988); activities building (1985); ESL program; drama; outdoor pool; two gyms.

Locale

Pop. 700; 25 miles west of Orlando and 35 miles from Disneyworld; water skiing and sailing on adjoining lake.

New Hampton School (Coed)

Founded 1821

New Hampton, NH 03256
(603) 744-5401
Airport: Boston, 100 miles

Students

Total: 290 Boys: 200 Girls: 90 Grades: 9-12 & PG
Boarding: 245 Day: 45 Local Students: 20%
Number of States: 30 Countries: 8 Foreign Students: 6%

Costs and Aid

Tuition: $14,900 School Extras: $700
Student Aid Money Awarded: $325,000
Number Granted: 24% Avg. Per Student: $7000

Additional Support

Endowment: $1.2 million Per Student: $4000
Alumni: 4000 Annual Gifts: $85,000 Giving: 20%

Admission

Largest Grade Entry: 10 Applied: 62
Accepted: 40 Entered: 32
Median Percentile Entering 9th Grade: 45%
Application Deadline: Rolling Remedial Program: Yes

Academics

Advanced Placement Preparation in 7 Test Areas
Class Size: 10-15 Student-Teacher Ratio: 6-1
Number of Seniors: 115 Combined SATS: 1000

Facilities

Rooms: Singles 20% Doubles: 80% Larger: 0%
Library Volumes: 36,000 Acres: 200 Plant: 8 million

Other Facts

Learning skills program; resource center; excellent arts and athletic programs; new arts/academic center 1987; radio station; skiing. New 1987 center for radio station, art studios, lounge, and 300-seat theatre.

Locale

100 miles from Boston and 35 north of Concord. Small colonial New England village in the center of the Lakes Region and at the base of the White Mountains; pop. 1250.

Northfield Mount Hermon School (Coed)

Founded 1879

Main St., Northfield, MA 01360
(413) 498-5311
Airport: Hartford, 80 miles

Students

Total: 1135 Boys: 570 Girls: 565 Grades: 9-PG
Boarding: 1015 Day: 120 Local Students: 10%
Number of States: 46 Countries: 67 Foreign Students: 20%

Costs and Aid

Tuition: $14,700 School Extras: $450
Student Aid Money Awarded: $2,248,300
Number Granted: 42% Avg. Per Student: $5525 + $1510 loans

Additional Support

Endowment: $48,000,000 Per Student: $44,000
Alumni: 23,000 Annual Gifts: $ Giving: %

Admission

Largest Grade Entry: 10 Applied: 1700
Accepted: 750 Entered: 465
Median Percentile Entering 9th Grade: 70%
Application Deadline: Rolling Remedial Program: No

Academics

Advanced Placement Preparation in All Test Areas
Class Size: 13.5 Student-Teacher Ratio: 7.6-1
Number of Seniors: 420 Combined SATS: 1150

Facilities

Rooms: Singles 2% Doubles: 98% Larger: 0%
Library Volumes: 110,000 Acres: 4900 Plant: 162 buildings

Other Facts

Two campuses — both coed 9-PG; all major facilities on both connected by shuttle; designated as exemplary school by U.S. Dept. of Education 1986-87.

Locale

Northern Mass. on VT/NH border — pop. 2400; two hours west of Boston, Mass; nearby lake resorts; Greenfield, 14 miles — pop. 18,000.

Northwood School (Coed)

Founded 1905

Lake Placid, NY 12946
(518) 523-3357
Airport: Albany, 120 miles

Students

Total: 150 Boys: 100 Girls: 50 Grades: 9-PG
Boarding: 130 Day: 20 Local Students: 9%
Number of States: 37 Countries: 4 Foreign Students: 2%

Costs and Aid

Tuition: $12,000 School Extras: $None
Student Aid Money Awarded: $80,000
Number Granted: 16% Avg. Per Student: $3000

Additional Support

Endowment: $2 mil. Per Student: $13,000
Alumni: 2000 Annual Gifts: $175,000 Giving: %

Admission

Largest Grade Entry: 9 Applied: 100
Accepted: 65 Entered: 23
Median Percentile Entering Grade: %
Application Deadline: rolling Remedial Program: No

Academics

Advanced Placement Preparation in 3 Test Areas
Class Size: 11 Student-Teacher Ratio: 8-1
Number of Seniors: 45 Combined SATS: 1030

Facilities

Rooms: Singles 75% Doubles: 25% Larger: 0%
Library Volumes: 20,000 Acres: 78 Plant: 1.5 Mil

Other Facts

New sports complex; two indoor tennis courts; computer room; new lecture hall.

Locale

Pop. 3000; near town that hosted winter Olympics; campus borders lake; ski lift 10 minutes away.

Oakwood School (Coed)

Founded 1796

515 South Road, Poughkeepsie, NY 12601
(914) 462-4200
Airport: Albany, 70 miles

Students

Total: 145 Boys: 73 Girls: 72 Grades: 9-PG
Boarding: 122 Day: 23 Local Students: 20%
Number of States: 16 Countries: 6 Foreign Students: 13%

Costs and Aid

Tuition: $13,800 School Extras: $300
Student Aid Money Awarded: $400,000
Number Granted: 32% Avg. Per Student: $8000

Additional Support

Endowment: $4,600,000 Per Student: $24,000
Alumni: 2600 Annual Gifts: $80,000 Giving: 14%

Admission

Largest Grade Entry: 10 Applied: 200
Accepted: 110 Entered: 70
Median Percentile Entering Grade: %
Application Deadline: Rolling Remedial Program:

Academics

Advanced Placement Preparation in 3 Test Areas
Class Size: 12 Student-Teacher Ratio: 6-1
Number of Seniors: 53 Combined SATS: 960

Facilities

Rooms: Singles 15% Doubles: 85% Larger: 0%
Library Volumes: 12,000 Acres: 45 Plant: 5 Mil

Other Facts

A friends school; international students program and English as a second language; a learning center for mild learning disabilities; rich ethnic diversity.

Locale

Pop. 30,000; 85 miles from NYC; Vassar College nearby; suburban location.

Ojai Valley School (Coed)

Founded 1911

723 El Paso Rd., Ojai, CA 93023
(805) 646-1423
Airport: L.A., 80 miles

Students

Total: 120 Boys: 60 Girls: 60 Grades: 1-12
Boarding: 108 Day: 12 Local Students: %
Number of States: 9 Countries: 17 Foreign Students: 20%

Costs and Aid

Tuition: $14,960 School Extras: $1000
Student Aid Money Awarded: $155,000
Number Granted: 22% Avg. Per Student: $6500

Additional Support

Endowment: $none Per Student: $
Alumni: 1500 Annual Gifts: $ Giving: %

Admission

Largest Grade Entry: 9 Applied: 32
Accepted: 23 Entered: 13
Median Percentile Entering Grade: %
Application Deadline: Rolling Remedial Program: No

Academics

Advanced Placement Preparation in Test Areas
Class Size: 7-12 Student-Teacher Ratio: 5-1
Number of Seniors: 30 Combined SATS: 950

Facilities

Rooms: Singles 0% Doubles: 100% Larger: 0%
Library Volumes: 21,000 Acres: 200 Plant: 3.5 M

Other Facts

Boarding grades start at Grade 3; riding ring on campus; lower school on separate nearby campus.

Locale

Pop. 7000; 40 miles southeast of Santa Barbara; in Ojai Valley; 65 miles north of Los Angeles.

Oldfields School (Girls)

Founded 1867

1500 Glencoe Rd., Glencoe, MD 21152
(301) 472-4800
Airport: Baltimore, 40 miles

Students

Total: 180 Boys: 0 Girls: 180 Grades: 8-12
Boarding: 144 Day: 36 Local Students: 34%
Number of States: 28 Countries: 6 Foreign Students: 5%

Costs and Aid

Tuition: $15,200 School Extras: $400
Student Aid Money Awarded: $181,350
Number Granted: 10% Avg. Per Student: $9,550

Additional Support

Endowment: $1,928,000 Per Student: $11,000
Alumni: 1554 Annual Gifts: $250,000 Giving: 30%

Admission

Largest Grade Entry: 9th Applied: 144
Accepted: 113 Entered: 75
Median Percentile Entering Grade: 50%
Application Deadline: March 1st Remedial Program:

Academics

Advanced Placement Preparation in 7 Test Areas
Class Size: 10 Student-Teacher Ratio: 5-1
Number of Seniors: 46 Combined SATS:

Facilities

Rooms: Singles 1 Doubles: 120 Larger: %
Library Volumes: 8,000 Acres: 250 Plant: 4,352,000

Other Facts

3 playing fields; optional 3-week study abroad; dance studio; riding facilities — include stables, 3 riding rings, indoor riding rings.

Locale

Pop. 215; rural setting amidst estates; 1½ hours from Washington; 30 minutes from cultural events in Baltimore.

Orme School (Coed)

Founded 1929

H.C. 63, Box 3040, Mayer, Arizona 86333-9990
(602) 632-7601
Airport: Phoenix, 80 miles

Students

Total: 145 Boys: 68 Girls: 77 Grades: 9-PG
Boarding: 145 Day: 0 Local Students: %
Number of States: 20 Countries: 10 Foreign Students: 8%

Costs and Aid

Tuition: $13,500 School Extras: $1000
Student Aid Money Awarded: $215,000
Number Granted: 24% Avg. Per Student: $9000

Additional Support

Endowment: $3,000,000 Per Student: $21,000
Alumni: 2000 Annual Gifts: $500,000 Giving: %

Admission

Largest Grade Entry: 9 Applied: 45
Accepted: 36 Entered: 34
Median Percentile Entering Grade: %
Application Deadline: Rolling Remedial Program: No

Academics

Advanced Placement Preparation in 8 Test Areas
Class Size: 12 Student-Teacher Ratio: 7-1
Number of Seniors: 49 Combined SATS: 950

Facilities

Rooms: Singles % Doubles: all% Larger: %
Library Volumes: 23,000 Acres: 235 Plant: 7 Mil

Other Facts

New math center; school has horses, 2 riding rings; ranch environment; a lighted rodeo arena; large swimming pool; "Frontier village" motif provides classroom, etc., and "Horsellar" theatre.

Locale

The School is located halfway between Phoenix and Flagstaff at an altitude of almost 4,000 ft. in a high desert area. The Orme ranch (40,000 acres) surrounds the campus (235 acres) which is located along Ash Creek.

Patterson School (Coed)

Founded 1909

Rt. 5, Box 170, Lenoir, NC 28645
(800) 367-4921
Airport: Charlotte, 85 miles

Students

Total: 97
Boys: 47 Girls: 50 Grades: 7-12
Boarding: 88 Day: 9 Local Students: 15%
Number of States: 13 Countries: 4 Foreign Students: 1%

Costs and Aid

Tuition: $9485 School Extras: $1200
Student Aid Money Awarded: $88,800
Number Granted: 20% Avg. Per Student: $3550

Additional Support

Endowment: $150,000 Per Student: $1500
Alumni: Annual Gifts: $ Giving: %

Admission

Largest Grade Entry: 9 Applied: 74
Accepted: 21 Entered: 21
Median Percentile Entering 9 Grade: 22%
Application Deadline: Rolling Remedial Program: Yes

Academics

Advanced Placement Preparation in 0 Test Areas
Class Size: Avg. 10 Student-Teacher Ratio: 7-1
Number of Seniors: 28 Combined SATS: 750

Facilities

Rooms: Singles 15% Doubles: 85% Larger: 0%
Library Volumes: 6700 Acres: 1450 Plant: 4 Mil

Other Facts

Episcopal affiliation; all denominations accepted; "Close-up" trips to Washington, D.C., NYC offered; Horizon's program on weekends; hiking; white-water rafting; snow-skiing; rock climbing, etc.

Locale

8 mi. from center of Lenoir — pop. 8000; 85 mi. NE of Charlotte; 1 hr. south of Appalchian State University in Boone; Art/Science Museum in Hickory — 25 miles.

Peddie School (Coed)

Founded 1864

S. Main St., Hightstown, NJ 08520
(609) 448-0997
Airport: Newark, 25 miles

Students

Total: 510 Boys: 300 Girls: 210 Grades: 8-PG
Boarding: 300 Day: 210 Local Students: 40%
Number of States: 35 Countries: 20 Foreign Students: 10%

Costs and Aid

Tuition: $14,000 School Extras: $400
Student Aid Money Awarded: $700,000
Number Granted: 20% Avg. Per Student: $7500

Additional Support

Endowment: $8,000,000 Per Student: $15,600
Alumni: 6000 Annual Gifts: $400,000 Giving: 30%

Admission

Largest Grade Entry: 9 Applied: 200
Accepted: 130 Entered: 102
Median Percentile Entering 9th Grade: 59%
Application Deadline: ASAP Remedial Program: No

Academics

Advanced Placement Preparation in All Test Areas
Class Size: 13 Student-Teacher Ratio: 8-1
Number of Seniors: 150 Combined SATS: 1100

Facilities

Rooms: Singles 2% Doubles: 98% Larger: 0%
Library Volumes: 30,000 Acres: 280 Plant: 20 M

Other Facts

New $6 million arts complex; 18 hole golf course, swimming program of national status; 1 mil. a year additional income received from benefactor.

Locale

4000 pop.; 4 motels; near Princeton (12 miles) on bus; train line to NYC (50 miles).

The Pennington School (Coed)

Founded 1838

112 W. Delaware Ave., Pennington, NJ 08534
(609) 737-1838
Airport: Philadelphia, 40 miles

Students

Total: 332 Boys: 225 Girls: 107 Grades: 7-12
Boarding: 156 Day: 176 Local Students: 53%
Number of States: 16 Countries: 11 Foreign Students: 10%

Costs and Aid

Tuition: $13,800 School Extras: $550 (B)
Student Aid Money Awarded: $325,000
Number Granted: 23% Avg. Per Student: $3500

Additional Support

Endowment: $3 mil. Per Student: $9000
Alumni: 3000 Annual Gifts: $162,000 Giving: 45%

Admission

Largest Grade Entry: 11 Applied: 235
Accepted: 214 Entered: 113
Median Percentile Entering Grade: 49%
Application Deadline: rolling Remedial Program: No

Academics

Advanced Placement Preparation in 2 Test Areas
Class Size: 12 Student-Teacher Ratio: 9-1
Number of Seniors: 81 Combined SATS: 1000

Facilities

Rooms: Singles 25% Doubles: 75% Larger: 0%
Library Volumes: 15,000 Acres: 54 Plant: 6 M

Other Facts

2.3 mil. classroom and administration building (1981); dress code; center for learning disabilities — limit 40 students.

Locale

Suburban small town of 2500 pop.; 1¼ hrs. from NYC; 10 miles from Trenton & Princeton.

Perkiomen School (Coed)

Founded 1875

Box 130, Pennsburg, PA 18073
(215) 679-9511
Airport: Phila., 45 miles

Students

Total: 210 Boys: 120 Girls: 90 Grades: 7-PG
Boarding: 150 Day: 60 Local Students: 20%
Number of States: 19 Countries: 11 Foreign Students: 10%

Costs and Aid

Tuition: $13,100 School Extras: $600-1000
Student Aid Money Awarded: $231,000
Number Granted: 24% Avg. Per Student: $3065

Additional Support

Endowment: $1,700,000 Per Student: $8000
Alumni: 3400 Annual Gifts: $125,000 Giving: 40%

Admission

Largest Grade Entry: 9th Applied: 50
Accepted: 35 Entered: 18
Median Percentile Entering 9th Grade: 45%
Application Deadline: Rolling Remedial Program: Developmental- Not Remedial

Academics

Advanced Placement Preparation in 7 Test Areas
Class Size: 8 Student-Teacher Ratio: 6-1
Number of Seniors: 73 Combined SATS: 980

Facilities

Rooms: Singles 10% Doubles: 90% Larger: 0%
Library Volumes: 18,000 Acres: 120 Plant: 3,500,000

Other Facts

D.V.L. program for reading/dyslexia; individualized math program; new fine arts facility renovation.

Locale

Small town of 2000; 17 miles from Allentown; 45 miles from Phila.; rural setting.

Phillips Academy (Coed)

Founded 1778

Andover, MA 01810
(508) 475-3400
Airport: Boston, 25 miles

Students

Total: 1215 Boys: 639 Girls: 576 Grades: 9-PG
Boarding: 943 Day: 272 Local Students: 22%
Number of States: 43 Countries: 30 Foreign Students: 8%

Costs and Aid

Tuition: $13,500 School Extras: $books
Student Aid Money Awarded: $3,897,121
Number Granted: 37% Avg. Per Student: $9191

Additional Support

Endowment: $150,900,000 Per Student: $125,000
Alumni: 21,000 Annual Gifts: $2,305,168 Giving: 45%

Admission

Largest Grade Entry: 9th Applied: 986
Accepted: 248 Entered: 168
Median Percentile Entering 9th Grade: 85%
Application Deadline: 2/1 Remedial Program: No

Academics

Advanced Placement Preparation in All Test Areas
Class Size: 14 Student-Teacher Ratio: 6-1
Number of Seniors: 400 Combined SATS: 1208

Facilities

Rooms: Singles 45% Doubles: 55% Larger: 0%
Library Volumes: 104,000 Acres: 500 Plant:

Other Facts

Newly renovated library (1988) doubled in size; new computer center; Soviet Exchange Program; Addison Gallery of American Art; new crew boathouse.

Locale

½ mile from town center, population 26,000; 25 miles north of Boston; nearby skiing.

Phillips Exeter Academy (Coed)

Founded 1781

Exeter, NH 03833
(603) 772-4311
Airport: Boston, 50 miles

Students

Total: 980 Boys: 541 Girls: 439 Grades: 9-PG
Boarding: 863 Day: 117 Local Students: 12%
Number of States: 44 Countries: 29 Foreign Students: 7%

Costs and Aid

Tuition: $13,500 School Extras: $625
Student Aid Money Awarded: $2,607,650
Number Granted: 31% Avg. Per Student: $8750

Additional Support

Endowment: $120,000,000 Per Student: $122,450
Alumni: 17,625 Annual Gifts: $2,800,000 Giving: 54%

Admission

Largest Grade Entry: 9 Applied: 540
Accepted: 216 Entered: 147
Median Percentile Entering 9th Grade: 87%
Application Deadline: Jan. 31 Remedial Program: No

Academics

Advanced Placement Preparation in All Test Areas
Class Size: 12-13 Student-Teacher Ratio: 8-1
Number of Seniors: 293 Combined SATS: 1255

Facilities

Rooms: Singles 73% Doubles: 27 Larger: 0%
Library Volumes: 125,000 Acres: 140 Plant: 100 Mil

Other Facts

New observatory (1989); drama, music, art buildings; gym with 2 pools; 2 hockey rinks; squash courts; programs in France, Spain, Mexico, Washington, D.C.

Locale

Pop. of Exeter 14,000; 10 minutes from N.H. Seacoast; 1½ hours from White Mountains; one hour from Boston.

Pine Crest School (Coed)

Founded 1934

1501 Northeast 62nd Street, Fort Lauderdale, FL 33334
(305) 492-4103
Airport: Fort Lauderdale, 8 miles

Students

Total: 800 Boys: 400 Girls: 400 Grades: 7-12
Boarding: 130 Day: 670 Local Students: 20%
Number of States: 18 Countries: 20 Foreign Students: 20%

Costs and Aid

Tuition: $11,900 School Extras: $0
Student Aid Money Awarded: $320,000
Number Granted: 14% Avg. Per Student: $3000

Additional Support

Endowment: $2,500,000 Per Student: $2000
Alumni: 3000 Annual Gifts: $1,000,000 Giving: 30%

Admission

Largest Grade Entry: 9 Applied: 97
Accepted: 50 Entered: 39
Median Percentile Entering Grade: %
Application Deadline: rolling Remedial Program: No

Academics

Advanced Placement Preparation in 16 Test Areas
Class Size: 4-24 Student-Teacher Ratio: 14-1
Number of Seniors: 152 Combined SATS: 1160

Facilities

Rooms: Singles 0% Doubles: 65% Larger: 0%
Library Volumes: 37,000 Acres: 47 Plant: 15 Million

Other Facts

Strong academic preparation enriched with variety of fine arts offerings, clubs, and over 50 sports teams including internationally known USS and school swimming and diving teams.

Locale

Fifty minute drive from Miami International Airport; located in residential area; about 10 minute drive from beaches; exceptional fine arts offerings; championship school and USS swim team (year round practice).

Pomfret School (Coed)

Founded 1894

Route 44, Pomfret, CT 06258
(203) 928-7969
Airport: Hartford, 50 miles

Students

Total: 307 Boys: 167 Girls: 140 Grades: 9-12
Boarding: 247 Day: 60 Local Students: 19%
Number of States: 28 Countries: 8 Foreign Students: 4%

Costs and Aid

Tuition: $15,500 School Extras: $400
Student Aid Money Awarded: $550,000
Number Granted: 26% Avg. Per Student: $6,800

Additional Support

Endowment: $10,750,000 Per Student: $35,000
Alumni: 3,100 Annual Gifts: $460,000 Giving: 60%

Admission

Largest Grade Entry: 10 Applied: 287
Accepted: 107 Entered: 59
Median Percentile Entering 10th Grade: 71%
Application Deadline: Feb. 1 Remedial Program: No

Academics

Advanced Placement Preparation in 11 Test Areas
Class Size: 12-15 Student-Teacher Ratio: 8-1
Number of Seniors: 87 Combined SATS: 1080

Facilities

Rooms: Singles 30% Doubles: 65% Larger: 5%
Library Volumes: 19,000 Acres: 500 Plant: 8 M

Other Facts

4 indoor tennis courts; championship basketball, field hockey, lacrosse, tennis and crew teams; new field house and student center in 1982; outstanding arts facility and program.

Locale

4 miles from town center — pop. 2800; multi B & B; 3 motels; 21 miles from U. of Connecticutt; 35 miles from Providence.

Portsmouth Abbey School (Boys)

Founded 1926

Cory's Lane, Portsmouth, Rhode Island 02871
(401) 683-2005
Airport: Providence, 30 miles

Students

Total: 265 Boys: 265 Girls: 0 Grades: 9-12
Boarding: 210 Day: 55 Local Students: 30%
Number of States: 26 Countries: 13 Foreign Students: 10%

Costs and Aid

Tuition: $14,230 School Extras: $700
Student Aid Money Awarded: $440,000
Number Granted: 25% Avg. Per Student: $6,000

Additional Support

Endowment: $9,000,000 Per Student: $34,000
Alumni: 2,000 Annual Gifts: $400,000 Giving: 45%

Admission

Largest Grade Entry: 9 Applied: 150
Accepted: 90 Entered: 60
Median Percentile Entering 10 Grade: 65%
Application Deadline: February 1 Remedial Program: No

Academics

Advanced Placement Preparation in 13 Test Areas
Class Size: 8-12 Student-Teacher Ratio: 8-1
Number of Seniors: 61 Combined SATS: 1110

Facilities

Rooms: Singles 50% Doubles: 50% Larger: 0%
Library Volumes: 25,000 Acres: 500 Plant: 22 M

Other Facts

New library (1989); two gyms (enclosed); hockey rink; squash courts; Roman Catholic; community service program.

Locale

½ mile of frontage on Narragansett Bay; eight miles from Newport; 60 miles from Boston; 30 miles from Providence and Brown University.

The Principia (Coed)

Founded 1898

13201 Clayton Rd., St. Louis, MO 63131
(314) 434-2100
Airport: St. Louis, 10 miles

Students

Total: 355 Boys: 175 Girls: 180 Grades: K-12
Boarding: 210 Day: 145 Local Students: 40%
Number of States: 40 Countries: 12 Foreign Students: 5%

Costs and Aid

Tuition: $11,600 School Extras: $
Student Aid Money Awarded: $1 million
Number Granted: 66% Avg. Per Student: $4000

Additional Support

Endowment: $60 million Per Student: $90,000
Alumni: 13,000 Annual Gifts: $ Giving: %

Admission

Largest Grade Entry: 9 Applied: 128
Accepted: 109 Entered: 40
Median Percentile Entering Grade: %
Application Deadline: Rolling Remedial Program: No

Academics

Advanced Placement Preparation in 5 Test Areas
Class Size: 15-20 Student-Teacher Ratio: 8-1
Number of Seniors: 105 Combined SATS: 1000

Facilities

Rooms: Singles 10% Doubles: 90% Larger: 0%
Library Volumes: 30,000 Acres: 360 Plant: 22 M

Other Facts

Christian Science background required. New computer lab and radio station as well as a TV station. Periodic trips to Tetons, Mexico, and Europe.

Locale

10 miles from downtown. In fine residential urban neighborhood.

Proctor Academy (Coed)
Founded 1848

Andover, NH 03216
(603) 735-5126
Airport: Boston, 100 miles

Students
Total: 285 Boys: 190 Girls: 95 Grades: 9-12
Boarding: 240 Day: 45 Local Students: 16%
Number of States: 28 Countries: 7 Foreign Students: 3%

Costs and Aid
Tuition: $14,900 School Extras: $500-1000
Student Aid Money Awarded: $353,000
Number Granted: 16% Avg. Per Student: $6000

Additional Support
Endowment: $5,375,000 Per Student: $19,000
Alumni: 2400 Annual Gifts: $353,156 Giving: 18%

Admission
Largest Grade Entry: 9/10 Even Applied: 245
Accepted: 137 Entered: 86
Median Percentile Entering 9/10 Grade: 45%
Application Deadline: N/A Remedial Program: N/A

Academics
Advanced Placement Preparation in 8 Test Areas
Class Size: 10-12 Student-Teacher Ratio: 6-1
Number of Seniors: 87 Combined SATS: 900

Facilities
Rooms: Singles 25% Doubles: 75% Larger: 0%
Library Volumes: 15,000 Acres: 2000 Plant: 5 M

Other Facts
Mountain classroom; 9-week Outward Bound Experience for academic credit in History, English, Science; overseas program in Avignon, France and Madrid, Spain.

Locale
1900 pop.; several B & Bs in area; ½ hour from Concord, NH near Lake Sunapee Lakes Region and Ski areas; Blackwater ski area with snow-making capabilities owned and operated by school; enclosed ice hockey rink.

Purnell School (Girls)

Founded 1963

Pottersville, NJ 07979
(701) 439-2154
Airport: Newark, 30 miles

Students

Total: 125 Boys: 0 Girls: 125 Grades: 10-12
Boarding: 125 Day: 0 Local Students: 0%
Number of States: 33 Countries: 10 Foreign Students: 10%

Costs and Aid

Tuition: $15,900 School Extras: $none
Student Aid Money Awarded: $110,000
Number Granted: 10% Avg. Per Student: $9000

Additional Support

Endowment: $3 million Per Student: $24,000
Alumni: Annual Gifts: $180,000 Giving: %

Admission

Largest Grade Entry: 10 Applied: 75
Accepted: 60 Entered: 36
Median Percentile Entering Grade: %
Application Deadline: Rolling Remedial Program: No

Academics

Advanced Placement Preparation in Test Areas
Class Size: 9 Student-Teacher Ratio: 5-1
Number of Seniors: 45 Combined SATS:

Facilities

Rooms: Singles 5% Doubles: 70% Larger: 25%
Library Volumes: 15,000 Acres: 80 Plant: 9 M

Other Facts

200 seat theater; art and computer centers with 20 Apple computers; 140 courses offered. Study programs in Canada and Mexico for seniors.

Locale

Pop. 500; horse farm in country, Somerset Hills; rural setting; 35 miles from Princeton.

Putney School (Coed)

Founded 1935

West Hill, Putney, VT 05346
(802) 387-5566
Airport: Hartford, 95 miles

Students

Total: 130 Boys: 65 Girls: 65 Grades: 9-12
Boarding: 110 Day: 20 Local Students: 20%
Number of States: 75 Countries: 7 Foreign Students: 7%

Costs and Aid

Tuition: $15,500 School Extras: $400
Student Aid Money Awarded: $400,000
Number Granted: 33% Avg. Per Student: $6000

Additional Support

Endowment: $1 million Per Student: $
Alumni: 2500 Annual Gifts: $962,102 Giving: 42%

Admission

Largest Grade Entry: 11th Applied: 123
Accepted: 78 Entered: 50
Median Percentile Entering Grade: %
Application Deadline: Feb. 1 Remedial Program: No

Academics

Advanced Placement Preparation in Test Areas
Class Size: 6 to 13 Student-Teacher Ratio: 6-1
Number of Seniors: 50 Combined SATS: 1010

Facilities

Rooms: Singles 30% Doubles: 70%
Larger: %
Library Volumes: 25,000 Acres: 1000 Plant: 4 Mil

Other Facts

Farm-based school; work program (care for horses, farm products and buildings). World-class cross country skiing.

Locale

Rural southern Vermont hilltop; 2 miles to town (pop. 1850); 9 miles north of Brattleboro.

Rabun Gap — Nacoochee School (Coed)

Founded 1903

Rabun Gap, GA 30568
(404) 746-5736
Airport: Atlanta, 100 miles

Students

Total: 226 Boys: 126 Girls: 100 Grades: 7-12
Boarding: 186 Day: 40 Local Students: 17%
Number of States: 15 Countries: 9 Foreign Students: 10%

Costs and Aid

Tuition: $8000 School Extras: $400
Student Aid Money Awarded: $385,000
Number Granted: 30% Avg. Per Student: $5500

Additional Support

Endowment: $35,800,000 Per Student: $160,000
Alumni: 3,500 Annual Gifts: $500,000 Giving: %

Admission

Largest Grade Entry: 10 Applied: 58
Accepted: 35 Entered: 30
Median Percentile Entering 10th Grade: 60%
Application Deadline: Aug. 1 Remedial Program: No

Academics

Advanced Placement Preparation in N/A Test Areas
Class Size: Avg. 12 Student-Teacher Ratio: 10-1
Number of Seniors: 62 Combined SATS: 890

Facilities

Rooms: Singles 0% Doubles: 100% Larger: 0%
Library Volumes: 9,000 Acres: 1200 Plant: 4.5 Million

Other Facts

Affiliated with Presbyterian Church (USA); work program requires participation of all students, regardless of need; interscholastic sports; outdoor program; ESL; equestrian competition.

Locale

Northeast Georgia mountains (2,200 ft.); 100 miles from Atlanta, 90 miles from Greenville, SC and Asheville, SC.

Robert Louis Stevenson School (Coed)

Founded 1952

Forest Lake Road, Pebble Beach, CA 93953
(408) 624-1257
Airport: Monterey, 7 miles

Students

Total: 505 Boys: 300 Girls: 205 Grades: 9-12
Boarding: 210 Day: 290 Local Students: 60%
Number of States: 15 Countries: 17 Foreign Students: 5%

Costs and Aid

Tuition: $15,500 School Extras: $none
Student Aid Money Awarded: $550,000
Number Granted: 17% Avg. Per Student: $7500

Additional Support

Endowment: $1.5 mil Per Student: $3000
Alumni: 1800 Annual Gifts: $500,000 Giving: %

Admission

Largest Grade Entry: 9 Applied: 195
Accepted: 135 Entered: 105
Median Percentile Entering 9th Grade: 58%
Application Deadline: 3/10 Remedial Program: No

Academics

Advanced Placement Preparation in 12 Test Areas
Class Size: 15 Student-Teacher Ratio: 9-1
Number of Seniors: 130 Combined SATS: 1100

Facilities

Rooms: Singles 25% Doubles: 74% Larger: 1%
Library Volumes: 18,000 Acres: 60 Plant: 40 M

Other Facts

New coed dorms; AFS and ESV Swiss programs; only boarding school in California with football; student operated radio station.

Locale

125 miles south of San Francisco. On Monterey Peninsula; adjoining golf course.

Saint Andrew's School (Coed)

Founded 1962

2707 Northwest 37th St., Boca Raton, FL 33434
(407) 483-8900
Airport: W. Palm Beach, 20 miles

Students

Total: 400 Boys: 202 Girls: 200 Grades: 6-12
Boarding: 87 Day: 313 Local Students: %
Number of States: 15 Countries: 14 Foreign Students: 16%

Costs and Aid

Tuition: $13,000 School Extras: $None
Student Aid Money Awarded: $220,000
Number Granted: 13% Avg. Per Student: $5000

Additional Support

Endowment: $500,000 Per Student: $1200
Alumni: 1600 Annual Gifts: $250,000 Giving: %

Admission

Largest Grade Entry: 9th Applied: 75
Accepted: 52 Entered: 50
Median Percentile Entering 9th Grade: 59%
Application Deadline: rolling Remedial Program: No

Academics

Advanced Placement Preparation in 13 Test Areas
Class Size: 14 Student-Teacher Ratio: 9-1
Number of Seniors: 100 Combined SATS: 1150

Facilities

Rooms: Singles 5% Doubles: 95% Larger: 0%
Library Volumes: 15,000 Acres: 95 Plant: 5 M

Other Facts

Only 1/3 of students from Florida; new library; new classroom — administration bldg. (1989); numerous golf courses nearby.

Locale

Pop. 100,000; 10 minutes from ocean; Mission Bay Aquatic Center.

St. Andrew's School (Coed)

Founded 1930

Middletown, Del 19709
(302) 834-5350
Airport: Philadelphia, 40 miles

Students

Total: 250 Boys: 150 Girls: 100 Grades: 9-12
Boarding: 250 Day: 0 Local Students: 10%
Number of States: 26 Countries: 13 Foreign Students: 6%

Costs and Aid

Tuition: $13,500 School Extras: $700
Student Aid Money Awarded: $950,000
Number Granted: 42% Avg. Per Student: $9,000

Additional Support

Endowment: $50,000,000 Per Student: $200,000
Alumni: 2300 Annual Gifts: $330,000 Giving: 45%

Admission

Largest Grade Entry: 9th Applied: 150
Accepted: 65 Entered: 42
Median Percentile Entering 9th Grade: 78%
Application Deadline: Jan. 31 Remedial Program: None

Academics

Advanced Placement Preparation in 11 Test Areas
Class Size: 12 Student-Teacher Ratio: 7-1
Number of Seniors: 65 Combined SATS: 1230

Facilities

Rooms: Singles 15% Doubles: 70% Larger: 15%
Library Volumes: 28,000 Acres: 2000 Plant: 30 Mil

Other Facts

New boat house and student center (1989); adding girls' soccer in 1989 ASA varsity sport.

Locale

Farming community; 1 mile from town; pop. 3000; 25 minutes from Wilmington and Amtrack; 1¼ hrs from Baltimore; 1 hr. from Philadelphia; 2 hrs. from Washington, D.C.

St. Andrew's — Sewanee School (Coed)

Founded 1981

St. Andrew's, TN 37372
(615) 598-5666
Airport: Chattanooga, 100 miles

Students

Total: 216 Boys: 115 Girls: 101 Grades: 7-12
Boarding: 90 Day: 126 Local Students: 60%
Number of States: 18 Countries: 3 Foreign Students: 5%

Costs and Aid

Tuition: $11,500 School Extras: $650
Student Aid Money Awarded: $196,000
Number Granted: 36% Avg. Per Student: $2500

Additional Support

Endowment: $3.6 mil Per Student: $15,000
Alumni: 5000 Annual Gifts: $300,000 Giving: %

Admission

Largest Grade Entry: 9th Applied: 32
Accepted: 25 Entered: 20
Median Percentile Entering Grade: %
Application Deadline: Rolling Remedial Program: No

Academics

Advanced Placement Preparation in No Test Areas
Class Size: 15 Student-Teacher Ratio: 8-1
Number of Seniors: 38 Combined SATS: 1070

Facilities

Rooms: Singles 16% Doubles: 84% Larger: No%
Library Volumes: 15,000 Acres: 450 Plant: 5 Mil

Other Facts

Very strong in arts (studio art, clay, drama, music); an outstanding outing program; students may take University classes at the University of the South.

Locale

Located on the Cumberland Plateau (2100 ft.elevation) between Chattanooga and Nashville; just 2 miles to University of the South (Sewanee).

St. Catherine's School (Girls)

Founded 1890

6001 Grove Avenue, Richmond, VA 23226
(804) 288-2804
Airport: 15 miles

Students

Total: 288 Boys: 0 Girls: 288 Grades: 9-12
Boarding: 105 Day: 185 Local Students: 64%
Number of States: 17 Countries: 7 Foreign Students: 02%

Costs and Aid

Tuition: $13,420 School Extras: $250
Student Aid Money Awarded: $110,468
Number Granted: 15% Avg. Per Student: $7365

Additional Support

Endowment: $6.8 million Per Student: $24,000
Alumni: 4100 Annual Gifts: $197,000 Giving: 49%

Admission

Largest Grade Entry: 10 Applied: 44
Accepted: 30 Entered: 17
Median Percentile Entering 10 Grade: 50%
Application Deadline: rolling Remedial Program: No

Academics

Advanced Placement Preparation in 14 Test Areas
Class Size: 14 Student-Teacher Ratio: 7-1
Number of Seniors: 97 Combined SATS: 1110

Facilities

Rooms: Singles 16% Doubles: 81% Larger: 03%
Library Volumes: 21,000 Acres: 16 Plant: 10 Mil

Other Facts

Coordinate program; coed classes with brother school, St. Christopher's, 3 blocks away.

Locale

In residential suburban Richmond — pop. 591,000 (219,000 city) — state capitol; many cultural opportunities.

St. George's School (Coed)

Founded 1896

Newport, RI 02840
(401) 847-7565
Airport: Boston, 70 miles

Students

Total: 323 Boys: 179 Girls: 144 Grades: 9-12
Boarding: 285 Day: 38 Local Students: 11%
Number of States: 36 Countries: 16 Foreign Students: 10%

Costs and Aid

Tuition: $15,200 School Extras: $Books, laundry
Student Aid Money Awarded: $640,000
Number Granted: 25% Avg. Per Student: $8000

Additional Support

Endowment: $21,000,000 Per Student: $66,000
Alumni: 2400 Annual Gifts: $693,000 Giving: 52%

Admission

Largest Grade Entry: 9 Applied: 240
Accepted: 90 Entered: 54
Median Percentile Entering 9th Grade: 75%
Application Deadline: February 1 Remedial Program: No

Academics

Advanced Placement Preparation in 13 Test Areas
Class Size: 10-12 Student-Teacher Ratio: 6-1
Number of Seniors: 85 Combined SATS: 1180

Facilities

Rooms: Singles 70% Doubles: 25% Larger: 5%
Library Volumes: 27,000 Acres: 240 Plant: 25 M

Other Facts

Semester at sea aboard school-owned marine research vessel; new fieldhouse includes 4 tennis courts, indoor track, and basketball courts; indoor pool; hockey rink; community service program.

Locale

Overlooks Atlantic Ocean and city of Newport (pop. 35,000); 14 movie theatres; numerous hotels; restaurants; 30 miles from Providence.

St. James School (Boys)

Founded 1842

St. James, MD 21781
(301) 733-9330
Airport: Washington, 60 miles

Students

Total: 155 Boys: 133 Girls: 22 Grades: 8-12
Boarding: 95 Day: 60 Local Students: 40%
Number of States: 15 Countries: 8 Foreign Students: 5%

Costs and Aid

Tuition: $12,500 School Extras: $250 books
Student Aid Money Awarded: $130,000
Number Granted: 15% Avg. Per Student: $5416.66

Additional Support

Endowment: $2.6 million Per Student: $22,580
Alumni: 1366 Annual Gifts: $75,000 Giving: 70%

Admission

Largest Grade Entry: 9th Applied: 25
Accepted: 17 Entered: 16
Median Percentile Entering 9th Grade: 60%
Application Deadline: March 15th Remedial Program: No

Academics

Advanced Placement Preparation in All Test Areas
Class Size: 12 Student-Teacher Ratio: 6-1
Number of Seniors: 42 Combined SATS: 1090

Facilities

Rooms: Singles 50% Doubles: 28% Larger: %
Library Volumes: 15,000 Acres: 155 Plant: 8.2 M

Other Facts

New indoor athletic center (1986); ski program every Wednesday; golf course near campus; Episcopal/English boarding program; trustees chaired by Bishop of Maryland.

Locale

Hamlet of 100, developed around the school; 5 miles south of Hagerstown, MD — 50,000; several hotels; 1 hour, 55 miles from Baltimore and Washington DC, due west.

St. Johnsbury Academy (Coed)

Founded 1842

7 Main Street, St. Johnsbury, VT 05819
(802) 748-8171
Airport: Burlington, 75 miles

Students

Total: 756 Boys: 385 Girls: 371 Grades: 9-PG
Boarding: 124 Day: 632 Local Students: 80%
Number of States: 15 Countries: 13 Foreign Students: 8%

Costs and Aid

Tuition: $13,000 School Extras: $
Student Aid Money Awarded: $125,000
Number Granted: 15% Avg. Per Student: $5000

Additional Support

Endowment: $7,200,000 Per Student: $9,600
Alumni: 7,380 Annual Gifts: $440,000 Giving: %

Admission

Largest Grade Entry: 9 Applied: 201
Accepted: 194 Entered: 194
Median Percentile Entering Grade: %
Application Deadline: rolling Remedial Program: yes

Academics

Advanced Placement Preparation in 10 Test Areas
Class Size: 15 Student-Teacher Ratio: 10-1
Number of Seniors: 160 Combined SATS: 970

Facilities

Rooms: Singles 7% Doubles: 63% Larger: 30%
Library Volumes: 15,000 Acres: 75 Plant: 22,000,000

Other Facts

750 seat theater; art and computer center; comprehensive curriculum for students of varying abilities; new field house (1986) with indoor track and pool.

Locale

Small town (pop. 7000) in the heart of Vermont ski center — three hours from Boston or Montreal; near Dartmouth and University of Vermont.

Saint John's Preparatory School (Boys)

Founded 1856

Collegeville, MN 56321
(612) 363-3317
Airport: Minneapolis/St. Paul, 80 miles

Students

Total: 227 Boys: 159 Girls: 68 Grades: 9-12
Boarding: 106 Day: 121 Local Students: 60%
Number of States: 20 Countries: 8 Foreign Students: 10%

Costs and Aid

Tuition: $9930 School Extras: $500
Student Aid Money Awarded: $210,000
Number Granted: 60% Avg. Per Student: $1800

Additional Support

Endowment: $2,000,000 Per Student: $9000
Alumni: 5000 Annual Gifts: $259,000 Giving: 24%

Admission

Largest Grade Entry: 9th Applied: 100
Accepted: 60 Entered: 45
Median Percentile Entering 9th Grade: 85%
Application Deadline: Rolling Remedial Program: No

Academics

Advanced Placement Preparation in 3 Test Areas
Class Size: 12-20 Student-Teacher Ratio: 12-1
Number of Seniors: 50 Combined SATS: 1000

Facilities

Rooms: Singles 15% Doubles: 85% Larger: 0%
Library Volumes: Acres: 2200 Plant: 2 M

Other Facts

Affiliated with Roman Catholic Church; study abroad in Austria for academic year; college credits available at St. John's University.

Locale

Pop. 100; 15 miles west of St. Cloud; 75 miles NW of Minneapolis. Near university.

St. Margaret's School (Girls)

Founded 1921

444 Water Lane, Tappahannock, VA 22560
(804) 443-3357
Airport: Richmond, 45 miles

Students

Total: 127 Boys: 0 Girls: 127 Grades: 8-12
Boarding: 100 Day: 27 Local Students: 21%
Number of States: 15 Countries: 3 Foreign Students: 3%

Costs and Aid

Tuition: $13,000 School Extras: $600
Student Aid Money Awarded: $118,700
Number Granted: 24% Avg. Per Student: $4000

Additional Support

Endowment: $1.8 million Per Student: $14,000
Alumni: 2,000 Annual Gifts: $260,561 Giving: 43%

Admission

Largest Grade Entry: 10 Applied: 85
Accepted: 74 Entered: 50
Median Percentile Entering 10th Grade: 26%
Application Deadline: Rolling Remedial Program: Some

Academics

Advanced Placement Preparation in 5 Test Areas
Class Size: 9 Student-Teacher Ratio: 6-1
Number of Seniors: 40 Combined SATS: 900

Facilities

Rooms: Singles % Doubles: 100% Larger: %
Library Volumes: 8,000 Acres: 8 Plant: 4 million

Other Facts

The academic resource center; writing lab; the mathematics resource center; honors courses in every discipline; a senior independent study program; sailing on Chesapeake Bay.

Locale

In a small town in the historic Tidewater area with convenient access to Richmond, VA (45 miles), Washington, DC (100 miles), and Williamsburg (50 miles).

Saint Mark's School (Coed)

Founded 1865

Southborough, MA 01772
(508) 485-0050
Airport: Boston, 26 miles

Students

Total: 318 Boys: 186 Girls: 132 Grades: 9-12
Boarding: 271 Day: 47 Local Students: 15%
Number of States: 31 Countries: 11 Foreign Students: 3%

Costs and Aid

Tuition: $15,500 School Extras: $
Student Aid Money Awarded: $600,000
Number Granted: 23% Avg. Per Student: $8000

Additional Support

Endowment: $24,000,000 Per Student: $75,000
Alumni: 3000 Annual Gifts: $700,000 Giving: %

Admission

Largest Grade Entry: 10th Applied: 229
Accepted: 150 Entered: 46
Median Percentile Entering 10th Grade: 77%
Application Deadline: Jan. 31 Remedial Program: No

Academics

Advanced Placement Preparation in 12 Test Areas
Class Size: 8-15 Student-Teacher Ratio: 7-1
Number of Seniors: 90 Combined SATS: 1200

Facilities

Rooms: Singles 20% Doubles: 80% Larger: 0%
Library Volumes: 27,000 Acres: 3000 Plant: 20 Mil

Other Facts

New dorms in 1984; new library (1986); arts center (1988); new sports complex being constructed.

Locale

Pop. 6200; golf course and main street within walking distance; suburban setting; Fay Junior Boarding School nearby.

St. Mary's Academy (Girls)

Founded 1874

Nauvoo, IL 62354
(217) 453-6619
Airport: Burlington, Iowa, 30 miles

Students

Total: 116 Boys: 0 Girls: 116 Grades: 9-12
Boarding: 114 Day: 2 Local Students: 2%
Number of States: 12 Countries: 6 Foreign Students: 23%

Costs and Aid

Tuition: $7850 School Extras: $450
Student Aid Money Awarded: $85,000
Number Granted: 35% Avg. Per Student: $2000

Additional Support

Endowment: $500,000 Per Student: $4000
Alumni: 3000 Annual Gifts: $75,000 Giving: %

Admission

Largest Grade Entry: 10th Applied: 50
Accepted: Entered: 40
Median Percentile Entering Grade: %
Application Deadline: rolling Remedial Program: No

Academics

Advanced Placement Preparation in Test Areas
Class Size: 10 Student-Teacher Ratio: 5-1
Number of Seniors: 34 Combined SATS: 830

Facilities

Rooms: Singles 5% Doubles: 95% Larger: 0%
Library Volumes: 9000 Acres: 17 Plant: 4 Mil

Other Facts

Owned and operated by Benedictine sisters; students 50% Catholic; trip abroad offered in spring; 650 seat auditorium.

Locale

Pop. 1150; 2 blocks from town; overlooks the Mississippi River; 60 miles north of Quincy, IL; rural setting.

Saint Mary's College (Girls)

Founded 1842

900 Hillsborough St., Raleigh, NC 27603-1689
(919) 828-2521
Airport: Raleigh, 12 miles

Students

Total: 157 Boys: 0 Girls: 157 Grades: 10-12
Boarding: 130 Day: 33 Local Students: %
Number of States: 11 Countries: 4 Foreign Students: 3%

Costs and Aid

Tuition: $10,600 School Extras: $
Student Aid Money Awarded: $192,200
Number Granted: 40% Avg. Per Student: $3100

Additional Support

Endowment: $4 Mil Per Student: $10,000
Alumni: 8,500 Annual Gifts: $250,000 Giving: 41%

Admission

Largest Grade Entry: 11th Applied: 85
Accepted: 70 Entered: 53
Median Percentile Entering 10th Grade: 45%
Application Deadline: None Remedial Program: None

Academics

Advanced Placement Preparation in Test Areas
Class Size: 15-17 Student-Teacher Ratio: 14-1
Number of Seniors: 94 Combined SATS: 900

Facilities

Rooms: Singles 30% Doubles: 45% Larger: 25%
Library Volumes: 38,109 Acres: 23 Plant: 12 Mil

Other Facts

Shakespeare Abroad Program; accelerated program for seniors to receive one year college credit; affiliated with Episcopal Church.

Locale

Pop. 150,000; near downtown and North Carolina State; operated in conjunction with junior college.

Saint Mary's Hall (Coed)

Founded 1879

9401 Starcrest Drive, San Antonio, TX 78265
(512) 655-7721
Airport: San Antonio, 3 miles

Students

Total: 177 Boys: 29 Girls: 148 Grades: K-12
Boarding: 75 Day: 102 Local Students: %
Number of States: 10 Countries: 5 Foreign Students: %

Costs and Aid

Tuition: $12,680 School Extras: $600
Student Aid Money Awarded: $225,000
Number Granted: 40% Avg. Per Student: $3,000

Additional Support

Endowment: $6.5 mil Per Student: $10,000
Alumni: 2500 Annual Gifts: $ Giving: %

Admission

Largest Grade Entry: 9th Applied:
Accepted: Entered: 54
Median Percentile Entering Grade: %
Application Deadline: Rolling Remedial Program: No

Academics

Advanced Placement Preparation in 8 Test Areas
Class Size: 14 Student-Teacher Ratio:
Number of Seniors: 46 Combined SATS: 1060

Facilities

Rooms: Singles 0% Doubles: 100% Larger: 0%
Library Volumes: 20,000 Acres: 55 Plant: 15 Mil

Other Facts

Became coed in 1987; new fine arts facility and gymnasium.

Locale

10 minutes to downtown; in residential suburbs; near five universities.

St. Mary's Preparatory School (Boys)

Founded 1886

Indian Trail, Orchard Lake, MI 48033
(313) 682-1885
Airport: Detroit, 30 miles

Students

Total: 185 Boys: 185 Girls: 0 Grades: 9-12
Boarding: 95 Day: 90 Local Students: %
Number of States: 8 Countries: 2 Foreign Students: 0%

Costs and Aid

Tuition: $5,500 School Extras: $400
Student Aid Money Awarded: $40,000
Number Granted: 15% Avg. Per Student: $

Additional Support

Endowment: $ Per Student: $
Alumni: Annual Gifts: $ Giving: %

Admission

Largest Grade Entry: 9th Applied: 48
Accepted: 48 Entered: 48
Median Percentile Entering Grade: %
Application Deadline: rolling Remedial Program: No

Academics

Advanced Placement Preparation in 2 Test Areas
Class Size: 15 Student-Teacher Ratio: 15-1
Number of Seniors: 47 Combined SATS: 1000

Facilities

Rooms: Singles 0% Doubles: 100% Larger: 0%
Library Volumes: Acres: 120 Plant:

Other Facts

Affiliated with Roman Catholic Church; interscholastic and intramural crew and rugby sports.

Locale

Pop. 1800; suburban area.

St. Paul's School (Coed)

Founded 1856

325 Pleasant St., Concord, NH 03301
(603) 225-3341
Airport: Boston, 70 miles

Students

Total: 499 Boys: 289 Girls: 210 Grades: 9-12
Boarding: 499 Day: 0 Local Students: 8%
Number of States: 40 Countries: 14 Foreign Students: 8%

Costs and Aid

Tuition: $13,500 School Extras: $None
Student Aid Money Awarded: $1.3 mil
Number Granted: 30% Avg. Per Student: $9000

Additional Support

Endowment: $135 mil Per Student: $270,000
Alumni: 6500 Annual Gifts: $1 mil Giving: %

Admission

Largest Grade Entry: 9th Applied: 600
Accepted: 90 Entered: 80
Median Percentile Entering 9th Grade: 85%
Application Deadline: Jan. 31 Remedial Program: No

Academics

Advanced Placement Preparation in 13 Test Areas
Class Size: 12 Student-Teacher Ratio: 6-1
Number of Seniors: 135 Combined SATS: N/A

Facilities

Rooms: Singles 40% Doubles: 60% Larger: 0%
Library Volumes: 60,000 Acres: 1800 Plant: 18 M

Other Facts

New enlarged library opening in 1990; 3 new indoor tennis courts; school year abroad program for 11th graders.

Locale

2 miles from downtown; capital city; pop. 30,000; campus encompasses ponds and extensive woodlands.

St. Scholastica Academy (Girls)

Founded 1889

615 Pike Ave., Canon City, CO 81212
(719) 275-7461
Airport: Colorado Springs, 50 miles

Students

Total: 110 Boys: 0 Girls: 110 Grades: 7-12
Boarding: 95 Day: 15 Local Students: 11%
Number of States: 13 Countries: 6 Foreign Students: 47%

Costs and Aid

Tuition: $7800 School Extras: $550
Student Aid Money Awarded: $12,000
Number Granted: 8% Avg. Per Student: $1000

Additional Support

Endowment: $ Per Student: $
Alumni: Annual Gifts: $ Giving: %

Admission

Largest Grade Entry: 9th Applied: 19
Accepted: 13 Entered: 13
Median Percentile Entering Grade: NA%
Application Deadline: 12/10 Remedial Program: No

Academics

Advanced Placement Preparation in Test Areas
Class Size: 16-18 Student-Teacher Ratio: 7-1
Number of Seniors: 12 Combined SATS: 900

Facilities

Rooms: Singles % Doubles: 56% Larger: %
Library Volumes: 10,000 Acres: 4 Plant:

Other Facts

In H.S. — intensive learning program; modular block system; Catholic school; fine arts emphasized; skiing; large swimming pool; new Learning Center/Theater, Gymnasium and Chapel/Library complex since 1979.

Locale

Canon City, Colorado; residential area of; pop. 13,000; mild climate; 50 miles from Colorado Springs; 45 miles from Pueblo; 115 miles so. west of Denver area; near famous Royal Gorge Bridge.

St. Stephen's Episcopal School (Coed)

Founded 1950

Austin, TX 78767
(512) 327-1213
Airport: Austin, 20 miles

Students

Total: 275 Boys: 140 Girls: 135 Grades: 7-12
Boarding: 132 Day: 151 Local Students: 12%
Number of States: 10 Countries: 19 Foreign Students: 11%

Costs and Aid

Tuition: $12,470 School Extras: $None
Student Aid Money Awarded: $300,000
Number Granted: 15% Avg. Per Student: $6000

Additional Support

Endowment: $2 mil Per Student: $7000
Alumni: 1800 Annual Gifts: $N/A Giving: %

Admission

Largest Grade Entry: 9th Applied: 75
Accepted: 55 Entered: 38
Median Percentile Entering 9th Grade: 64%
Application Deadline: rolling Remedial Program: No

Academics

Advanced Placement Preparation in 8 Test Areas
Class Size: 14 Student-Teacher Ratio: 7-1
Number of Seniors: 75 Combined SATS: 1130

Facilities

Rooms: Singles 5% Doubles: 95% Larger: 0%
Library Volumes: 16,000 Acres: 400 Plant: 5.5 M

Other Facts

Trip to Spain or France by language students; 6 weeks in summer school with school credit.

Locale

20 minutes from downtown; Austin 350,000 pop.; U. of Texas campus 20 minutes away.

St. Timothy's School (Girls)
Founded 1882

Stevenson, MD 21153
(301) 486-7400
Airport: Baltimore, 22 miles

Students
Total: 119 Boys: NA Girls: 119 Grades: 9-12
Boarding: 100 Day: 21 Local Students: %
Number of States: 22 Countries: 10 Foreign Students: 8%

Costs and Aid
Tuition: $14,900 School Extras: $325
Student Aid Money Awarded: $180,000
Number Granted: 25% Avg. Per Student: $6500

Additional Support
Endowment: $6.5 million Per Student: $50,000
Alumni: 3000 Annual Gifts: $338,429 Giving: 56%

Admission
Largest Grade Entry: 9 Applied: 43
Accepted: 32 Entered: 16
Median Percentile Entering 9th Grade: 56%
Application Deadline: Rolling Remedial Program: No

Academics
Advanced Placement Preparation in 6 Test Areas
Class Size: 10 Student-Teacher Ratio: 5-1
Number of Seniors: 39 Combined SATS: 1065

Facilities
Rooms: Singles 0% Doubles: 75% Larger: 25%
Library Volumes: 20,000 Acres: 234 Plant: 6.6 Mil

Other Facts
Indoor riding facilities; excellent arts facility and program; student school in England.

Locale
23 acre campus located 10 miles north of Baltimore and one hour from Washington.

Salem Academy (Girls)

Founded 1772

500 Salem Ave., Winston-Salem, NC 27108
(919) 721-2644
Airport: Greensboro, 25 miles

Students

Total: 170 Boys: 0 Girls: 170 Grades: 9-12
Boarding: 109 Day: 61 Local Students: 36%
Number of States: 13 Countries: 7 Foreign Students: 4%

Costs and Aid

Tuition: $13,600 School Extras: $300
Student Aid Money Awarded: $99,000
Number Granted: 20% Avg. Per Student: $4613

Additional Support

Endowment: $1.5 mil Per Student: $8823
Alumni: 2000 Annual Gifts: $63,500 Giving: 36%

Admission

Largest Grade Entry: 9 Applied: 42
Accepted: 33 Entered: 24
Median Percentile Entering 9th Grade: 50%
Application Deadline: Rolling Remedial Program: No

Academics

Advanced Placement Preparation in 7 Test Areas
Class Size: 10-12 Student-Teacher Ratio: 8-1
Number of Seniors: 55 Combined SATS: 1070

Facilities

Rooms: Singles 17% Doubles: 77% Larger: 6%
Library Volumes: 21,000 Acres: 57 Plant: 6 M

Other Facts

January term program; 2 year Latin req.; shares campus with Salem College; affiliated with Moravian Church.

Locale

Restored 18th Cent. village within culturally rich Winston-Salem, pop. 130,000; near Wake Forest College.

Salisbury School (Boys)
Founded 1901

Salisbury, CT 06068
(203) 435-2531
Airport: Hartford, 45 miles

Students
Total: 230 Boys: 230 Girls: 0 Grades: 9-12
Boarding: 217 Day: 13 Local Students: %
Number of States: 31 Countries: 11 Foreign Students: 11%

Costs and Aid
Tuition: $15,500 School Extras: $400
Student Aid Money Awarded: $400,000
Number Granted: 22% Avg. Per Student: $8000

Additional Support
Endowment: $4,500,000 Per Student: $19,000
Alumni: 2200 Annual Gifts: $412,000 Giving: 37%

Admission
Largest Grade Entry: 10 Applied: 150
Accepted: 70 Entered: 37
Median Percentile Entering Grade: 65%
Application Deadline: Feb. 1st Remedial Program: No

Academics
Advanced Placement Preparation in 8 Test Areas
Class Size: 12 Student-Teacher Ratio: 7-1
Number of Seniors: 75 Combined SATS: 1100

Facilities
Rooms: Singles 30% Doubles: 70% Larger: 0%
Library Volumes: 19,000 Acres: 520 Plant: 13,000,000

Other Facts
Harris Science Center (1978); new facilities; Olympic size hockey rink; dining hall; dormitory renovation.

Locale
1000 ft.elevation; situated on hilltop — overlooks Berkshire Mtns.; 520 acres owned by school, including lake-front property in village — pop. 4000

San Domenico School (Girls)

Founded 1850

1500 Butterfield Rd., San Anselmo, CA 94960
(415) 454-0200
Airport: San Francisco, 25 miles

Students

Total: 160 Boys: None Girls: 160 Grades: 9-12
Boarding: 80 Day: 80 Local Students: 14%
Number of States: 6 Countries: 7 Foreign Students: 14%

Costs and Aid

Tuition: $14,500 School Extras: $425
Student Aid Money Awarded: $270,000
Number Granted: 25% Avg. Per Student: $4000

Additional Support

Endowment: $none Per Student: $
Alumni: 3000 Annual Gifts: $ Giving: 25%

Admission

Largest Grade Entry: 9 Applied: 150
Accepted: 60 Entered: 30
Median Percentile Entering 9th Grade: 65%
Application Deadline: rolling Remedial Program: No

Academics

Advanced Placement Preparation in 7 Test Areas
Class Size: 10 Student-Teacher Ratio: 8-1
Number of Seniors: 45 Combined SATS: 1020

Facilities

Rooms: Singles 35% Doubles: 65% Larger: 0%
Library Volumes: 12,000 Acres: 500 Plant: 14 Mil

Other Facts

New 2 million-dollar library (1987); extensive music program; stables; covered arena on campus; 50% are Roman Catholic.

Locale

Pop. 3000; suburban location; 20 miles west of Berkeley.

San Marcos Baptist Academy (Coed)

Founded 1907

San Marcos, TX 78666-9406
(512) 353-2400
Airport: Austin, 30 miles

Students

Total: 270 Boys: 177 Girls: 93 Grades: 6-12
Boarding: 250 Day: 20 Local Students: 8%
Number of States: 9 Countries: 11 Foreign Students: 18%

Costs and Aid

Tuition: $9800 School Extras: $750
Student Aid Money Awarded: $150,000
Number Granted: 17% Avg. Per Student: $3300

Additional Support

Endowment: $1,800,000 Per Student: $6500
Alumni: 4300 Annual Gifts: $ Giving: %

Admission

Largest Grade Entry: 10 Applied: 38
Accepted: 30 Entered: 28
Median Percentile Entering Grade: 45%
Application Deadline: Sept. 1 Remedial Program: Yes

Academics

Advanced Placement Preparation in Test Areas
Class Size: Av. 12 Student-Teacher Ratio: 9-1
Number of Seniors: 76 Combined SATS: 783

Facilities

Rooms: Singles 0% Doubles: 100% Larger: 0%
Library Volumes: 16,000 Acres: 200 Plant: Assets 18 Mil

Other Facts

New campus occupied in Dec. 1982; indoor swimming pool; indoor rifle range; junior ROTC program required for boys in grades 9-12; Christian school accepting of all faiths.

Locale

School located about midway between Austin and San Antonio; 2 miles from San Marcos (pop. 25,000); Southwest Texas State University is located in San Marcos (alma mater of Lyndon Johnson).

Santa Catalina School (Girls)

Founded 1950

1500 Mark Thomas Dr., Monterey, CA 93940
(408) 649-1432
Airport: San Francisco, 117 miles

Students

Total: 241 Boys: 0 Girls: 241 Grades: 9-12
Boarding: Day: Local Students: 33%
Number of States: 13 Countries: 11 Foreign Students: 16%

Costs and Aid

Tuition: $15,000 School Extras: $
Student Aid Money Awarded: $238,375
Number Granted: 20% Avg. Per Student: $5,500

Additional Support

Endowment: $1,000,000 Per Student: $4000
Alumni: 2000 Annual Gifts: $60,014 Giving: 17%

Admission

Largest Grade Entry: 9 Applied: 172
Accepted: 123 Entered: 96
Median Percentile Entering 9th Grade: 70%
Application Deadline: rolling **Remedial Program: No**

Academics

Advanced Placement Preparation in 10 Test Areas
Class Size: 15 Student-Teacher Ratio: 7-1
Number of Seniors: 63 Combined SATS: N/A

Facilities

Rooms: Singles 0% Doubles: 100% Larger: 0%
Library Volumes: 22,537 Acres: 36 Plant:

Other Facts

Gymnasium complex under construction; professional theatre facility; Roman Catholic School; frequent visits to San Francisco and Stanford area.

Locale

Located on Monterey Peninsula; town pop. 30,000; 5 minutes from Carmel/ Pebble Beach; 15 minutes from Pt. Lobos and other outdoor recreation.

Shattuck - St. Mary's School (Coed)

Founded 1858

P.O. Box 218, Faribault, Minnesota 55021
(507) 332-7527 / (507) 334-6466
Airport: Minneapolis - St. Paul, 45 miles

Students

Total: 154 Boys: 82 Girls: 72 Grades: 7-12
Boarding: 135 Day: 19 Local Students: 12%
Number of States: 23 Countries: 10 Foreign Students: 6%

Costs and Aid

Tuition: $13,500 School Extras: $
Student Aid Money Awarded: $360,000
Number Granted: 42% Avg. Per Student: $5900

Additional Support

Endowment: $10,000,000 Per Student: $62,000
Alumni: 5000 Annual Gifts: $281,000 Giving: 36%

Admission

Largest Grade Entry: 9 Applied: 97
Accepted: 80 Entered: 62
Median Percentile Entering 9th Grade: %
Application Deadline: rolling Remedial Program: None

Academics

Advanced Placement Preparation in 8 Test Areas
Class Size: 7-14 Student-Teacher Ratio: 7-1
Number of Seniors: 33 Combined SATS: 1031

Facilities

Rooms: Singles 20% Doubles: 75% Larger: 5%
Library Volumes: 20,000 Acres: 250 Plant: 31 Million

Other Facts

One of the most complete athletic complexes in Minnesota; indoor ice arena; 9 hole golf course; 2 private lakefront properties.

Locale

50 miles south of Minneapolis/St. Paul; located in Faribault, Minnesota. Entire campus listed on the Nat'l Register of Historic Places.

South Kent School (Boys)

Founded 1923

South Kent, CT 06785
(203) 927-3530
Airport: Hartford, 45 miles

Students

Total: 150 Boys: 150 Girls: 0 Grades: 9-12
Boarding: 150 Day: 0 Local Students: %
Number of States: 18 Countries: 7 Foreign Students: 8%

Costs and Aid

Tuition: $14,500 School Extras: $370
Student Aid Money Awarded: $240,000
Number Granted: 24% Avg. Per Student: $7500

Additional Support

Endowment: $2 mil Per Student: $19,000
Alumni: 1650 Annual Gifts: $350,000 Giving: %

Admission

Largest Grade Entry: 10th Applied: 120
Accepted: 80 Entered: 40
Median Percentile Entering Grade: 45%
Application Deadline: rolling Remedial Program: No

Academics

Advanced Placement Preparation in 4 Test Areas
Class Size: 8 Student-Teacher Ratio: 6-1
Number of Seniors: 48 Combined SATS: 1050

Facilities

Rooms: Singles 10% Doubles: 60% Larger: 30%
Library Volumes: 27,000 Acres: 600 Plant:

Other Facts

Newly covered hockey rink; new gymnasium; radio station; job program applies to all students; trips abroad; skiing within 30 minutes.

Locale

Northwestern Connecticut/Housatonic River Valley; 4 miles from Kent — pop. 2500. Foothills of the Berkshires.

Southwestern Academy (Coed)

Founded 1924

2800 Monterey Road, San Marino, CA 91108
(818) 799-5010
Airport: Los Angeles, 10 miles

Students

Total: 125 Boys: 99 Girls: 26 Grades: 1-12
Boarding: 91 Day: 34 Local Students: 10%
Number of States: 20 Countries: 34 Foreign Students: 50%

Costs and Aid

Tuition: $13,900 School Extras: $500
Student Aid Money Awarded: $225,000
Number Granted: 42% Avg. Per Student: $5000

Additional Support

Endowment: $1.8 M Per Student: $
Alumni: 3300 Annual Gifts: $165,000 Giving: %

Admission

Largest Grade Entry: 9th Applied: 31
Accepted: 13 Entered: 13
Median Percentile Entering Grade: %
Application Deadline: rolling Remedial Program: No

Academics

Advanced Placement Preparation in 4 Test Areas
Class Size: 10-12 Student-Teacher Ratio: 5-1
Number of Seniors: 22 Combined SATS:

Facilities

Rooms: Singles 0% Doubles: 100% Larger: 0%
Library Volumes: 12,800 Acres: 135 Plant: 7 M

Other Facts

Separate school-owned 180 acre ranch in Arizona for week-long study trips; highly international student body.

Locale

In fine residential suburb of L.A. right next to Pasadena; second campus in northern Arizona.

Stoneleigh-Burnham School (Girls)

Founded 1869

Greenfield, MA 01301
(413) 774-2711
Airport: Hartford, 65 miles

Students

Total: 183 Boys: 0 Girls: 183 Grades: 9-PG
Boarding: 162 Day: 21 Local Students: 12%
Number of States: 29 Countries: 14 Foreign Students: 33%

Costs and Aid

Tuition: $14,300 School Extras: $500
Student Aid Money Awarded: $237,057
Number Granted: 21% Avg. Per Student: $6000

Additional Support

Endowment: $900,000 Per Student: $4,900
Alumni: 3600 Annual Gifts: $5400 Giving: 20%

Admission

Largest Grade Entry: 11 Applied: 41
Accepted: 36 Entered: 23
Median Percentile Entering Grade: N/A%
Application Deadline: rolling Remedial Program:

Academics

Advanced Placement Preparation in 6 Test Areas
Class Size: 10-15 Student-Teacher Ratio: 8-1
Number of Seniors: 65 Combined SATS: 900

Facilities

Rooms: Singles 30% Doubles: 70% Larger: .1%
Library Volumes: 10,000 Acres: 100 Plant: 4.5 M

Other Facts

A.P. courses; debate club; intersession program; riding; dance; 18-hole golf course; art gallery and student art center.

Locale

Located in five-college area; 2 miles from city (pop. 18,000) in rural setting.

The Stony Brook School (Coed)

Founded 1922

Route 25A, Stony Brook, NY 11790
(516) 751-1800
Airport: JFK/LaGuardia, 50 miles

Students

Total: 349 Boys: 187 Girls: 162 Grades: 7-12
Boarding: 181 Day: 168 Local Students: 48%
Number of States: 28 Countries: 14 Foreign Students: 22%

Costs and Aid

Tuition: $12,900 School Extras: $125
Student Aid Money Awarded: $592,900
Number Granted: 31% Avg. Per Student: $5489

Additional Support

Endowment: $6,250,000 Per Student: $20,000
Alumni: 2500 Annual Gifts: $700,000 Giving: 35%

Admission

Largest Grade Entry: 9 Applied: 294
Accepted: 179 Entered: 142
Median Percentile Entering 9th Grade: 44%
Application Deadline: rolling Remedial Program: no

Academics

Advanced Placement Preparation in 8 Test Areas
Class Size: 15 Student-Teacher Ratio: 10-1
Number of Seniors: 81 Combined SATS: 1039

Facilities

Rooms: Singles 3% Doubles: 94% Larger: 3%
Library Volumes: 14,100 Acres: 50 Plant: 20 M

Other Facts

Advanced Placement courses offered; trips abroad — 3; T.A.S., Art Guild; Choir Chamber Singers; interscholastic sports; new lacrosse field; indoor pool; new tennis courts; new classroom and library (1983).

Locale

1 mile from village of Stony Brook, pop. 6500; 50 miles east of New York City.

Storm King School (Coed)

Founded 1867

314 Mountain Rd., Cornwall-on-Hudson, NY 12520
(914) 534-7892
Airport: Newark, 65 miles

Students

Total: 135 Boys: 90 Girls: 45 Grades: 9-PG
Boarding: 125 Day: 10 Local Students: 7%
Number of States: 19 Countries: 8 Foreign Students: 8%

Costs and Aid

Tuition: $14,950 School Extras: $None
Student Aid Money Awarded: $250,000
Number Granted: 24% Avg. Per Student: $9000

Additional Support

Endowment: $2.5 mil Per Student: $18,000
Alumni: Annual Gifts: $90,000 Giving: %

Admission

Largest Grade Entry: 11 Applied: 65
Accepted: 45 Entered: 36
Median Percentile Entering Grade: %
Application Deadline: rolling Remedial Program: yes

Academics

Advanced Placement Preparation in 4 Test Areas
Class Size: 10 Student-Teacher Ratio: 7-1
Number of Seniors: 43 Combined SATS: 910

Facilities

Rooms: Singles 10% Doubles: 90% Larger: 0%
Library Volumes: 25,000 Acres: 65 Plant: 4 Mil

Other Facts

350 seat theater; professional programs directed by Broadway producer; wilderness program.

Locale

Pop. 30,000; 4 miles from downtown; on bluff overlooking Hudson River.

Stuart Hall (Girls)

Founded 1844

Box 210, Staunton, VA 24401
(703) 885-0356
Airport: Shenandoah Valley, 15 miles

Students

Total: 105 Boys: None Girls: 105 Grades: 8-12
Boarding: 91 Day: 14 Local Students: %
Number of States: 23 Countries: 7 Foreign Students: 12%

Costs and Aid

Tuition: $12,500 School Extras: $None
Student Aid Money Awarded: $100,000
Number Granted: % Avg. Per Student: $4500

Additional Support

Endowment: $1.4 mil Per Student: $14,000
Alumni: 2400 Annual Gifts: $150,000 Giving: %

Admission

Largest Grade Entry: 10th Applied:
Accepted: Entered:
Median Percentile Entering Grade: 5%
Application Deadline: rolling Remedial Program: No

Academics

Advanced Placement Preparation in 5 Test Areas
Class Size: 8-12 Student-Teacher Ratio: 7-1
Number of Seniors: 33 Combined SATS: 930

Facilities

Rooms: Singles 30% Doubles: 70% Larger: 0%
Library Volumes: 12,000 Acres: 8 Plant: 6 Mil

Other Facts

New one-million-dollar library opening in 1990; Stuart Scholars program abroad; affiliated with Episcopal Church.

Locale

Pop. 22,000; located right in town; 40 minutes from Charlottesville.

Suffield Academy (Coed)

Founded 1833

Suffield, CT 06078
(203) 668-7315
Airport: Hartford, 5 miles

Students

Total: 332 Boys: 191 Girls: 141 Grades: 9-PG
Boarding: 220 Day: 112 Local Students: 35%
Number of States: 23 Countries: 17 Foreign Students: 12%

Costs and Aid

Tuition: $14,800 School Extras: $500
Student Aid Money Awarded: $574,070
Number Granted: 23% Avg. Per Student: $7,176

Additional Support

Endowment: $8,902,184 Per Student: $25,882
Alumni: 3000 Annual Gifts: $250,000 Giving: %

Admission

Largest Grade Entry: 10 Applied: 250
Accepted: 118 Entered: 38
Median Percentile Entering 10 Grade: 55%
Application Deadline: Feb. 15th Remedial Program:

Academics

Advanced Placement Preparation in 10 Test Areas
Class Size: 13 Student-Teacher Ratio: 7-1
Number of Seniors: 119 Combined SATS: N/A

Facilities

Rooms: Singles 2% Doubles: 96% Larger: 2%
Library Volumes: 29,000 Acres: 300 Plant: 11 M

Other Facts

New performing arts center (1989); new computer center (25 Macs, 3 laser printers).

Locale

2 blocks from center of town — pop. 10,000; 10 miles from Springfield; 1½ hours from Boston.

Tabor Academy (Coed)

Founded 1876

Front St., Marion, MA 02738
(508) 748-2000
Airport: Providence, RI, 50 miles

Students

Total: 500 Boys: 300 Girls: 200 Grades: 9-12
Boarding: 340 Day: 160 Local Students: %
Number of States: 27 Countries: 11 Foreign Students: 8%

Costs and Aid

Tuition: $14,800 School Extras: $350
Student Aid Money Awarded: $800,000
Number Granted: 25% Avg. Per Student: $8000

Additional Support

Endowment: $8,000,000 Per Student: $16,000
Alumni: 6500 Annual Gifts: $400,000 Giving: 40%

Admission

Largest Grade Entry: 9 Applied: 300
Accepted: 185 Entered: 84
Median Percentile Entering 9 Grade: 61%
Application Deadline: Jan. 31 Remedial Program: No

Academics

Advanced Placement Preparation in 12 Test Areas
Class Size: 12-15 Student-Teacher Ratio: 8-1
Number of Seniors: 140 Combined SATS: 1120

Facilities

Rooms: Singles 25% Doubles: 75% Larger: 0%
Library Volumes: 20,000 Acres: 80 Plant: 23 Mil

Other Facts

Located right on Buzzard's Bay. Extensive sailing program; performing arts center completed in 1989.

Locale

Located in the center of a small village — pop. 4000; one hour south of Boston; 2000 feet of waterfront on harbor.

The Taft School (Coed)

Founded 1890

Watertown, CT 06795
(203) 274-2516
Airport: Hartford, 45 miles

Students

Total: 543 Boys: 311 Girls: 232 Grades: 9-PG
Boarding: 430 Day: 113 Local Students: %
Number of States: 38 Countries: 21 Foreign Students: 6%

Costs and Aid

Tuition: $14,300 School Extras: $200 (general fee)
Student Aid Money Awarded: $955,650
Number Granted: 25% Avg. Per Student: $7585

Additional Support

Endowment: $34,679,539 Per Student: $65,000
Alumni: 5866 Annual Gifts: $1,350,000 Giving: 50%

Admission

Largest Grade Entry: 9/10 Applied: 850
Accepted: 350 Entered: 173
Median Percentile Entering 78 Grade: 84%
Application Deadline: Feb. 1 Remedial Program: None

Academics

Advanced Placement Preparation in 20 Test Areas
Class Size: 12 Student-Teacher Ratio: 8-1
Number of Seniors: 149 Combined SATS: 1205

Facilities

Rooms: Singles 25% Doubles: 75% Larger: 0%
Library Volumes: 50,000 Acres: 200+ Plant: 36 Million

Other Facts

Arts and Humanity Center; 70th Anniversary Science Center; Hulbert Taft Junior Library; two theatres; Farwell Computer Center; two field houses; eighteen hole golf course; indoor ice hockey arena.

Locale

Walking distance of town — pop. 20,000; suburban location; 30 miles from New Haven; 90 miles from NYC.

Thacher School (Coed)

Founded 1889

5025 Thacher Road, Ojai, CA 93023
(805) 646-4377
Airport: Santa Barbara, 60 miles

Students

Total: 228 Boys: 120 Girls: 108 Grades: 9-12
Boarding: 204 Day: 24 Local Students: 10%
Number of States: 15 Countries: 13 Foreign Students: 8%

Costs and Aid

Tuition: $15,350 School Extras: $750
Student Aid Money Awarded: $366,900
Number Granted: 20% Avg. Per Student: $8700

Additional Support

Endowment: $12,000,000 Per Student: $52,000
Alumni: 2150 Annual Gifts: $520,000 Giving: 59%

Admission

Largest Grade Entry: 9th Applied: 224
Accepted: 115 Entered: 70
Median Percentile Entering 9th Grade: 76%
Application Deadline: Feb. 1 Remedial Program: No

Academics

Advanced Placement Preparation in 13 Test Areas
Class Size: 11 Student-Teacher Ratio: 5-1
Number of Seniors: 55 Combined SATS: 1200 (Median)

Facilities

Rooms: Singles 65% Doubles: 35% Larger: 0%
Library Volumes: 30,000 Acres: 400 Plant: 16 Mil

Other Facts

1 million dollar expansion of library; extensive riding facilities; outdoor theater; radio station; Spanish ranch architecture.

Locale

Southern California mountains of Los Padres; National Forest abuts school property; 10 miles to coast.

Tilton School (Coed)

Founded 1845

School Street, Tilton, NH 03276
(603) 286-4342
Airport: Boston, 76 miles

Students

Total: 228 Boys: 147 Girls: 81 Grades: 9-PG
Boarding: 176 Day: 52 Local Students: 30%
Number of States: 25 Countries: 7 Foreign Students: 3%

Costs and Aid

Tuition: $14,500 School Extras: $400
Student Aid Money Awarded: $350,000
Number Granted: 24% Avg. Per Student: $6500

Additional Support

Endowment: $3.7 mil Per Student: $16,228
Alumni: 5,200 Annual Gifts: $194,494 Giving: 20%

Admission

Largest Grade Entry: 11th Applied: 67
Accepted: 39 Entered: 20
Median Percentile Entering 11th Grade: N/A%
Application Deadline: rolling Remedial Program: yes

Academics

Advanced Placement Preparation in 4 Test Areas
Class Size: 8-12 Student-Teacher Ratio: 7-1
Number of Seniors: 88 Combined SATS: 950

Facilities

Rooms: Singles 28% Doubles: 72% Larger: 0%
Library Volumes: 14,100 Acres: 140 Plant: 7 Million

Other Facts

New girls dorm (Sept. 1988); Plus 5 program; learning center; renovation and expansion of library (1989); computer center.

Locale

Foothills of White Mountains; 20 miles north of Concord; Center of Tilton — pop. 3400.

Trinity-Pawling School (Boys)

Founded 1907

161 Rt. 22, Pawling, NY 12564
(914) 855-3100
Airport: Hartford, 65 miles

Students

Total: 298 Boys: 298 Girls: 0 Grades: 9-12
Boarding: 280 Day: 18 Local Students: 7%
Number of States: 18 Countries: 3 Foreign Students: 1%

Costs and Aid

Tuition: $14,900 School Extras: $None
Student Aid Money Awarded: $293,550
Number Granted: 17% Avg. Per Student: $5756

Additional Support

Endowment: $43,000,00 Per Student: $14,300
Alumni: 2500 Annual Gifts: $230,000 Giving: 35%

Admission

Largest Grade Entry: 9th/46 Applied: 104
Accepted: 76 Entered: 46
Median Percentile Entering Grade: 45%
Application Deadline: rolling Remedial Program: 20%

Academics

Advanced Placement Preparation in 12 Test Areas
Class Size: 15 Student-Teacher Ratio: 8-1
Number of Seniors: 88 Combined SATS: N/A

Facilities

Rooms: Singles 2% Doubles: 97% Larger: 1%
Library Volumes: 16,000 Acres: 143 Plant: 16 Million

Other Facts

New dorms and science center; language retraining program for dyslexia, limited to 50 students, 9th and 10th grades only.

Locale

Pop. 3000; rural setting; school ½ mile from train station to NYC (62 miles).

United World College (Coed)

Founded 1982

Box 248, Montezuma, NM 87731
(505) 454-1461
Airport: Albuquerque, NM, 126 miles

Students

Total: 200 Boys: 100 Girls: 100 Grades: 11 & 12
Boarding: 200 Day: Local Students: %
Number of States: 15 Countries: 67 Foreign Students: 70%

Costs and Aid

Tuition: $11,000 School Extras: $500
Student Aid Money Awarded: $330,000
Number Granted: 50% Avg. Per Student: $5,500

Additional Support

Endowment: $15,000,000 Per Student: $75,000
Alumni: Annual Gifts: $ Giving: %

Admission

Largest Grade Entry: 11 Applied: 150
Accepted: 26 Entered: 26
Median Percentile Entering Grade: %
Application Deadline: Feb. 1 Remedial Program: No

Academics

Advanced Placement Preparation in Test Areas
Class Size: Student-Teacher Ratio: 12-1
Number of Seniors: Combined SATS: 1140

Facilities

Rooms: Singles 0% Doubles: 100% Larger: 0%
Library Volumes: 11,000 Acres: 140 Plant: 15 Mil

Other Facts

New cultural arts center Jan. 1989; international baccalaureate curriculum.

Locale

Rural; 5 miles from Las Vegas, NM — pop. 25,000; 60 miles from Santa Fe; adjacent to Pecos wilderness area — Sangare De Christo Mts.; elevation 6,800 ft.

Verde Valley School (Coed)

Founded 1948

3511 Verde Valley School Rd., Sedona, AZ 86336
(602) 282-7148
Airport: Phoenix, 110 miles

Students

Total: 78 Boys: 39 Girls: 39 Grades: 9-PG
Boarding: 71 Day: 7 Local Students: 16%
Number of States: 17 Countries: 7 Foreign Students: 21%

Costs and Aid

Tuition: $13,750 School Extras: $900
Student Aid Money Awarded: $207,000
Number Granted: 31% Avg. Per Student: $6677

Additional Support

Endowment: $180,000 Per Student: $2,300
Alumni: 1,200 Annual Gifts: $75,000 Giving: 26%

Admission

Largest Grade Entry: 10 Applied: 65 (total)
Accepted: 44 (total) Entered: 38 (total)
Median Percentile Entering 10th Grade: NA%
Application Deadline: 9/1 Remedial Program: No

Academics

Advanced Placement Preparation in 6 Test Areas
Class Size: 8-9 Student-Teacher Ratio: 5-1
Number of Seniors: 21 Combined SATS: 1000

Facilities

Rooms: Singles 50% Doubles: 50% Larger: 0%
Library Volumes: 10,000 Acres: 200 Plant: 5 Mil

Other Facts

Performing arts building; art studios; music studio; ESL; riding program; three golf courses within 5 minutes; intercultural field trips to Mexico and Indian Reservations.

Locale

12,000 pop.; 50 miles south of Flagstaff (50,000 pop.); 110 miles north of Phoenix (1,000,000 pop.); 4,300 ft. elevation; 1 hour to ski area.

Vermont Academy (Coed)

Founded 1876

Saxtons River, VT 05154
(802) 869-2121
Airport: Hartford, 110 miles

Students

Total: 253 Boys: 185 Girls: 68 Grades: 9-PG
Boarding: 195 Day: 58 Local Students: 20%
Number of States: 27 Countries: 5 Foreign Students: 3%

Costs and Aid

Tuition: $14,300 School Extras: $500-900
Student Aid Money Awarded: $350,000
Number Granted: 35% Avg. Per Student: $4,000

Additional Support

Endowment: $1.2 mil Per Student: $4,700
Alumni: 3200 Annual Gifts: $225,000 Giving: 25%

Admission

Largest Grade Entry: 9, 11 Applied: 74/83
Accepted: 64/64 Entered: 37/37
Median Percentile Entering 9th Grade: 54%
Application Deadline: rolling Remedial Program: No

Academics

Advanced Placement Preparation in 0 Test Areas
Class Size: 10-13 Student-Teacher Ratio: 9-1
Number of Seniors: 85 Combined SATS: 970

Facilities

Rooms: Singles 24% Doubles: 73% Larger: 3%
Library Volumes: 12,000 Acres: 500 Plant: 8 Mil

Other Facts

New learning skills center; ski tow and grip right on campus; 30 km nordic and x-country trails; indoor hockey rink.

Locale

½ miles from town center — pop. 700; Inn, B & B's; 45 minutes to Dartmouth and Amherst; 2½ hours to Boston; foothills of Green Mountains.

Virginia Episcopal School (Coed)

Founded 1916

P.O. Box 408, 400 VES Road, Lynchburg, VA 24505
(804) 384-6221
Airport: Lynchburg, 10 miles

Students

Total: 260 Boys: 195 Girls: 65 Grades: 9-12
Boarding: 190 Day: 70 Local Students: 27%
Number of States: 18 Countries: 6 Foreign Students: 2%

Costs and Aid

Tuition: $12,550 School Extras: $125
Student Aid Money Awarded: $230,000
Number Granted: 19% Avg. Per Student: $4,600

Additional Support

Endowment: $4,000,000 Per Student: $16,000
Alumni: 2,800 Annual Gifts: $765,000 Giving: 43%

Admission

Largest Grade Entry: 10 Applied: 80
Accepted: 60 Entered: 47
Median Percentile Entering 9-12 Grade: 48%
Application Deadline: rolling Remedial Program: no

Academics

Advanced Placement Preparation in 8 Test Areas
Class Size: 12-15 Student-Teacher Ratio: 6-1
Number of Seniors: 70 Combined SATS: 1010

Facilities

Rooms: Singles 0% Doubles: 90% Larger: 10%
Library Volumes: 16,000 Acres: 160 Plant: 14 M

Other Facts

New girls dorm (1987); participation in English-Speaking-Union; year abroad program; member of Virginia's Preparatory League in Athletics.

Locale

Residential suburb of Lynchburg — Population 66,000; five colleges in 30 mile radius.

Vivian Webb School (Girls)

Founded 1981

1175 West Base Line Rd., Claremont, CA 91711
(714) 626-3587
Airport: Ontario(LA), 10 miles

Students

Total: 160 Boys: 0 Girls: 160 Grades: 9-12
Boarding: 90 Day: 70 Local Students: 55%
Number of States: 9 Countries: 9 Foreign Students: 10%

Costs and Aid

Tuition: $16,300 School Extras: $800
Student Aid Money Awarded: $450,000
Number Granted: 15% Avg. Per Student: $7460

Additional Support

Endowment: $1.5 mil Per Student: $9000
Alumni: 100 Annual Gifts: $235,000 Giving:

Admission

Largest Grade Entry: 9 Applied: 59
Accepted: 40 Entered: 28
Median Percentile Entering Grade: NA%
Application Deadline: rolling Remedial Program: No

Academics

Advanced Placement Preparation in 13 Test Areas
Class Size: 14 Student-Teacher Ratio: 9-1
Number of Seniors: 32 Combined SATS: 1110

Facilities

Rooms: Singles 10% Doubles: 90% Larger: 0%
Library Volumes: 16,000 Acres: 66 Plant: 10 Mil

Other Facts

New library (1988); pool; tennis courts; athletic fields; large gymnasium; track; museum on campus very much part of science prog. (open to public).

Locale

Located in foothills of San Gabriel Mtns.; 1 mile from town — pop. 34,000; home of Claremont Colleges; 1 hr. from beach; 40 mins. from downtown L.A.; share campus with boy's school.

Walnut Hill School of the Performing Arts (Coed)

Founded 1893

412 Highland St., Natick, MA 01760
(508) 653-4312
Airport: Boston, 30 miles

Students

Total: 208 Boys: 36 Girls: 172 Grades: 8-12
Boarding: 155 Day: 50 Local Students: 22%
Number of States: 33 Countries: 19 Foreign Students: 17%

Costs and Aid

Tuition: $14,500 School Extras: $210
Student Aid Money Awarded: $340,000
Number Granted: 34% Avg. Per Student: $5500

Additional Support

Endowment: $2 mil Per Student: $10,000
Alumni: 4500 Annual Gifts: $ Giving: %

Admission

Largest Grade Entry: 10 Applied: NA
Accepted: Entered:
Median Percentile Entering Grade: %
Application Deadline: rolling Remedial Program: No

Academics

Advanced Placement Preparation in Test Areas
Class Size: 10-15 Student-Teacher Ratio: 6-1
Number of Seniors: 72 Combined SATS: NA

Facilities

Rooms: Singles 50% Doubles: 50% Larger: %
Library Volumes: 10,000 Acres: 65 Plant: 4 M

Other Facts

Excellent college conservatory placement; fully integrated arts and academics; joint program with New England Conservatory of Music.

Locale

Pop. 2000; walking distance of downtown; residential community.

Wasatch Academy (Coed)

Founded 1875

120 S. 100 W., Box 1, Mt. Pleasant, UT 84647
(801) 462-2411
Airport: Salt Lake, 100 miles

Students

Total: 117 Boys: 70 Girls: 47 Grades: 9-12
Boarding: 110 Day: 7 Local Students: %
Number of States: 18 Countries: 3 Foreign Students: 10%

Costs and Aid

Tuition: $13,700 School Extras: $400
Student Aid Money Awarded: $140,000
Number Granted: % Avg. Per Student: $600

Additional Support

Endowment: $800,000 Per Student: $6500
Alumni: 2500 Annual Gifts: $200,000 Giving: %

Admission

Largest Grade Entry: 9 Applied:
Accepted: Entered:
Median Percentile Entering Grade: %
Application Deadline: rolling Remedial Program: No

Academics

Advanced Placement Preparation in 2 Test Areas
Class Size: 7-15 Student-Teacher Ratio: 7-1
Number of Seniors: 35 Combined SATS:

Facilities

Rooms: Singles 0% Doubles: 100% Larger: 0%
Library Volumes: 7500 Acres: 13 Plant: 3 M

Other Facts

Riding at nearby ranch; use of nearby Snow Junior College facilities; music and art building (1970).

Locale

Pop. 2800; a few blocks from center; rural setting; 60 miles south of Provo; 100 miles south of Salt Lake City; right next to Rocky Mtns.

Wayland Academy (Coed)

Founded 1855

101 North University Avenue, Beaver Dam, WI 53916
(414) 885-3373
Airport: Milwaukee, 40 miles

Students

Total: 242 Boys: 136 Girls: 106 Grades: 9-12
Boarding: 203 Day: 39 Local Students: 19%
Number of States: 22 Countries: 11 Foreign Students: 9%

Costs and Aid

Tuition: $13,600 School Extras: $325
Student Aid Money Awarded: $430,000
Number Granted: 35% Avg. Per Student: $5,500

Additional Support

Endowment: $4,000,000 Per Student: $16,000
Alumni: 3450 Annual Gifts: $548,695 Giving: 9%

Admission

Largest Grade Entry: 10th Applied: 51
Accepted: 46 Entered: 36
Median Percentile Entering Grade: NA%
Application Deadline: rolling Remedial Program: No

Academics

Advanced Placement Preparation in 7 Test Areas
Class Size: 10 Student-Teacher Ratio: 11-1
Number of Seniors: 81 Combined SATS: 990

Facilities

Rooms: Singles 0% Doubles: 100% Larger: 0%
Library Volumes: 20,000 Acres: 55 Plant: 22 M

Other Facts

A new academic building (1988) with 15 classrooms, 21 faculty offices, and workrooms; the Swan Library (1989) houses a library/media center with electronic research aids, a computer center, and the Whiting Gallery.

Locale

Beaver Dam — population 15,000; 2 motels close to campus; 40 minutes from Madison — state capitol; 2½ hours from Chicago.

Webb School (Coed)

Founded 1870

Webb Highway, Bell Buckle, TN 37020
(615) 389-6003
Airport: Nashville, 50 miles

Students

Total: 150 Boys: 90 Girls: 60 Grades: 7-PG
Boarding: 78 Day: 72 Local Students: 50%
Number of States: 12 Countries: 8 Foreign Students: 12%

Costs and Aid

Tuition: $11,800 School Extras: $650
Student Aid Money Awarded: $190,000
Number Granted: 51% Avg. Per Student: $3,725

Additional Support

Endowment: $6.5 mil Per Student: $43,333
Alumni: 3200 Annual Gifts: $180,000 Giving: %

Admission

Largest Grade Entry: 7 Applied: 31
Accepted: 22 Entered: 20
Median Percentile Entering 7th Grade: %
Application Deadline: rolling Remedial Program: No

Academics

Advanced Placement Preparation in 5 Test Areas
Class Size: 10-12 Student-Teacher Ratio: 8-1
Number of Seniors: 34 Combined SATS: 1000

Facilities

Rooms: Singles 0% Doubles: 100% Larger: 0%
Library Volumes: 16,000 Acres: 150 Plant: 6 Million

Other Facts

New computer/science building (1987); out-door program; indoor pool; some air conditioned dorms; extensive outdoor programs.

Locale

500 population; 25 miles from Murfreesboro — population 30,000 — home of Middle Tennessee State University; 1 hour from Nashville; 1½ hours from Chattanooga.

Webb School of California (Boys)

Founded 1922

1175 West Base Line Rd., Claremont, CA 91711
(714) 626-3587
Airport: Ontario (LA), 10 miles

Students

Total: Boys: 230 Girls: Grades: 9-12
Boarding: 160 Day: 70 Local Students: 30%
Number of States: 9 Countries: 9 Foreign Students: 11%

Costs and Aid

Tuition: $15,300 School Extras: $800
Student Aid Money Awarded: $450,000
Number Granted: 15% Avg. Per Student: $7,460

Additional Support

Endowment: 1 Mil. Per Student: $4000
Alumni: 1900 Annual Gifts: $235,000 Giving: %

Admission

Largest Grade Entry: 9 Applied: 76
Accepted: 48 Entered: 38
Median Percentile Entering Grade: 65%
Application Deadline: Rolling Remedial Program: No

Academics

Advanced Placement Preparation in 13 Test Areas
Class Size: 14 Student-Teacher Ratio: 9-1
Number of Seniors: 60 Combined SATS: 1170

Facilities

Rooms: Singles 100% Doubles: 0% Larger: 0%
Library Volumes: 16,000 Acres: 66 Plant: 8 Mil

Other Facts

New library (1988); pool; tennis courts; athletic fields; large gymnasium; track; museum on campus very much part of science prog.; open to public.

Locale

Located in foothills of San Gabriel Mtns.; 1 mile from town; pop. 34,000; home of Claremont Colleges; 1 hr. from beach; 40 mins. from L.A.; share campus with girls' school.

West Nottingham Academy (Coed)

Founded 1744

Colora, MD 21917
(301) 658-5556
Airport: Philadelphia, 40 miles

Students

Total: 115 Boys: 80 Girls: 35 Grades: 9-PG
Boarding: 100 Day: 15 Local Students: 60%
Number of States: 20 Countries: 2 Foreign Students: 7%

Costs and Aid

Tuition: $13,100 School Extras: $0
Student Aid Money Awarded: $75,000
Number Granted: 25% Avg. Per Student: $

Additional Support

Endowment: 9 Mil Per Student: $
Alumni: 2000 Annual Gifts: $ Giving: %

Admission

Largest Grade Entry: 9 Applied: 20
Accepted: 14 Entered: 13
Median Percentile Entering Grade: 60%
Application Deadline: rolling Remedial Program: yes

Academics

Advanced Placement Preparation in 3 Test Areas
Class Size: 8 Student-Teacher Ratio: 5-1
Number of Seniors: 36 Combined SATS: 950

Facilities

Rooms: Singles 10% Doubles: 90% Larger: 0%
Library Volumes: 8000 Acres: 200 Plant: 4 Mil

Other Facts

New student union and dining hall; nearby riding stables and golf course; also has learning center for learning disabilities.

Locale

Pop. 25,000 in Rising Sun (3 miles away); in rural setting; 50 miles from downtown Baltimore.

Western Reserve Academy (Coed)

Founded 1826

College St., Hudson, OH 44236
(216) 650-4400
Airport: Cleveland, 30 miles

Students

Total: 365 Boys: 240 Girls: 125 Grades: 9-12
Boarding: 240 Day: 125 Local Students: 16%
Number of States: 24 Countries: 12 Foreign Students: 10%

Costs and Aid

Tuition: $12,700 School Extras: $400
Student Aid Money Awarded: $750,000
Number Granted: 33% Avg. Per Student: $6,500

Additional Support

Endowment: $30,000,000 Per Student: $80,000
Alumni: 5500 Annual Gifts: $350,000 Giving: 42%

Admission

Largest Grade Entry: 9 Applied: 250
Accepted: 95 Entered: 80
Median Percentile Entering 9 Grade: 74%
Application Deadline: 3/10 Remedial Program: No

Academics

Advanced Placement Preparation in 7 Test Areas
Class Size: 13 Student-Teacher Ratio: 8-1
Number of Seniors: 95 Combined SATS: 1200

Facilities

Rooms: Singles 15% Doubles: 60% Larger: 15%
Library Volumes: 25,000 Acres: 400 Plant: 40 M

Other Facts

Knight Fine Arts Center (1986); courses offered; 100% faculty reside on campus; family style meals; new observatory (1980).

Locale

One block from the Village of Hudson; 10 miles from Akron; 30 miles from Cleveland; 5 miles from Cleveland Colliseum; 5 miles from two ski slopes; 3 miles from Kenyon College.

Westminster School (Coed)

Founded 1888

995 Hopmeadow St., Simsbury, CT 06070
(203) 658-4444
Airport: Hartford, 8 miles

Students

Total: 339 Boys: 204 Girls: 135 Grades: 9-PG
Boarding: 244 Day: 95 Local Students: 28%
Number of States: 28 Countries: 14 Foreign Students: 4%

Costs and Aid

Tuition: $15,000 School Extras: $600
Student Aid Money Awarded: $519,000
Number Granted: 19% Avg. Per Student: $8373

Additional Support

Endowment: $12,000,000 Per Student: $36,000
Alumni: 2600 Annual Gifts: $600,000 Giving: 54%

Admission

Largest Grade Entry: 9 & 10 Applied: 525
Accepted: 247 Entered: 105
Median Percentile Entering 9 & 10 Grade: 65%
Application Deadline: Jan. 25 Remedial Program: No

Academics

Advanced Placement Preparation in 4 Test Areas
Class Size: 14 Student-Teacher Ratio: 7-1
Number of Seniors: 95 Combined SATS: 1100

Facilities

Rooms: Singles 23% Doubles: 75% Larger: 2%
Library Volumes: 21,000 Acres: 220 Plant: 38 M

Other Facts

Recent academic center has 20 classrooms, library, labs, computer center; new $6 million performing arts center (1989); kayaking on nearby river.

Locale

Rural; suburban town, pop. 21,000; rolling countryside; 15 miles from center of Hartford; 2 hrs. to Boston; 2½ to NYC.

Westover School (Girls)

Founded 1909

Whittemore Rd., Middlebury, CT 06762
(203) 758-2423
Airport: Hartford, 40 miles

Students

Total: 162 Boys: 0 Girls: 162 Grades: 9-12
Boarding: 122 Day: 40 Local Students: 24%
Number of States: 22 Countries: 10 Foreign Students: 10%

Costs and Aid

Tuition: $15,300 School Extras: $1000
Student Aid Money Awarded: $495,000
Number Granted: 34% Avg. Per Student: $9166

Additional Support

Endowment: $9.6 mil Per Student: $58,000
Alumni: 3100 Annual Gifts: $427,979 Giving: 55%

Admission

Largest Grade Entry: 9 Applied: 74
Accepted: 65 Entered:
Median Percentile Entering 9 Grade: 53%
Application Deadline: Feb. 15 Remedial Program: No

Academics

Advanced Placement Preparation in 8 Test Areas
Class Size: 11 Student-Teacher Ratio: 6-1
Number of Seniors: 46 Combined SATS: 1010

Facilities

Rooms: Singles 16% Doubles: 80% Larger: 4%
Library Volumes: 16,000 Acres: 100 Plant: 18 M

Other Facts

New award-winning science and library building, including computer facilities and a greenhouse; exchange program with Jordan, as well as other foreign countries.

Locale

On town green — pop. 6000; suburb of Waterbury; within easy reach of Hartford, Boston, New Haven, and New York City.

Westtown School (Coed)

Founded 1799

Westtown, PA 19395
(215) 399-0123
Airport: Philadelphia, 20 miles

Students

Total: 350 Boys: 180 Girls: 170 Grades: K-12
Boarding: 290 Day: 60 Local Students: 15%
Number of States: 38 Countries: 15 Foreign Students: 14%

Costs and Aid

Tuition: $12,400 School Extras: $200
Student Aid Money Awarded: $1,150,000
Number Granted: 30% Avg. Per Student: $

Additional Support

Endowment: $20 mil Per Student: $37,000
Alumni: 6500 Annual Gifts: $450,000 Giving: %

Admission

Largest Grade Entry: 9th Applied: 145
Accepted: 65 Entered: 30
Median Percentile Entering 9th Grade: 62%
Application Deadline: rolling Remedial Program: No

Academics

Advanced Placement Preparation in 12 Test Areas
Class Size: 14 Student-Teacher Ratio: 8-1
Number of Seniors: 92 Combined SATS: 1170

Facilities

Rooms: Singles 0% Doubles: 100% Larger: 0%
Library Volumes: 34,000 Acres: 600 Plant: 35 M

Other Facts

In historic Chester County; 23% of students are Quakers; longstanding Quaker heritage; lake provides canoeing, fishing and skating in the winter.

Locale

In suburban — rural setting; numerous cultural opportunities in nearby Wilmington and Delaware; two colleges within 10 minutes.

Whiteman School (Coed)

Founded 1957

42605 RCR 36G, Steamboat Springs, CO 80487
(303) 879-1350
Airport: Steamboat Springs, 6 miles

Students

Total: 63 Boys: 44 Girls: 19 Grades:
Boarding: 60 Day: 3 Local Students: 5%
Number of States: 16 Countries: 5 Foreign Students: 10%

Costs and Aid

Tuition: $13,300 School Extras: $
Student Aid Money Awarded: $110,580
Number Granted: 34% Avg. Per Student: $5900

Additional Support

Endowment: $0 Per Student: $
Alumni: 360 Annual Gifts: $40,000 Giving: 40%

Admission

Largest Grade Entry: 11 Applied: 27
Accepted: 18 Entered: 12
Median Percentile Entering 11 Grade: 37%
Application Deadline: rolling Remedial Program: No

Academics

Advanced Placement Preparation in Test Areas
Class Size: 8 (Av) Student-Teacher Ratio: 6-1
Number of Seniors: 12 Combined SATS: 1000

Facilities

Rooms: Singles 5% Doubles: 60% Larger: 35%
Library Volumes: 3000 Acres: 180 Plant: 1.4 Mil

Other Facts

Annual foreign trip; new gym (1984); camping; riding; soccer; daily skiing; special program for competitive skiers.

Locale

Rural mountain setting; resort town of 6000 pop.; 6 miles to ski area; 160 NW of Denver.

White Mountain School (Coed)

Founded 1886

West Farm Road, Littleton, NH 03561
(603) 444-2928
Airport: Boston, MA, 150 miles

Students

Total: 100 Boys: 60 Girls: 40 Grades: 9-PG
Boarding: 90 Day: 10 Local Students: 10%
Number of States: 20 Countries: 3 Foreign Students: 13%

Costs and Aid

Tuition: $14,500 School Extras: $750
Student Aid Money Awarded: $140,000
Number Granted: 25% Avg. Per Student: $7000

Additional Support

Endowment: $660,000 Per Student: $6600
Alumni: 1400 Annual Gifts: $ Giving: 9%

Admission

Largest Grade Entry: 11th Applied: 90
Accepted: 67 Entered: 50
Median Percentile Entering Grade: %
Application Deadline: rolling Remedial Program: Yes

Academics

Advanced Placement Preparation in 6 Test Areas
Class Size: avg. 6 Student-Teacher Ratio: 5-1
Number of Seniors: 20 Combined SATS: 880

Facilities

Rooms: Singles 30% Doubles: 70% Larger: %
Library Volumes: 13,000 Acres: 320 Plant: 6 Mil

Other Facts

Outdoor wilderness program includes white water canoeing, kayaking, rock climbing and hiking; daily alpine skiing; barn theatre for dramatic productions.

Locale

In heart of the White Mountains; 150 miles north of Boston, and 150 miles south of Montreal; 2 miles from Littleton, NH, population 5,000; 6 miles north of Franconia Notch, NH; 30 motels/hotels in area.

Wilbraham & Monson Academy (Coed)

Founded 1804

Main Street, Wilbraham, Massachusetts 01095
(413) 596-6811
Airport: Hartford, 23 miles

Students

Total: 308 Boys: 240 Girls: 68 Grades: 7-PG
Boarding: 156 Day: 152 Local Students: 66%
Number of States: 17 Countries: 11 Foreign Students: 6%

Costs and Aid

Tuition: $14,450 School Extras: $300
Student Aid Money Awarded: $450,000
Number Granted: 33% Avg. Per Student: $4,400

Additional Support

Endowment: $2 million Per Student: $6,300
Alumni: 7000 Annual Gifts: $127,383 Giving: 30%

Admission

Largest Grade Entry: pg Applied: 112
Accepted: 92 Entered: 46
Median Percentile Entering 11th Grade: 20%
Application Deadline: rolling Remedial Program: yes

Academics

Advanced Placement Preparation in 5 Test Areas
Class Size: 12-15 Student-Teacher Ratio: 10-1
Number of Seniors: 90 Combined SATS: 925

Facilities

Rooms: Singles 20% Doubles: 80% Larger: %
Library Volumes: 27,000 Acres: 350 Plant: 5 Mil

Other Facts

A program for students with a diagnosed learning disability; academy listed in National Register of Historic Sites.

Locale

Located in center of town (pop. 12,000); 8 miles from Springfield; Smith, Amherst, Hampshire, Mt. Holyoke and U Mass are nearby.

The Williston Northampton School (Coed)

Founded 1841

19 Payson Avenue, Easthampton , MA 01027
(413) 527-1520
Airport: Hartford, 45 miles

Students

Total: 450 Boys: 227 Girls: 223 Grades: 9-PG
Boarding: 285 Day: 165 Local Students: 30%
Number of States: 28 Countries: 13 Foreign Students: 4%

Costs and Aid

Tuition: $15,400 School Extras: $500
Student Aid Money Awarded: $650,000
Number Granted: 30% Avg. Per Student: $4400

Additional Support

Endowment: $6,600,000 Per Student: $14,600
Alumni: 7,500 Annual Gifts: $483,000 Giving: 35%

Admission

Largest Grade Entry: Applied:
Accepted: Entered:
Median Percentile Entering 9th Grade: 55%
Application Deadline: 2/15 Remedial Program: No

Academics

Advanced Placement Preparation in 7 Test Areas
Class Size: 13 Student-Teacher Ratio: 8-1
Number of Seniors: 150 Combined SATS: 1000

Facilities

Rooms: Singles 10% Doubles: 90% Larger: %
Library Volumes: 30,000 Acres: 100 Plant: 25 Mil

Other Facts

A multi-talented, diverse student body; Intersession (65 minicourses, internships, tutorials, world travel, and SAT prep); School-Year abroad and English-Speaking union program.

Locale

Pop. 15,000; walking distance; skiing; a few miles from the base of Mount Tom; 85 miles west of Boston; within a 15-mile radius are Smith, Mount Holyoke, Amherst, and University of Massachusetts.

Woodberry Forest (Boys)
Founded 1889

Woodberry Forest, Virginia 22989
(703) 672-3900
Airport: Charlottesville, 35 miles

Students
Total: 361 Boys: 361 Girls: 0 Grades: 9-12
Boarding: 359 Day: 2 Local Students: %
Number of States: 28 Countries: 9 Foreign Students: 3%

Costs and Aid
Tuition: $12,200 School Extras: $
Student Aid Money Awarded: $574,730
Number Granted: 22% Avg. Per Student: $7096

Additional Support
Endowment: $34,000,000 Per Student: $94,000
Alumni: 5457 Annual Gifts: $1,109,792 Giving: 63%

Admission
Largest Grade Entry: 9 Applied: 141
Accepted: 90 Entered: 71
Median Percentile Entering 9th Grade: 60%
Application Deadline: Feb. 15 Remedial Program: No

Academics
Advanced Placement Preparation in 17 Test Areas
Class Size: 13 Student-Teacher Ratio: 7-1
Number of Seniors: 99 Combined SATS: 1160

Facilities
Rooms: Singles 19% Doubles: 71% Larger: 10%
Library Volumes: 44,000 Acres: 1400 Plant: 34 Mil

Other Facts
Campus in England; 4 years of Japanese and European languages; multi-million dollar athletic complex (1986); math-science building (1970's); Fine Arts Building (1960's); school's golf course is oldest course in Virginia.

Locale
2 miles north of town of Orange on U.S. 15; ½ hour drive from Charlottesville; 1½ hour drive from Washington and Richmond.

Woodside Priory (Boys)
Founded 1957

302 Portola Road, Portola Valley, CA 94025
(415) 851-8221
Airport: San Francisco, 25 miles

Students
Total: 100 Boys: 100 Girls: 0 Grades: 7-12
Boarding: 60 Day: 40 Local Students: %
Number of States: 6 Countries: 8 Foreign Students: 30%

Costs and Aid
Tuition: $16,800 School Extras: $None
Student Aid Money Awarded: $60,000
Number Granted: 20% Avg. Per Student: $3000

Additional Support
Endowment: $ Per Student: $
Alumni: 670 Annual Gifts: $400,000 Giving: %

Admission
Largest Grade Entry: 9th Applied: 30
Accepted: 25 Entered: 17
Median Percentile Entering Grade: 75%
Application Deadline: rolling Remedial Program: No

Academics
Advanced Placement Preparation in 11 Test Areas
Class Size: 12-14 Student-Teacher Ratio: 7-1
Number of Seniors: 30 Combined SATS: 1000

Facilities
Rooms: Singles 0% Doubles: 100% Larger: 0%
Library Volumes: 18,000 Acres: 70 Plant: 4 Mil

Other Facts
Work grant program; million dollar new campus center; European trip each year for 15 students.

Locale
Pop. 4500; located in town; 6 miles from Stanford University; Palo Alto 7 miles.

Worcester Academy (Coed)

Founded 1854

81 Providence, Worcester, MA 01604
(508) 754-5302
Airport: Boston, 45 miles

Students

Total: 370 Boys: 240 Girls: 130 Grades: 7-12-PG
Boarding: 140 Day: 230 Local Students: 70%
Number of States: 17 Countries: 14 Foreign Students: 20%

Costs and Aid

Tuition: $15,400 School Extras: $500
Student Aid Money Awarded: $512,000
Number Granted: 15% Avg. Per Student: $5000

Additional Support

Endowment: $8,000,000 Per Student: $21,000
Alumni: 5600 Annual Gifts: $300,000 Giving: %

Admission

Largest Grade Entry: 8 Applied: 60
Accepted: 48 Entered: 43
Median Percentile Entering 10 Grade: 60%
Application Deadline: rolling Remedial Program: No

Academics

Advanced Placement Preparation in 11 Test Areas
Class Size: 12 Student-Teacher Ratio: 10-1
Number of Seniors: 140 Combined SATS: 1000

Facilities

Rooms: Singles 40% Doubles: 40% Larger: %
Library Volumes: 16,000 Acres: 14 Plant: 12 Mil

Other Facts

Indoor pool; theater building also contains music facilities; 11 acre athletic field just off campus.

Locale

Close to city center — pop. 160,000; location of Holy Cross College, Worcester Polytechnic Institute; 55 miles from Hartford.

Wyoming Seminary (Coed)

Founded 1844

201 North Sprague Ave., Kingston, PA 18704
(717) 283-6060
Airport: Wilkes-Barre-Scranton, 20 miles

Students

Total: 330 Boys: 178 Girls: 160 Grades: 9-PG
Boarding: 105 Day: 225 Local Students: 60%
Number of States: 10 Countries: 9 Foreign Students: 9%

Costs and Aid

Tuition: $13,100 School Extras: $100
Student Aid Money Awarded: $660,000
Number Granted: 25% Avg. Per Student: $4500

Additional Support

Endowment: 9 Mil Per Student: $800
Alumni: 8000 Annual Gifts: $625,000 Giving: %

Admission

Largest Grade Entry: 9 Applied: 90
Accepted: 75 Entered: 69
Median Percentile Entering Grade: 60%
Application Deadline: rolling Remedial Program: No

Academics

Advanced Placement Preparation in Test Areas
Class Size: 18 Student-Teacher Ratio: 8-1
Number of Seniors: 87 Combined SATS: 1080

Facilities

Rooms: Singles 50% Doubles: 50% Larger: 0%
Library Volumes: 18,000 Acres: 17.5 Plant: 13 Mil

Other Facts

1.2 million renovation of science building in 1988; music group travels abroad each year.

Locale

Pop. 23,000; located downtown; 2 hours from Philadelphia; 3 hours from NY; 4 hours from Washington.

Church Farm School (Boys)

Founded 1918

Paoli, PA, 19301
(215) 363-7500
Airport: Philadelphia, 26 miles

Students

Total: 200 Boys: 200 Girls: 0 Grades: 1-12
Boarding: 170 Day: 0 Local Students: 15%
Number of States: 23 Countries: 3 Foreign Students: %

Costs and Aid

Tuition: $2500 School Extras: $
Student Aid Money Awarded: $
Number Granted: % Avg. Per Student: $

Additional Support

Endowment: $ Per Student: $
Alumni: Annual Gifts: $ Giving: %

Admission

Largest Grade Entry: 9 Applied: 65
Accepted: 15 Entered:
Median Percentile Entering Grade: %
Application Deadline: Rolling Remedial Program: Yes

Academics

Advanced Placement Preparation in Test Areas
Class Size: Student-Teacher Ratio: 8-1
Number of Seniors: 16 Combined SATS: 900

Facilities

Rooms: Singles % Doubles: % Larger: %
Library Volumes: 20,000 Acres: 1500 Plant: 10M

Other Facts

2- hour work program in farming, machinery, plumbing; live in cottages; preference given to those with single parents, minister's sons, etc.

Locale

Pop. 6000; campus has lake, farmland, and woods; can walk to nearby shopping center; 10 miles from Valley Forge.

Milton Hershey School (Coed)

Founded 1909

Box 830, Hershey, PA 17033
(717) 534-3546
Airport: Harrisburg, 8 miles

Students

Total: 1150 Boys: 650 Girls: 500 Grades: K-12
Boarding: 550 Day: 0 Local Students: 0%
Number of States: 30 Countries: 2 Foreign Students: 1%

Costs and Aid

Tuition: $0 School Extras: $0
Student Aid Money Awarded: $
Number Granted: 100% Avg. Per Student: $

Additional Support

Endowment: $privately funded Per Student: $All costs
Alumni: 5000 Annual Gifts: $ Giving: %

Admission

Largest Grade Entry: 9 Applied:
Accepted: Entered:
Median Percentile Entering Grade: %
Application Deadline: rolling Remedial Program: No

Academics

Advanced Placement Preparation in Test Areas
Class Size: 18-20 Student-Teacher Ratio: 11-1
Number of Seniors: 108 Combined SATS: 950

Facilities

Rooms: Singles 0% Doubles: 95% Larger: 5%
Library Volumes: 25,000 Acres: 10,000 Plant:

Other Facts

Boarders from 1st grade; children admitted from disrupted families; endowed by Hershey Chocolate Family to provide 100% free education.

Locale

Pop. 9000; Hershey Chocolate Factory; Hotel Hershey within walking distance; 450 in secondary school.

Oneida Institute (Coed)

Founded 1899

Box 67, Oneida, KY 40972
(606) 847-4111
Airport: Lexington, 120 miles

Students

Total: 550 Boys: 310 Girls: 240 Grades: 6-PG
Boarding: 500 Day: 50 Local Students: 10%
Number of States: 23 Countries: 9 Foreign Students: 15%

Costs and Aid

Tuition: $3100 School Extras: $
Student Aid Money Awarded: $
Number Granted: % Avg. Per Student: $

Additional Support

Endowment: $1.3 Mil Per Student: $2200
Alumni: 2000 Annual Gifts: $2 Mil Giving: %

Admission

Largest Grade Entry: 9 Applied: 150
Accepted: 90 Entered:
Median Percentile Entering Grade: %
Application Deadline: Rolling Remedial Program: Yes

Academics

Advanced Placement Preparation in 5 Test Areas
Class Size: 13 Student-Teacher Ratio: 13-1
Number of Seniors: 100 Combined SATS:

Facilities

Rooms: Singles 0% Doubles: 0% Larger: 100%
Library Volumes: 16,000 Acres: 200 Plant: 12M

Other Facts

Affiliated with Baptist Church; over 50% of students are Baptist; plant has quadrupled in last 10 years; work program of 1½ hours a day; most of food consumed is grown by school farm.

Locale

Pop. 60; rural; nearest town of any size is 40 miles; school operates its own water and sewer facilities.

The Piney Woods School (Coed)

Founded 1909

Piney Woods, MS 39148
(601) 845-2214
Airport: Jackson, 21 miles

Students

Total: 211 Boys: 115 Girls: 96 Grades: K-12
Boarding: 211 Day: 0 Local Students: %
Number of States: 21 Countries: 6 Foreign Students: 6%

Costs and Aid

Tuition: $3400 School Extras: $
Student Aid Money Awarded: $185,000
Number Granted: 100% Avg. Per Student: $

Additional Support

Endowment: $23 Mil Per Student: $33,000
Alumni: Annual Gifts: $ Giving: %

Admission

Largest Grade Entry: 9th Applied: 55
Accepted: 45 Entered: 45
Median Percentile Entering Grade: %
Application Deadline: Rolling Remedial Program: Yes

Academics

Advanced Placement Preparation in Test Areas
Class Size: 15 Student-Teacher Ratio: 15-1
Number of Seniors: 56 Combined SATS: ACT 13

Facilities

Rooms: Singles 0% Doubles: 50% Larger: 50%
Library Volumes: 30,000 Acres: 2000 Plant:

Other Facts

All students work 15 hours a week; new student center in 1985; 90% enter college.

Locale

Pop. 500; rural; campus has a farm, lakes, and timber.

Subiaco Academy (Boys)

Founded 1887

Subiaco, AR 72865
(501) 934-4292
Airport: Fort Smith, 50 miles

Students

Total: 188 Boys: All Girls: 0 Grades: 9-12
Boarding: 161 Day: 27 Local Students: 14%
Number of States: 16 Countries: 2 Foreign Students: 5%

Costs and Aid

Tuition: $3,950 School Extras: $200
Student Aid Money Awarded: $130,830.00
Number Granted: 32% Avg. Per Student: $2000

Additional Support

Endowment: $750,000 Per Student: $4000
Alumni: $20,000 Annual Gifts: $12,000.00 Giving: %

Admission

Largest Grade Entry: 11th Applied: 85
Accepted: 74 Entered: 72
Median Percentile Entering Grade: %
Application Deadline: None Remedial Program: No

Academics

Advanced Placement Preparation in 2 Test Areas
Class Size: 12 Student-Teacher Ratio: 6-1
Number of Seniors: 38 Combined SATS: 1016

Facilities

Rooms: Singles 0% Doubles: 30% Larger: 70%
Library Volumes: 13,100 Acres: 100 Plant: 10 Mil

Other Facts

Modern performing arts center; supervised study; varied sports; state championship tennis team 1988; pool; campsite; picturesque rural setting.

Locale

47 miles east of Fort Smith, Arkansas, and 110 miles northwest of Little Rock, Arkansas.

Admiral Farragut Academy (North) (Boys)

Founded 1933

Pine Beach, NJ 08741
(201) 349-1121
Airport: Newark, N.J., 60 miles

Students

Total: 230 Boys: 230 Girls: 0 Grades: 7-PG
Boarding: 200 Day: 30 Local Students: 12%
Number of States: 16 Countries: 8 Foreign Students: 4%

Costs and Aid

Tuition: $9875 School Extras: $2,300
Student Aid Money Awarded: $87,000
Number Granted: 18% Avg. Per Student: $2,240

Additional Support

Endowment: $2 Mil Per Student: $9000
Alumni: 3300 Annual Gifts: $ Giving: %

Admission

Largest Grade Entry: 9 Applied: 40
Accepted: 40 Entered: 30
Median Percentile Entering Grade: %
Application Deadline: August 31 Remedial Program: No

Academics

Advanced Placement Preparation in 3 Test Areas
Class Size: 14 Student-Teacher Ratio: 12-1
Number of Seniors: 50 Combined SATS: 890

Facilities

Rooms: Singles 0% Doubles: 60% Larger: 40%
Library Volumes: 20,000 Acres: 30 Plant: 5M

Other Facts

N.J. R.O.T.C.; 100% college placement; naval honor school; cum laude society.

Locale

Pop. 2000; near Toms River; Pop. 68,000; campus right on Toms River; waterfront; docks with various boats; 55 miles from Phila.

Admiral Farragut Academy (South) (Boys)

Founded 1945

501 Park St. N., St. Petersburg, FL 33710
(813) 384-5500
Airport: Tampa, 20 miles

Students

Total: 228 Boys: 228 Girls: 0 Grades: 5-12
Boarding: 172 Day: 56 Local Students: 20%
Number of States: 21 Countries: 15 Foreign Students: 15%

Costs and Aid

Tuition: $9100 School Extras: $1500
Student Aid Money Awarded: $75,000
Number Granted: 20% Avg. Per Student: $2000

Additional Support

Endowment: $ Per Student: $
Alumni: 1500 Annual Gifts: $ Giving: %

Admission

Largest Grade Entry: 9 Applied: 30
Accepted: 25 Entered:
Median Percentile Entering Grade: %
Application Deadline: Rolling Remedial Program: No

Academics

Advanced Placement Preparation in 4 Test Areas
Class Size: 16 Student-Teacher Ratio: 10-1
Number of Seniors: 42 Combined SATS:

Facilities

Rooms: Singles 0% Doubles: 50% Larger: 50%
Library Volumes: 12,000 Acres: 55 Plant: 5M

Other Facts

Originally a resort hotel; incorporates all facilities; a naval honors school permitting special appointment eligibility to academies.

Locale

Pop. 250,000; on the bay; has sail boats, power boats, etc.; minutes from beaches.

Army and Navy Academy (Boys)

Founded 1910

2605 Carlsbad Blvd., Carlsbad, CA 92008
(619) 729-2385
Airport: San Diego, 35 miles

Students

Total: 330 Boys: 330 Girls: 0 Grades: 7-12
Boarding: 290 Day: 40 Local Students: ?%
Number of States: 9 Countries: 16 Foreign Students: 15%

Costs and Aid

Tuition: $9300 School Extras: $3390
Student Aid Money Awarded: $NA
Number Granted: % Avg. Per Student: $

Additional Support

Endowment: $230,000 Per Student: $750
Alumni: 1679 Annual Gifts: $16,080 Giving: 10.5%

Admission

Largest Grade Entry: 9 Applied: 66
Accepted: 56 Entered: 44
Median Percentile Entering 29 Grade: ?%
Application Deadline: 8/15/89 Remedial Program: yes

Academics

Advanced Placement Preparation in Test Areas
Class Size: 15 Student-Teacher Ratio: 12-1
Number of Seniors: 58 Combined SATS: 870

Facilities

Rooms: Singles 0% Doubles: 100% Larger: 0%
Library Volumes: 7000 Acres: 16 Plant: $1,647,000

Other Facts

Participates in 11 varsity sports, including golf and water polo; campus located on Pacific Ocean; adjoins beach.

Locale

1 mile from town center; pop. 45,000; 100 miles from Los Angeles.

Camden Military Academy (Boys)

Founded 1950

Camden, SC 29020
(803) 432-6001
Airport: Charlotte, 75 miles

Students

Total: 240 Boys: 240 Girls: 0 Grades: 7-PG
Boarding: 240 Day: 0 Local Students: 2%
Number of States: 22 Countries: 5 Foreign Students: 3%

Costs and Aid

Tuition: $7900 School Extras: $1000
Student Aid Money Awarded: $10,400
Number Granted: 4% Avg. Per Student: $1500

Additional Support

Endowment: $ Per Student: $
Alumni: 6000 Annual Gifts: $250,000 Giving: 19%

Admission

Largest Grade Entry: 9 Applied: 85
Accepted: 75 Entered: 63
Median Percentile Entering Grade: %
Application Deadline: none Remedial Program: Math & English

Academics

Advanced Placement Preparation in 4 Test Areas
Class Size: 8-12 Student-Teacher Ratio: 12/1
Number of Seniors: 45 Combined SATS: 950

Facilities

Rooms: Singles 0% Doubles: 90% Larger: 10%
Library Volumes: 7800 Acres: 30 Plant: 4M

Other Facts

JROTC Honor Unit with Distinction; 11 varsity sports plus horsemanship and flight instruction; two buildings recently renovated and additional land purchased at cost of $300,000.

Locale

4 miles from center of town; 30 miles from Columbia; 1:45 from Myrtle Beach; 3 hours from ski area.

Carson Long Military Institute (Boys)

Founded 1837

New Bloomfield, PA 17068
(717) 582-2121
Airport: Harrisburg, 40 miles

Students

Total: 220 Boys: 220 Girls: 0 Grades: 6-12
Boarding: 220 Day: 0 Local Students: %
Number of States: 25 Countries: 12 Foreign Students: 9%

Costs and Aid

Tuition: $6100 School Extras: $500
Student Aid Money Awarded: $0
Number Granted: % Avg. Per Student: $

Additional Support

Endowment: $ Per Student: $
Alumni: 1100 Annual Gifts: $ Giving: %

Admission

Largest Grade Entry: 10 Applied: 70
Accepted: 43 Entered: 42
Median Percentile Entering Grade: %
Application Deadline: Rolling Remedial Program: No

Academics

Advanced Placement Preparation in Test Areas
Class Size: 16 Student-Teacher Ratio: 10-1
Number of Seniors: 30 Combined SATS: 1000

Facilities

Rooms: Singles 0% Doubles: 60% Larger: 40%
Library Volumes: 8000 Acres: 50 Plant: 2.5 Mil

Other Facts

ESL program; new science classrooms; chapel and assembly room added; military honor school with distinction.

Locale

Pop. 1000; 2 blocks from center; rural country town; community in the mountains; skiing 30 minutes away.

Florida Air Academy (Boys)

Founded 1961

1950 South Academy Drive, Melbourne, FL 32901
(407) 723-3211
Airport: Melbourne, 2 miles

Students

Total: 250 Boys: 250 Girls: 0 Grades: 7-PG
Boarding: 235 Day: 15 Local Students: %
Number of States: 27 Countries: 20 Foreign Students: 25%

Costs and Aid

Tuition: $8800 School Extras: $1500
Student Aid Money Awarded: $50,000
Number Granted: 20% Avg. Per Student: $1000

Additional Support

Endowment: $0 Per Student: $
Alumni: 800 Annual Gifts: $ Giving: %

Admission

Largest Grade Entry: 10 Applied: 50
Accepted: 47 Entered:
Median Percentile Entering Grade: %
Application Deadline: Rolling Remedial Program: Yes

Academics

Advanced Placement Preparation in Test Areas
Class Size: 17-20 Student-Teacher Ratio: 17-1
Number of Seniors: 50 Combined SATS: 780

Facilities

Rooms: Singles 0% Doubles: 0% Larger: 100%
Library Volumes: 8000 Acres: 25 Plant: 3 Mil

Other Facts

Golf course next to campus; scuba diving; flying courses up to commercial rating; airfield just two miles away.

Locale

Pop. 45,000; suburban location; three miles from downtown; 60 miles south of Orlando.

Fork Union Military Academy (Boys)

Founded 1898

P.O. Box 278, Fork Union, Virginia 23055
(804) 842-3212
Airport: Richmond, 50 miles

Students

Total: 650 Boys: 650 Girls: 0 Grades: 6-PG
Boarding: 635 Day: 15 Local Students: 2%
Number of States: 31 Countries: 21 Foreign Students: 3%

Costs and Aid

Tuition: $8300 School Extras: $600
Student Aid Money Awarded: $312,000
Number Granted: 32% Avg. Per Student: $1500

Additional Support

Endowment: $2 Mil Per Student: $3000
Alumni: 7,270 Annual Gifts: $560,000 Giving: 18%

Admission

Largest Grade Entry: 10 Applied: 106
Accepted: 85 Entered: 72
Median Percentile Entering 10 Grade: 67%
Application Deadline: N/A Remedial Program: Reading

Academics

Advanced Placement Preparation in 3 Test Areas
Class Size: 17 Student-Teacher Ratio: 12-1
Number of Seniors: 115 Combined SATS: NA

Facilities

Rooms: Singles 3% Doubles: 77% Larger: 20%
Library Volumes: 17,000 Acres: 500 Plant: 12 Mil

Other Facts

Separate Junior School (6-8); new athletic center complex (1988); computer facilities; interscholastic and intramural sports; band, chorus, clubs.

Locale

2 miles from town; pop. 2500; rural setting; 50 miles west of Richmond, Virginia; 120 miles south of Washington, D.C.; 30 miles south of Charlottesville.

Hargrave Military Academy (Boys)

Founded 1909

Hargrave Blvd., Chatham, VA 24531
(804) 432-2481
Airport: Greensboro, 55 miles

Students

Total: 330 Boys: 330 Girls: 0 Grades: 6-PG
Boarding: 310 Day: 20 Local Students: 15%
Number of States: 26 Countries: 10 Foreign Students: 8%

Costs and Aid

Tuition: $8600 School Extras: $1400
Student Aid Money Awarded: $50,000
Number Granted: 20% Avg. Per Student: $1500

Additional Support

Endowment: $1 Mil Per Student: $3000
Alumni: 3600 Annual Gifts: $260,000 Giving: %

Admission

Largest Grade Entry: 10 Applied: 50
Accepted: 40 Entered: 30
Median Percentile Entering Grade: %
Application Deadline: Rolling Remedial Program: No

Academics

Advanced Placement Preparation in 2 Test Areas
Class Size: 13 Student-Teacher Ratio:
Number of Seniors: 75 Combined SATS: 910

Facilities

Rooms: Singles 0% Doubles: 100% Larger: 0%
Library Volumes: 17,000 Acres: 220 Plant: 8 Mil

Other Facts

Air strip on campus; flight instruction given; also, horses and horsemanship taught; 20 day girls.

Locale

Pop. 1400; Chatham Girls School in same town.

Howe Military Academy (Coed)

Founded 1884

783 Academy Place, Howe, IN 46746
(219) 562-2131
Airport: South Bend, 45 miles

Students

Total: 170 Boys: 136 Girls: 34 Grades: 5-12
Boarding: 170 Day: 0 Local Students: %
Number of States: 10 Countries: 2 Foreign Students: 2%

Costs and Aid

Tuition: $11,300 School Extras: $None
Student Aid Money Awarded: $150,000
Number Granted: 30% Avg. Per Student: $2500

Additional Support

Endowment: $8 Mil Per Student: $45,000
Alumni: 7000 Annual Gifts: $ Giving: %

Admission

Largest Grade Entry: 10 Applied: 35
Accepted: 30 Entered: 25
Median Percentile Entering Grade: %
Application Deadline: Rolling Remedial Program: No

Academics

Advanced Placement Preparation in 4 Test Areas
Class Size: 12 Student-Teacher Ratio: 10-1
Number of Seniors: 31 Combined SATS: 900

Facilities

Rooms: Singles 0% Doubles: 100% Larger: 0%
Library Volumes: 18,000 Acres: 120 Plant:

Other Facts

Became Coed in 1989; new science lab; affiliated with Episcopal Church; only 10% are Episcopalians.

Locale

Pop. 500; rural; skiing 40 miles away; school is halfway between Detroit and Chicago.

Kemper Military School (Coed)

Founded 1844

700 3rd St., Boonville, MO 65233
(816) 882-5623
Airport: Kansas City, 100 miles

Students

Total: 160 Boys: 130 Girls: 30 Grades: 7-12
Boarding: 160 Day: 0 Local Students: %
Number of States: 30 Countries: 9 Foreign Students: 7%

Costs and Aid

Tuition: $9800 School Extras: $1500
Student Aid Money Awarded: $0
Number Granted: % Avg. Per Student: $

Additional Support

Endowment: $0 Per Student: $
Alumni: 12,000 Annual Gifts: $ Giving: %

Admission

Largest Grade Entry: Applied:
Accepted: Entered:
Median Percentile Entering Grade: %
Application Deadline: Remedial Program:

Academics

Advanced Placement Preparation in Test Areas
Class Size: 15-17 Student-Teacher Ratio: 15-1
Number of Seniors: 45 Combined SATS: 870

Facilities

Rooms: Singles 0% Doubles: 100% Larger: 0%
Library Volumes: 20,000 Acres: 140 Plant: 18 Mil

Other Facts

New computer learning center; school sponsored trips.

Locale

Pop. 7000; U. of Missouri 20 minutes away; lake on campus; 9 hole golf course.

Marine Military Academy (Boys)

Founded 1965

320 B Iwo Jima Blvd., Harlingen, TX 78550
(512) 423-6006
Airport: Harlingen, 0 miles

Students

Total: 380 Boys: 380 Girls: 0 Grades: 8-PG
Boarding: 380 Day: 0 Local Students: %
Number of States: 33 Countries: 7 Foreign Students: 18%

Costs and Aid

Tuition: $8400 School Extras: $1600
Student Aid Money Awarded: $105,000
Number Granted: 18% Avg. Per Student: $3000

Additional Support

Endowment: $10 Mil Per Student: $28,000
Alumni: 1800 Annual Gifts: $200,000 Giving: %

Admission

Largest Grade Entry: 10 Applied: 80
Accepted: 59 Entered: 50
Median Percentile Entering Grade: %
Application Deadline: Rolling Remedial Program: No

Academics

Advanced Placement Preparation in Test Areas
Class Size: 12-15 Student-Teacher Ratio: 13-1
Number of Seniors: 90 Combined SATS: 1030

Facilities

Rooms: Singles 0% Doubles: 100% Larger: 0%
Library Volumes: 11,000 Acres: 150 Plant: 14 Mil

Other Facts

New library and tennis center (1989); also, new administration building; Marine ROTC.

Locale

Pop. 45,000; 3 miles from downtown; 100 miles southwest of Corpus Christi; campus right next to airport.

Marion Military Institute (Coed)

Founded 1842

Washington St., Marion, AL 36756
(205) 683-6173
Airport: Birmingham, 75 miles

Students

Total: 250 Boys: 200 Girls: 50 Grades: 9-12
Boarding: 200 Day: 50 Local Students: %
Number of States: 35 Countries: 6 Foreign Students: 3%

Costs and Aid

Tuition: $8000 School Extras: $400
Student Aid Money Awarded: $
Number Granted: % Avg. Per Student: $

Additional Support

Endowment: $3 Mil Per Student: $12,000
Alumni: 9500 Annual Gifts: $50,000 Giving: %

Admission

Largest Grade Entry: 11 Applied: 65
Accepted: 63 Entered: 58
Median Percentile Entering Grade: %
Application Deadline: Rolling Remedial Program: No

Academics

Advanced Placement Preparation in Test Areas
Class Size: 15 Student-Teacher Ratio: 16-1
Number of Seniors: 55 Combined SATS: 1000

Facilities

Rooms: Singles 0% Doubles: 100% Larger: 0%
Library Volumes: 30,000 Acres: 125 Plant: 8 Mil

Other Facts

Golf course on campus; service academy program; as many as 14% go on to the Academy.

Locale

Pop. 4000; rural setting; 80 miles west of Montgomery; walking distance of downtown.

Marmion Military Academy (Boys)

Founded 1933

Butterfield Road, Aurora, IL 60504
(312) 897-6936
Airport: O'Hare, 25 miles

Students

Total: 350 Boys: 350 Girls: Grades: 9-12
Boarding: 175 Day: 175 Local Students: %
Number of States: 16 Countries: 4 Foreign Students: 6%

Costs and Aid

Tuition: $7250 School Extras: $
Student Aid Money Awarded: $40,000
Number Granted: 16% Avg. Per Student: $1000

Additional Support

Endowment: $400,000 Per Student: $1100
Alumni: 6000 Annual Gifts: $ Giving: %

Admission

Largest Grade Entry: 9 Applied: 130
Accepted: 100 Entered: 100
Median Percentile Entering Grade: %
Application Deadline: Rolling Remedial Program: No

Academics

Advanced Placement Preparation in 6 Test Areas
Class Size: 22 Student-Teacher Ratio: 10-1
Number of Seniors: 76 Combined SATS: 1050

Facilities

Rooms: Singles 0% Doubles: 60% Larger: 40%
Library Volumes: 9000 Acres: 350 Plant: 13 Mil

Other Facts

In last 15 years, 81 merit scholarship finalists; ski club; 71% of faculty have masters degrees or better; 85% Catholic; operated by Benedictine Monks.

Locale

Pop. 85,000; campus in high tech corridor; suburban location.

Missouri Military Academy (Boys)

Founded 1889

204 Grand Ave., Mexico, MO 65265
(314) 581-1776
Airport: St. Louis, 105 miles

Students

Total: 330 Boys: 330 Girls: 0 Grades: 4-12
Boarding: 330 Day: 0 Local Students: %
Number of States: 31 Countries: 12 Foreign Students: 33%

Costs and Aid

Tuition: $9,530 School Extras: $3,470
Student Aid Money Awarded: $25,000
Number Granted: 3% Avg. Per Student: $1,250

Additional Support

Endowment: $ Per Student: $
Alumni: 20,000 Annual Gifts: $190,000 Giving: %

Admission

Largest Grade Entry: 10 Applied: 55
Accepted: 45 Entered: 40
Median Percentile Entering Grade: %
Application Deadline: Rolling Remedial Program: Yes

Academics

Advanced Placement Preparation in 2 Test Areas
Class Size: 13 Student-Teacher Ratio: 9-1
Number of Seniors: 60 Combined SATS:

Facilities

Rooms: Singles 0% Doubles: 98% Larger: 2%
Library Volumes: 8000 Acres: 288 Plant: 14M

Other Facts

English as second language available; new field house; natatorium; library.

Locale

12,500 pop.; 4 motels; 50 miles from Jefferson City.

New York Military Academy (Coed)

Founded 1889

Academy Avenue, Cornwall-on-Hudson, New York 12520
(914) 534-3710
Airport: La Guardia, 67 miles

Students

Total: 315 Boys: 265 Girls: 50 Grades: 5-PG
Boarding: 290 Day: 25 Local Students: 7%
Number of States: 22 Countries: 20 Foreign Students: 6%

Costs and Aid

Tuition: $8400 School Extras: $3400
Student Aid Money Awarded: $143,500
Number Granted: 22% Avg. Per Student: $1500

Additional Support

Endowment: $800,000 Per Student: $2500
Alumni: 3.6 M Annual Gifts: $N/A Giving: 7%

Admission

Largest Grade Entry: 10 Applied: 215
Accepted: 178 Entered: 138
Median Percentile Entering 10th Grade: 15%
Application Deadline: Rolling Remedial Program: No

Academics

Advanced Placement Preparation in 6 Test Areas
Class Size: 10-12 Student-Teacher Ratio: 10:1
Number of Seniors: 81 Combined SATS: 940

Facilities

Rooms: Singles 0% Doubles: 100% Larger: 0%
Library Volumes: 17,000 Acres: 325 Plant: 12.3M

Other Facts

3 swimming pools (2 indoor); gym; weight room (Nautilus); stables, academic summer session available (2,4, and 6 week programs).

Locale

Pop. 3300; 60 miles north of NYC and 6 miles north of the USMA; West Point on outskirts of town.

Northwestern Military Academy (Boys)

Founded 1888

550 Southshore Drive, Lake Geneva, WI 53147
(414) 248-4465
Airport: Milwaukee, 50 miles

Students

Total: 130 Boys: 130 Girls: 0 Grades: 7-12
Boarding: 125 Day: 5 Local Students: %
Number of States: 15 Countries: 6 Foreign Students: 7%

Costs and Aid

Tuition: $12,950 School Extras: $None
Student Aid Money Awarded: $25,000
Number Granted: % Avg. Per Student: $1250

Additional Support

Endowment: $400,000 Per Student: $3000
Alumni: 2800 Annual Gifts: $ Giving: %

Admission

Largest Grade Entry: 9 Applied: 40
Accepted: 25 Entered: 20
Median Percentile Entering Grade: %
Application Deadline: Rolling Remedial Program: No

Academics

Advanced Placement Preparation in 3 Test Areas
Class Size: 9 Student-Teacher Ratio: 9-1
Number of Seniors: 35 Combined SATS:

Facilities

Rooms: Singles 0% Doubles: 100% Larger: 0%
Library Volumes: 9000 Acres: 43 Plant: 4M

Other Facts

Miniature golf course on campus; numerous golf courses nearby.

Locale

Pop. 5500. 5 miles from Geneva; rural setting; on Lake Geneva; sailing.

Oak Ridge Military Academy (Coed)

Founded 1852

Hwy. 150, Box 498, Oak Ridge, NC 27310
(919) 643-4131
Airport: Greensboro, 6 miles

Students

Total: 160 Boys: 125 Girls: 35 Grades: 7-12 & PG
Boarding: 146 Day: 14 Local Students: 30%
Number of States: 24 Countries: 12 Foreign Students: 9%

Costs and Aid

Tuition: $8400 School Extras: $845
Student Aid Money Awarded: $87,240
Number Granted: 34% Avg. Per Student: $1586

Additional Support

Endowment: $800,000 Per Student: $5000
Alumni: 7,500 Annual Gifts: $208,996 Giving: 8%

Admission

Largest Grade Entry: 10th Applied: 89
Accepted: 67 Entered: 56
Median Percentile Entering 10th Grade: 32%
Application Deadline: 1 Aug. & 1 Jan. Remedial Program: LD only in 7th, 8th, 9th

Academics

Advanced Placement Preparation in 6 Test Areas
Class Size: 10-12 Student-Teacher Ratio: 8-1
Number of Seniors: 27 Combined SATS: 980

Facilities

Rooms: Singles 0% Doubles: 100% Larger: 0%
Library Volumes: 18,000 Acres: 101 Plant: 4.7M

Other Facts

25% in Gifted and Talented Program; 10% in LD; N.C.'s oldest male and coed school. N.C.'s first accredited school and only Military Academy; indoor pool.

Locale

Pop. 1000; rural; 15 miles equidistant — Greensboro, Winston-Salem, High Point. Entire campus is a National Historic District with 11 buildings on National Register.

Randolph-Macon Academy (Coed)

Founded 1892

1st & 3rd Streets, Front Royal, VA 22630
(703) 635-4141
Airport: Washington, 70 miles

Students

Total: 325 Boys: 280 Girls: 45 Grades: 7-PG
Boarding: 285 Day: 40 Local Students: 13%
Number of States: 25 Countries: 15 Foreign Students: 10%

Costs and Aid

Tuition: $7600 School Extras: $1300
Student Aid Money Awarded: $80,000
Number Granted: 25% Avg. Per Student: $1000

Additional Support

Endowment: $400,000 Per Student: $
Alumni: 4700 Annual Gifts: $ Giving: %

Admission

Largest Grade Entry: 9 Applied:
Accepted: Entered:
Median Percentile Entering Grade: %
Application Deadline: Rolling Remedial Program: Yes

Academics

Advanced Placement Preparation in Test Areas
Class Size: 14 Student-Teacher Ratio: 10-1
Number of Seniors: 60 Combined SATS: 925

Facilities

Rooms: Singles 0% Doubles: 100% Larger: 0%
Library Volumes: 7500 Acres: 130 Plant: 6 Mil

Other Facts

An Air Force Junior ROTC; flight instruction; new math and science bldg.; also, new 500 seat chapel; ESL offered; new girls' dorm and dining hall (1990).

Locale

Pop. 12,000; rural setting next to Shenandoah National Park; 18 miles from Winchester.

Riverside Military Academy (Boys)

Founded 1907

Gainesville, GA. 30501
(404) 532-6251
Airport: Atlanta, 65 miles

Students

Total: 540 Boys: 540 Girls: 0 Grades: 8-PG
Boarding: 540 Day: 0 Local Students: 5%
Number of States: 35 Countries: 16 Foreign Students: 19%

Costs and Aid

Tuition: $6875 School Extras: $None
Student Aid Money Awarded: $
Number Granted: % Avg. Per Student: $

Additional Support

Endowment: $50,000,000 Per Student: $95,000
Alumni: 4000 Annual Gifts: $0 Giving: 0%

Admission

Largest Grade Entry: 9 Applied:
Accepted: Entered:
Median Percentile Entering Grade: %
Application Deadline: Rolling Remedial Program: No

Academics

Advanced Placement Preparation in Test Areas
Class Size: 15 Student-Teacher Ratio: 15-1
Number of Seniors: 125 Combined SATS: 980

Facilities

Rooms: Singles 0% Doubles: 50% Larger: 50%
Library Volumes: 23,000 Acres: 200 Plant: 16M

Other Facts

ESL offered; indoor Olympic pool (1984); 1.5 million dollar field house (1982) with a running track; new barracks (1988); fencing program.

Locale

Pop. 35,000; ¼ mile from Lake Lanier; Brenau Girls' School also in Gainesville.

St. John's Military Academy (Boys)

Founded 1885

Delafield, WI 53018
(414) 646-3311
Airport: Milwaukee, 30 miles

Students

Total: 200 Boys: 200 Girls: 0 Grades: 7-12
Boarding: 200 Day: 0 Local Students: %
Number of States: 17 Countries: 4 Foreign Students: 13%

Costs and Aid

Tuition: $13,250 School Extras: $None
Student Aid Money Awarded: $75,000
Number Granted: % Avg. Per Student: $

Additional Support

Endowment: $4 Mil Per Student: $8000
Alumni: 3500 Annual Gifts: $ Giving: %

Admission

Largest Grade Entry: 9th Applied:
Accepted: Entered:
Median Percentile Entering Grade: %
Application Deadline: Rolling Remedial Program: No

Academics

Advanced Placement Preparation in Test Areas
Class Size: 6-10 Student-Teacher Ratio: 6-1
Number of Seniors: 45 Combined SATS: 1010

Facilities

Rooms: Singles 10% Doubles: 90% Larger: 0%
Library Volumes: 15,000 Acres: 150 Plant: 20 Mil

Other Facts

Indoor pool; 9- hole golf course on campus; skiing 5 minutes away; Apple computer in every cadet room; skiing; indoor pool.

Locale

Pop. 2000; 1 block from downtown and borders on lake; 50 miles from Madison.

Valley Forge Junior Military Academy & Junior College (Boys)

Founded 1928

1001 Eagle Road, Wayne PA 19087
(215) 688-3151
Airport: Philadelphia, 15 miles

Students

Total: 720 Boys: 720 Girls: 0 Grades: 7-JC
Boarding: 720 Day: Local Students: 30%
Number of States: 25 Countries: 19 Foreign Students: 9%

Costs and Aid

Tuition: $8,615 School Extras: $3900
Student Aid Money Awarded: $400,000
Number Granted: 18% Avg. Per Student: $2300

Additional Support

Endowment: $1.6 Mil Per Student: $2400
Alumni: 12,000 Annual Gifts: $275,460 Giving: 15%

Admission

Largest Grade Entry: 11 Applied: 91
Accepted: 89 Entered: 49
Median Percentile Entering Grade: %
Application Deadline: Rolling Remedial Program: Yes

Academics

Advanced Placement Preparation in 6 Test Areas
Class Size: 10-15 Student-Teacher Ratio: 15-1
Number of Seniors: 124 Combined SATS: 860

Facilities

Rooms: Singles 0% Doubles: 100% Larger: 0%
Library Volumes: 69,000 Acres: 123 Plant: 17 Mil

Other Facts

Accreditation: Middle States Association of Colleges & Schools; Army ROTC Commissioning Program; full varsity sport program; band; and summer programs.

Locale

1 mile from the center of town and situated on a beautiful 123 acre campus; four miles from Valley Forge National Historical Park with access to 10 local motels/hotels.

Wentworth Military Academy (Boys)

Founded 1880

18th & Washington Ave., Lexington, MO 64067
(816) 259-2221
Airport: Kansas City, 45 miles

Students

Total: 250 Boys: 250 Girls: 0 Grades: 7-14
Boarding: 240 Day: 10 Local Students: 3%
Number of States: 25 Countries: 8 Foreign Students: 15%

Costs and Aid

Tuition: $10,100 School Extras: $2000
Student Aid Money Awarded: $300,000
Number Granted: 50% Avg. Per Student: $2000

Additional Support

Endowment: $300,000 Per Student: $1200
Alumni: 7000 Annual Gifts: $300,000 Giving: 15%

Admission

Largest Grade Entry: 9 Applied: 40
Accepted: 30 Entered: 30
Median Percentile Entering Grade: %
Application Deadline: Rolling Remedial Program: None

Academics

Advanced Placement Preparation in 2 Test Areas
Class Size: 15-20 Student-Teacher Ratio: 9-1
Number of Seniors: 40 CombinedACTS: 19

Facilities

Rooms: Singles 0% Doubles: 100% Larger: 0%
Library Volumes: 20,000 Acres: 137 Plant: 10M

Other Facts

Fieldhouse — 65,000 sq. ft.; indoor trk; 3 BB courts; Olympic pool; wt. lifting; 2 racquetball rooms; golf course; 10-court tennis complex.

Locale

5000 pop.; 2 motels; historical river town; many beautiful antebellum homes & antique shops; 45 miles from Truman Library; professional sports; dinner theatre.

For Those With Learning Differences

Blue Ridge School (Boys)

Founded 1909

Dyke, VA 22935
(804) 985-2811
Airport: Charlottesville, 18 miles

Students

Total: 230 Boys: 230 Girls: 0 Grades: 9-12
Boarding: 230 Day: 0 Local Students: %
Number of States: 27 Countries: 4 Foreign Students: %

Costs and Aid

Tuition: $12,300 School Extras: $1200-1500
Student Aid Money Awarded: $126,000
Number Granted: 10% Avg. Per Student: $5500

Additional Support

Endowment: $1,400,000 Per Student: $6000
Alumni: 1400 Annual Gifts: $212,000 Giving: 40%

Admission

Largest Grade Entry: 9th Applied: 80
Accepted: 45 Entered: 40
Median Percentile Entering 25% Grade: %
Application Deadline: Rolling Remedial Program: No

Academics

Advanced Placement Preparation in Test Areas
Class Size: 12 Student-Teacher Ratio: 7-1
Number of Seniors: 60 Combined SATS: 830

Facilities

Rooms: Singles 0% Doubles: 100% Larger: 0%
Library Volumes: 11,000 Acres: 1000 Plant: 6 Mil

Other Facts

Outstanding computer facility; extensive athletic facility; 100% college placement; 4 indoor tennis courts; golf nearby; lake on property.

Locale

Pop. 45,000; 2 hrs. from D.C.; 30 minutes from Charlottesville and U. of Virginia in Blue Ridge Mountains just below Skyline Drive;. rural setting.

Brandon Hall School (Boys)

Founded 1959

1701 Brandon Hall Drive, Atlanta, GA 30350
(404) 394-8177
Airport: Atlanta, 18 miles

Students

Total: 170 Boys: 120 Girls: 50 Grades: 5-12
Boarding: 65 Day: 105 Local Students: %
Number of States: 15 Countries: 1 Foreign Students: 1%

Costs and Aid

Tuition: $16-24,000 School Extras: $700
Student Aid Money Awarded: $
Number Granted: % Avg. Per Student: $

Additional Support

Endowment: $ Per Student: $
Alumni: 1200 Annual Gifts: $ Giving: %

Admission

Largest Grade Entry: 8th Applied:
Accepted: Entered:
Median Percentile Entering Grade: %
Application Deadline: Rolling Remedial Program: Yes

Academics

Advanced Placement Preparation in 4 Test Areas
Class Size: 3 Student-Teacher Ratio: 2-1
Number of Seniors: 40 Combined SATS: 950

Facilities

Rooms: Singles 10% Doubles: 90% Larger: %
Library Volumes: 3000 Acres: 25 Plant: 7M

Other Facts

100% attend colleges throughout U.S.; new classroom and dormitory building in 1988; new chapel and assembly hall planned.

Locale

Pop. 500,000; in residential area; just outside the perimeter; a wooded estate overlooking the Chattahoochee River; a Norman manor house.

Cedu School (Coed)

Founded 1966

Box 1176, Running Springs, CA
(714) 867-2722
Airport: Los Angeles, 90 miles

Students

Total: 120 Boys: 60 Girls: 60 Grades: Ungraded
Boarding: 120 Day: 0 Local Students: %
Number of States: 15 Countries: 3 Foreign Students: 3%

Costs and Aid

Tuition: $30,000 School Extras: $
Student Aid Money Awarded: $
Number Granted: % Avg. Per Student: $

Additional Support

Endowment: $ Per Student: $
Alumni: Annual Gifts: $ Giving: %

Admission

Largest Grade Entry: Applied:
Accepted: Entered:
Median Percentile Entering Grade: %
Application Deadline: Remedial Program: Yes

Academics

Advanced Placement Preparation in Test Areas
Class Size: 12 Student-Teacher Ratio: 5-1
Number of Seniors: Combined SATS:

Facilities

Rooms: Singles 0% Doubles: 60% Larger: 40%
Library Volumes: 12,000 Acres: 120 Plant: 5M

Other Facts

$3300 per month; targeted for special needs or problems; includes a farm.

Locale

Pop. 2000; surrounded by San Bernardino National Forest; 6000 feet altitude; near Lake Arrowhead.

Christchurch School (Boys)

Founded 1921

Christchurch, VA 23031
(804) 758-2306
Airport: Richmond, 40 miles

Students

Total: 220 Boys: 200 Girls: 20 Grades: 9-PG
Boarding: 170 Day: 50 Local Students: 29%
Number of States: 23 Countries: 2 Foreign Students: 2%

Costs and Aid

Tuition: $12,610 School Extras: $1,000
Student Aid Money Awarded: $300,000
Number Granted: 31% Avg. Per Student: $6,100

Additional Support

Endowment: $Not available. Per Student: $
Alumni: 1800 Annual Gifts: $ Giving: %

Admission

Largest Grade Entry: 9 Applied: 48
Accepted: 35 Entered: 30
Median Percentile Entering Grade: %
Application Deadline: rolling Remedial Program: Yes

Academics

Advanced Placement Preparation in 2 Test Areas
Class Size: 12 Student-Teacher Ratio: 6-1
Number of Seniors: 50 Combined SATS: 910

Facilities

Rooms: Singles 1% Doubles: 99% Larger: 0%
Library Volumes: 10,000 Acres: 125 Plant: 5 Mil

Other Facts

Excellent program in marine sciences; special program for learning or disabled students; sailing program as well as golf and lacrosse.

Locale

Pop. 100; located on the Chesapeake Bay; 30 minutes from Colonial Williamsburg; sailing program; famous old Christ Church (1663) used by students for required attendance.

Eagle Hill School (Coed)

Founded 1967

Hardwick, MA 01037
(413) 477-6000
Airport: Boston, 75 miles

Students

Total: 82 Boys: 60 Girls: 22 Grades: Ungraded
Boarding: 81 Day: 1 Local Students: %
Number of States: 22 Countries: 5 Foreign Students: 11%

Costs and Aid

Tuition: $24,400 School Extras: $
Student Aid Money Awarded: $
Number Granted: % Avg. Per Student: $

Additional Support

Endowment: $0 Per Student: $
Alumni: 1200 Annual Gifts: $45,000 Giving: %

Admission

Largest Grade Entry: Applied: 95
Accepted: 45 Entered:
Median Percentile Entering Grade: %
Application Deadline: Rolling Remedial Program: Yes

Academics

Advanced Placement Preparation in Test Areas
Class Size: 3-4 Student-Teacher Ratio: 3-1
Number of Seniors: 11 Combined SATS:

Facilities

Rooms: Singles 0% Doubles: 100% Larger: 0%
Library Volumes: 10,000 Acres: 150 Plant: 2M

Other Facts

For students with average or above average intelligence who are underachieving; skiing on and off campus; swimming; camping; interscholastic team sports.

Locale

Pop. 2300; rural setting; 20 miles from Worcester.

Forman School (Coed)

Founded 1930

Litchfield, CT 06759
(203) 567-0140
Airport: Hartford, 32 miles

Students

Total: 220 Boys: 155 Girls: 75 Grades: 9-12
Boarding: 190 Day: 30 Local Students: %
Number of States: 30 Countries: 10 Foreign Students: 6%

Costs and Aid

Tuition: $19,300 School Extras: $
Student Aid Money Awarded: $100,000
Number Granted: 7% Avg. Per Student: $6000

Additional Support

Endowment: $1 Mil Per Student: $5500
Alumni: 1800 Annual Gifts: $200,000 Giving: %

Admission

Largest Grade Entry: 9 Applied: 75
Accepted: 36 Entered: 36
Median Percentile Entering Grade: %
Application Deadline: March 1 Remedial Program: Yes

Academics

Advanced Placement Preparation in Test Areas
Class Size: 12 Student-Teacher Ratio: 4-1
Number of Seniors: 67 Combined SATS: 820

Facilities

Rooms: Singles 10% Doubles: 90% Larger: 0%
Library Volumes: 12,000 Acres: 140 Plant: 7 Mil

Other Facts

For dyslexic and learning disabled; new dining hall and gym as well as science center; indoor Olympic pool.

Locale

Historic town; pop. 1500; 100 miles from NYC and Boston.

Gow School (Boys)

Founded 1926

Emery Rd., South Wales, NY 14139
(716) 652-3450
Airport: Buffalo, 30 miles

Students

Total: 150 Boys: 150 Girls: Grades: 7-PG
Boarding: 150 Day: Local Students: %
Number of States: 28 Countries: 4 Foreign Students: 2%

Costs and Aid

Tuition: $13,900 School Extras: $650
Student Aid Money Awarded: $69,500
Number Granted: 7% Avg. Per Student: $

Additional Support

Endowment: $500,000 Per Student: $3300
Alumni: Annual Gifts: $ Giving: %

Admission

Largest Grade Entry: 10 Applied: 21
Accepted: 21 Entered:
Median Percentile Entering Grade: %
Application Deadline: None Remedial Program: Yes

Academics

Advanced Placement Preparation in Test Areas
Class Size: 3-6 Student-Teacher Ratio: 5-1
Number of Seniors: 28 Combined SATS: 762

Facilities

Rooms: Singles % Doubles: 85% Larger: 15%
Library Volumes: 6000 Acres: 100 Plant: 3.5m

Other Facts

Ski slope on campus; new dorm (1984); science lab; study hall and classroom bldg. (1987); nation's oldest college preparatory boarding school for boys with dyslexia and learning disabilities.

Locale

30 mi. southeast of Buffalo; 100 mi. south of Toronto, Canada; rural area with stream and woods; 1 motel.

Grand River Academy (Boys)

Founded 1831

3042 College Street, Austinburg, OH 44010
(216) 275-2811
Airport: Cleveland, 65 miles

Students

Total: 93 Boys: 91 Girls: 2 Grades: 9-12 (PG)
Boarding: 89 Day: 4 Local Students: 5%
Number of States: 9 Countries: 1 Foreign Students: 0%

Costs and Aid

Tuition: $10,500 School Extras: $800
Student Aid Money Awarded: $25,000
Number Granted: 40% Avg. Per Student: $600

Additional Support

Endowment: $450,000 Per Student: $5000
Alumni: 500 Annual Gifts: $75,000 Giving: 25%

Admission

Largest Grade Entry: 10 Applied: 28
Accepted: 20 Entered: 20
Median Percentile Entering Grade: %
Application Deadline: rolling Remedial Program: yes

Academics

Advanced Placement Preparation in Test Areas
Class Size: 7 Student-Teacher Ratio: 5-1
Number of Seniors: 22 Combined ACT: 18

Facilities

Rooms: Singles 5% Doubles: 95% Larger: 0%
Library Volumes: 7,000 Acres: 150 Plant: 5M

Other Facts

Specialized college prep program for students not working to their potential; new dining room, stage and infirmary in 1976.

Locale

Small rural community one hour east of Cleveland; 10 miles south of Lake Erie; pop. 1900; 50 miles east of Cleveland; near Lake Erie.

Highcroft School (Coed)

Founded 1978

Gale Road, Williamstown, MA 01267
(413) 458-8136
Airport: Albany, 40 miles

Students

Total: 80 Boys: 55 Girls: 25 Grades: 4-PG
Boarding: 80 Day: 0 Local Students: 0%
Number of States: 26 Countries: 8 Foreign Students: 10%

Costs and Aid

Tuition: $18,500 School Extras: $1000
Student Aid Money Awarded: $160,000
Number Granted: % Avg. Per Student: $4000

Additional Support

Endowment: $ Per Student: $
Alumni: 100 Annual Gifts: $ Giving: %

Admission

Largest Grade Entry: Applied:
Accepted: Entered:
Median Percentile Entering Grade: %
Application Deadline: Rolling Remedial Program:

Academics

Advanced Placement Preparation in 2 Test Areas
Class Size: 3-6 Student-Teacher Ratio: 4-1
Number of Seniors: 15 Combined SATS: 800

Facilities

Rooms: Singles 0% Doubles: 100% Larger: 0%
Library Volumes: 8000 Acres: 25 Plant: 4 Mil

Other Facts

Assists students to reach their potential; student lounge added in 1988; school occupies the former Cluett Estate.

Locale

Pop. 9000; 1 mile from village center; college town (Williams); 2½ hours from NYC and Boston; ski lift minutes away.

Hyde School (Coed)

Founded 1966

616 High St., Bath, ME 04530
(207) 443-5584
Airport: Portland, 30 miles

Students

Total: 140 Boys: 95 Girls: 45 Grades: 8-PG
Boarding: 138 Day: 2 Local Students: %
Number of States: 30 Countries: 4 Foreign Students: 2%

Costs and Aid

Tuition: $14,000 School Extras: $
Student Aid Money Awarded: $150,000
Number Granted: % Avg. Per Student: $3500

Additional Support

Endowment: $50,000 Per Student: $400
Alumni: 650 Annual Gifts: $6000 Giving: 9%

Admission

Largest Grade Entry: 10 Applied: 120
Accepted: 70 Entered: 60
Median Percentile Entering Grade:
Application Deadline: rolling Remedial Program: no

Academics

Advanced Placement Preparation in Test Areas
Class Size: 10-15 Student-Teacher Ratio: 6-1
Number of Seniors: 28 Combined SATS:

Facilities

Rooms: Singles 0% Doubles: 90% Larger: 10%
Library Volumes: 10,000 Acres: 140 Plant: 6 million

Other Facts

New academic/art building; three new dorms; performing arts required; parent involvement through Family Learning Center.

Locale

2½ hours from Boston; 45 min. from Portland Airport; 20 min. from beautiful beaches; 1 hr. 15 min. from ski areas.

Kildonan School (Boys)

Founded 1969

Amenia, NY 12501
(914) 373-8111
Airport: Hartford, 55 miles

Students

Total: 98 Boys: 96 Girls: 2 Grades: 5-PG
Boarding: 96 Day: 2 Local Students: 6%
Number of States: 21 Countries: 2 Foreign Students: 3%

Costs and Aid

Tuition: $22,000 School Extras: $400
Student Aid Money Awarded: $50,000
Number Granted: 8% Avg. Per Student: $7000

Additional Support

Endowment: $0 Per Student: $
Alumni: 5000 Annual Gifts: $ Giving: %

Admission

Largest Grade Entry: 10 Applied:
Accepted: Entered:
Median Percentile Entering Grade: %
Application Deadline: Rolling Remedial Program: Yes

Academics

Advanced Placement Preparation in Test Areas
Class Size: 5-7 Student-Teacher Ratio: 3-1
Number of Seniors: 20 Combined SATS: 720

Facilities

Rooms: Singles 10% Doubles: 90% Larger: %
Library Volumes: 8000 Acres: 450 Plant: 2 Mil

Other Facts

Acquired campus in 1980; for dyslexics of average or above average intelligence; students often go on to other "main stream" prep schools.

Locale

Pop. 6000. 25 miles from Poughkeepsie; 90 miles north of NYC.

Landmark School (Coed)

Founded 1971

412 Hale St., Prides Crossing, MA 01965
(508) 927-4440
Airport: Boston, 20 miles

Students

Total: 442 Boys: 364 Girls: 78 Grades: ungraded
Boarding: 299 Day: 143 Local Students: 25%
Number of States: 50 Countries: 10 Foreign Students: %

Costs and Aid

Tuition: $12-27K School Extras: $750
Student Aid Money Awarded: $40,000
Number Granted: 35% Avg. Per Student: $4000

Additional Support

Endowment: $ Per Student: $
Alumni: 1400 Annual Gifts: $500,000 Giving: %

Admission

Largest Grade Entry: Applied:
Accepted: Entered:
Median Percentile Entering Grade: %
Application Deadline: Remedial Program:

Academics

Advanced Placement Preparation in Test Areas
Class Size: Student-Teacher Ratio: 3-1
Number of Seniors: 75 Combined SATS:

Facilities

Rooms: Singles 0% Doubles: 80% Larger: 20%
Library Volumes: 13,000 Acres: 45 Plant: 4 M

Other Facts

For only emotionally sound, intellectually average or above with known dyslexia; Ages 8 to 18.

Locale

2 miles from Salem. North Shore of Boston on Atlantic Ocean and residential neighborhood; sailing; skiing.

Oak Creek School (Coed)

Founded 1972

P.O. Box NN, W. Sedona, AZ 86340
(602) 634-5571
Airport: Phoenix, 100 miles

Students

Total: 100 Boys: 55 Girls: 45 Grades: 5-PG
Boarding: 100 Day: 0 Local Students: 0%
Number of States: 20 Countries: 8 Foreign Students: 8%

Costs and Aid

Tuition: $12,400 School Extras: $800
Student Aid Money Awarded: $0
Number Granted: 0% Avg. Per Student: $0

Additional Support

Endowment: $0 Per Student: $0
Alumni: 0 Annual Gifts: $0 Giving: 0%

Admission

Largest Grade Entry: 11 Applied: 30
Accepted: 27 Entered: 26
Median Percentile Entering 11 Grade: %
Application Deadline: Rolling Remedial Program: Yes

Academics

Advanced Placement Preparation in Test Areas
Class Size: 8-10 Student-Teacher Ratio: 7-1
Number of Seniors: 25 Combined SATS: 980

Facilities

Rooms: Singles 0% Doubles: 80% Larger: 20%
Library Volumes: 15,000 Acres: 20 Plant: 3M

Other Facts

3 new dormitories; new science lab; ESL; structured environment for underachievers.

Locale

Adjoins Coconino Nat. Forest; 6 miles from town; Cottonwood. Modern hospitals; shopping centers; 100 miles north of Phoenix; 17 miles from Sedona.

Oak Hill Academy (Coed)

Founded 1878

Mouth of Wilson, Virginia 24363
(703) 579-2619
Airport: Tri-City

Students

Total: 182 Boys: 94 Girls: 88 Grades: 9-PG
Boarding: 180 Day: 0 Local Students: %
Number of States: 18 Countries: 7 Foreign Students: 12%

Costs and Aid

Tuition: $8100 School Extras: $
Student Aid Money Awarded: $40,000
Number Granted: 20% Avg. Per Student: $1000

Additional Support

Endowment: $30,000 Per Student: $
Alumni: Annual Gifts: $ Giving: %

Admission

Largest Grade Entry: 11 Applied: 35
Accepted: 28 Entered: 18
Median Percentile Entering Grade: %
Application Deadline: Rolling Remedial Program: Yes

Academics

Advanced Placement Preparation in Test Areas
Class Size: 14 Student-Teacher Ratio: 9-1
Number of Seniors: 60 Combined SATS:

Facilities

Rooms: Singles 5% Doubles: 95% Larger: %
Library Volumes: 8000 Acres: 160 Plant: 4M

Other Facts

Affiliated with Baptist Church; required Sunday School attendance; new 1-million-dollar classroom bldg.; primarily for underachievers; equestrian program; learning resource center.

Locale

Pop. 200; in farming area; near Jefferson National Forest; West Jefferson 14 miles away.

The Phelps School (Boys)
Founded 1946

Malvern, PA 19355
(215) 644-1754
Airport: Philadelphia, 22 miles

Students
Total: 135 Boys: 135 Girls: Grades: 7-PG
Boarding: 135 Day: NA Local Students: %
Number of States: 21 Countries: 13 Foreign Students: 13%

Costs and Aid
Tuition: $12,400 School Extras: $500
Student Aid Money Awarded: $42,000
Number Granted: 5% Avg. Per Student: $1500-4200

Additional Support
Endowment: $0 Per Student: $
Alumni: 750 Annual Gifts: $25,000 Giving: %

Admission
Largest Grade Entry: 10 Applied: 16
Accepted: 12 Entered: 12
Median Percentile Entering Grade: %
Application Deadline: Rolling Remedial Program: Yes

Academics
Advanced Placement Preparation in Test Areas
Class Size: 7 Student-Teacher Ratio: 7-1
Number of Seniors: 28 Combined SATS:

Facilities
Rooms: Singles 8% Doubles: 92% Larger: 0%
Library Volumes: 7000 Acres: 110 Plant: 4 million

Other Facts
Indoor equestrian arena; remedial/developmental reading; structured for boys with basic subject deficiencies.

Locale
Pop. 2700; suburban community; includes 75 acres of farmland.

Pine Ridge School (Coed)
Founded 1968

1075 Williston Road, Williston, VT 05495
(802) 434-2161
Airport: Burlington, 8 miles

Students
Total: 109 Boys: 106 Girls: 43 Grades: 13-18 Ages
Boarding: 109 Day: 0 Local Students: %
Number of States: 26 Countries: 5 Foreign Students: 5%

Costs and Aid
Tuition: $23,500 School Extras: $
Student Aid Money Awarded: $
Number Granted: % Avg. Per Student: $

Additional Support
Endowment: $ Per Student: $
Alumni: 700 Annual Gifts: $235,000 Giving: %

Admission
Largest Grade Entry: Applied:
Accepted: 55 Entered: 38
Median Percentile Entering Grade: %
Application Deadline: Rolling Remedial Program: Yes

Academics
Advanced Placement Preparation in Test Areas
Class Size: 5-8 Student-Teacher Ratio: 6-1
Number of Seniors: 21 Combined SATS:

Facilities
Rooms: Singles 0% Doubles: 83% Larger: 17%
Library Volumes: 15,000 Acres: 110 Plant: 2 Mil

Other Facts
For average to above average students who have a diagnosed learning disability but no emotional or behavioral problems.

Locale
Pop. 4000; 10 miles from downtown; at foot of Green Mountains; skiing nearby; also, canoeing, kayaking.

St. Andrew's School (Coed)

Founded 1893

63 Federal Rd., Barrington, RI 02806
(401) 246-1230
Airport: Providence, 15 miles

Students

Total: 125 Boys: 90 Girls: 35 Grades: 6-12
Boarding: 75 Day: 50 Local Students: 45%
Number of States: 22 Countries: 4 Foreign Students: 5%

Costs and Aid

Tuition: $19,950 School Extras: $
Student Aid Money Awarded: $150,000
Number Granted: 22% Avg. Per Student: $8000

Additional Support

Endowment: $2.6 Mil Per Student: $21,000
Alumni: 400 Annual Gifts: $ Giving: %

Admission

Largest Grade Entry: 9 Applied: 30
Accepted: 20 Entered:
Median Percentile Entering Grade: %
Application Deadline: Rolling Remedial Program: Yes

Academics

Advanced Placement Preparation in Test Areas
Class Size: 10 Student-Teacher Ratio: 5-1
Number of Seniors: 22 Combined SATS: 750

Facilities

Rooms: Singles 20% Doubles: 60% Larger: 20%
Library Volumes: 12,000 Acres: 95 Plant: 3 Mil

Other Facts

Episcopal school; for students who want less competitive atmosphere; small classes; and want to work hard; all students in work program.

Locale

Pop. 17,000; 50 miles south of Boston; 20 miles north of Newport; near Brown University.

Saint Thomas More School (Boys)

Founded 1962

85 Cottage Road, Oakdale, CT 06370
(203) 859-1900
Airport: Hartford, 35 miles

Students

Total: 180 Boys: 180 Girls: 0 Grades: 8-PG
Boarding: 180 Day: 0 Local Students: 16%
Number of States: 13 Countries: 6 Foreign Students: 14%

Costs and Aid

Tuition: $11,000 School Extras: $
Student Aid Money Awarded: $30,000
Number Granted: 15% Avg. Per Student: $1000

Additional Support

Endowment: $ Per Student: $
Alumni: 1900 Annual Gifts: $ Giving: %

Admission

Largest Grade Entry: 9 Applied:
Accepted: Entered:
Median Percentile Entering Grade: %
Application Deadline: Rolling Remedial Program: Yes

Academics

Advanced Placement Preparation in Test Areas
Class Size: 12 Student-Teacher Ratio: 10-1
Number of Seniors: 46 Combined SATS: 870

Facilities

Rooms: Singles 0% Doubles: 100% Larger: 0%
Library Volumes: 7500 Acres: 150 Plant: 4 Mil

Other Facts

Affiliated with Catholic Church; all faiths welcome; for those with learning differences.

Locale

Pop. 400; 50 miles from New Haven on large lake; sailing; swimming; water skiing.

Vanguard School (Coed)

Founded 1966

Highway 27 North, Lake Wales, FL 33853
(813) 676-6091
Airport: Orlando, 50 miles

Students

Total: 150 Boys: 100 Girls: 50 Grades: 1-12
Boarding: 145 Day: 5 Local Students: 25%
Number of States: 23 Countries: 14 Foreign Students: 15%

Costs and Aid

Tuition: $18,000 School Extras: $None
Student Aid Money Awarded: $60,000
Number Granted: % Avg. Per Student: $4000

Additional Support

Endowment: $1 Mil Per Student: $6500
Alumni: 140 Annual Gifts: $ Giving: %

Admission

Largest Grade Entry: Applied:
Accepted: Entered:
Median Percentile Entering Grade: %
Application Deadline: Rolling Remedial Program: Yes

Academics

Advanced Placement Preparation in Test Areas
Class Size: 7 Student-Teacher Ratio: 8-1
Number of Seniors: 22 Combined SATS:

Facilities

Rooms: Singles 0% Doubles: 100% Larger: 0%
Library Volumes: 10,000 Acres: 75 Plant: 5M

Other Facts

For those with learning problems and adjustment difficulties; new arts center (1987).

Locale

3 miles north of Lake Wales; pop. 4500; 45 miles south of Orlando.

The Winchendon School (Coed)

Founded 1960

Winchendon, MA 01475
(508) 297-1223
Airport: Boston, 65 miles

Students

Total: 120 Boys: 85 Girls: 35 Grades: 9-PG
Boarding: 115 Day: 5 Local Students: 4%
Number of States: 23 Countries: 14 Foreign Students: 20%

Costs and Aid

Tuition: $16,950 School Extras: $2000
Student Aid Money Awarded: $60,000
Number Granted: 9% Avg. Per Student: $5000

Additional Support

Endowment: $0 Per Student: $
Alumni: 1000 Annual Gifts: $80,000 Giving: %

Admission

Largest Grade Entry: 11 Applied: 60
Accepted: 50 Entered: 40
Median Percentile Entering 11 Grade: 45%
Application Deadline: Rolling Remedial Program: Yes

Academics

Advanced Placement Preparation in Test Areas
Class Size: 6-8 Student-Teacher Ratio: 5:1
Number of Seniors: 45 Combined SATS: 800

Facilities

Rooms: Singles 70% Doubles: 30% Larger: 0%
Library Volumes: 9000 Acres: 232 Plant: 4 Mil

Other Facts

For mild underachievers; dress code (tie and coat); new girls' dorm (1986); once a resort hotel; has 18-hole golf course.

Locale

Rural small town; 2000 pop.; 36 miles from Worcester; ski resorts nearby.

Cardigan Mountain School (Boys)

Founded 1945

Canaan, NH 03741
(603) 523-4321
Airport: Boston, 120 miles

Students
Total: 180 Boys: 180 Girls: 0 Grades: 6-9
Boarding: 170 Day: 10 Local Students: %
Number of States: 30 Countries: 8 Foreign: 10%

Costs and Aid
Tuition: $15,500 School Extras: $550
Student Aid Money Awarded: $315,000
Number Granted: 21% Avg. Per Student: $7000

Additional Support
Endowment: $3.5 Mil Per Student: $79,000
Alumni: 2300 Annual Giving: $130,000 Participate: %

Facilities
Rooms: Singles 10% Doubles 90% Larger 0%
Library: 11,000 Volumes Acres: 500 Plant: 9 Mil

Other Facts
Pop. 2500; rural setting on large lake; 18 miles from Dartmouth; campus ski slope and jump; 2.2 million dollar learning center and library theater complex.

Eaglebrook School (Boys)

Founded 1922

Deerfield, MA 01342
(413) 774-7411
Airport: Hartford, 60 miles

Students
Total: 248 Boys: 244 Girls: 4 Grades: 6-9
Boarding: 178 Day: 70 Local Students: 28%
Number of States: 25 Countries: 21 Foreign: 19%

Costs and Aid
Tuition: $16,700 School Extras: $1200
Student Aid Money Awarded: $370,000
Number Granted: 24% Avg. Per Student: $6000

Additional Support
Endowment: $6.5 M Per Student: $26,000
Alumni: 2650 Annual Giving: $170,000 Participate: 25%

Facilities
Rooms: Singles: 25% Doubles: 74% Larger: 1%
Library: 10,000 Volumes Acres: 500 Plant: 11M

Other Facts
Pop. 4500; ski lift on campus; new science bldg. (1988); Deerfield School ½ mile; adjoins historic village; 2 hours from Boston.

Fay School (Coed)

Founded 1866

48 Main St., Southborough, MA 01772
(508) 485-0100
Airport: Boston, 30 miles

Students
Total: 350 Boys: 200 Girls: 150 Grades: 1-9
Boarding: 120 Day: 230 Local Students: 64%
Number of States: 24 Countries: 20 Foreign: 15%

Costs and Aid
Tuition: $17,600 School Extras: $None
Student Aid Money Awarded: $270,000
Number Granted: 20% Avg. Per Student: $5500

Additional Support
Endowment: $2.5 Mil Per Student: $7000
Alumni: 2500 Annual Giving: $300,000 Participate: 75%

Facilities
Rooms: Singles 40% Doubles: 58% Larger: 2%
Library: 12,000 volumes Acres: 45 Plant: 8 Mil

Other Facts
1 block from town center; pop. 6000; beautiful residential community; next to St. Mark's golf course within walking distance; new arts bldg.

The Fessenden School (Boys)

Founded 1903

250 Waltham St., West Newton, MA 02165
(617) 964-5350
Airport: Boston, 15 miles

Students
Total: 330 Boys: 330 Girls: 0 Grades: 1-9
Boarding: 90 Day: 240 Local Students: 85%
Number of States: 10 Countries: 8 Foreign: 6%

Costs and Aid
Tuition: $16,800 School Extras: $400
Student Aid Money Awarded: $200,000
Number Granted: 10% Avg. Per Student: $6000

Additional Support
Endowment: $1.2 Mil Per Student: $3700
Alumni: 3400 Annual Giving: $245,000 Participate: 20%

Facilities
Rooms: Singles: 40% Doubles: 60% Larger: %
Library: 8000 Volumes Acres: 40 Plant: 3 Mil

Other Facts
Pop. 60,000; home of Brandeis University; indoor hockey rink; 2 gyms; indoor/outdoor pool; art and music bldg; dorms remodeled recently.

Indian Mountain School (Coed)

Founded 1922

Lakeville, CT 06039
(203) 435-0871
Airport: Hartford, 53 miles

Students
Total: 150 Boys: 110 Girls: 40 Grades: 6-9
Boarding: 70 Day: 80 Local Students: 35%
Number of States: 14 Countries: 6 Foreign: 4%

Costs and Aid
Tuition: $15,250 School Extras: $750
Student Aid Money Awarded: $150,000
Number Granted: 23% Avg. Per Student: $5000

Additional Support
Endowment: $750,000 Per Student: $5000
Alumni: 1500 Annual Giving: $20,000 Participate: 14%

Facilities
Rooms: Singles: 0% Doubles: 93% Larger: 7%
Library: 7000 Volumes Acres: 400 Plant: 3M

Other Facts
Pop. 1500; Hotchkiss and Salisbury schools nearby; 3 mi. from town; ski tows on campus; new dorm (1985); 2½ hours from NYC.

North Country (Coed)

Founded 1938

Box 187, Lake Placid, NY 12946
(518) 523-9329
Airport: Albany, 140 miles

Students
Total: 80 Boys: 45 Girls: 35 Grades: 4-8
Boarding: 70 Day: 10 Local Students: 15%
Number of States: 18 Countries: 9 Foreign: 11%

Costs and Aid
Tuition: $14,900 School Extras: $300
Student Aid Money Awarded: $130,000
Number Granted: 25% Avg. Per Student: $4000

Additional Support
Endowment: $750,000 Per Student: $9500
Alumni: 900 Annual Giving: $45,000 Participate: 27%

Facilities
Rooms: Singles: 0% Doubles: 100% Larger: 0%
Library: 8000 Volumes Acres: 165 Plant: 2.5 Mil

Other Facts
Pop. 2500; site of Winter Olympics; Northwood School nearby; 7 miles from downtown; working farm with all students involved.

The Rectory School (Boys)

Founded 1920

Pomfret, CT 06258
(203) 928-7759
Airport: Hartford, 50 miles

Students
Total: 170 Boys: 155 Girls: 14 Grades: 6-9
Boarding: 135 Day:135 Local Students: %
Number of States: Countries: Foreign: %

Costs and Aid
Tuition: $14,050 School Extras: None
Student Aid Money Awarded: $60,000
Number Granted: 6% Avg. Per Student: $6000

Additional Support
Endowment: $1.5M Per Student: $8500
Alumni: 2200 Annual Giving: $100,000 Participate: %

Facilities
Rooms: Singles: 75% Doubles: 25% Larger: 0%
Library: 8000 Volumes Acres: 135 Plant: 4 Mil

Other Facts
Pop. 2800; next to Pomfret School; rural setting; 1½ hours from Boston; new academic center and gymnasium.

Rumsey Hall (Coed)

Founded 1900

Romford Road, Washington, CT 06793
(203) 868-0535
Airport: Hartford, 55 miles

Students
Total: 170 Boys: 85 Girls: 85 Grades: 5-9
Boarding: 100 Day: 70 Local Students: %
Number of States: 27 Countries: 9 Foreign: 7%

Costs and Aid
Tuition: $15,300 School Extras: $500
Student Aid Money Awarded: $180,000
Number Granted: 22% Avg. Per Student: $3500

Additional Support
Endowment: $500,000 Per Student: $3000
Alumni: 2000 Annual Giving: $330,000 Participate: %

Facilities
Rooms: Singles: 5% Doubles: 85% Larger: 10%
Library: 6000 Volumes Acres: 55 Plant: 5 Mil

Other Facts
Pop. 4000; The Gunnery School nearby; rural setting; 2 hours north of NYC; new gym.

Narrowing The Choices

This guide enables readers to have detailed information in a handy form that a family needs in order to decide which boarding schools to visit or pursue further. Some of this information, of course, can be obtained by hours of research in the public library, going through a number of different books, school catalogues, etc. With these important facts and figures available in this one book in a concise form, the reader can eliminate that effort as well as costly unwarranted trips often undertaken to inappropriate schools.

No school should be chosen without such a personal visit, if at all possible, and some schools require it. Furthermore, the student and at least one parent should visit several boarding schools to make an intelligent selection and have a basis of comparison.

Choosing a boarding school is a major decision in the life of a student. Facts and figures need to be available on virtually every boarding school. No appropriate educational institution should be overlooked because of ignorance or lack of sufficient information to warrant further investigation.

Completion of the following two page chart on 10 or 12 boarding schools should be helpful in narrowing the choices to the 5 or 6 that call for more intensive exploration and a personal visit.

An Educational Consultant, who actually visits a number of schools on a regular basis, can be of considerable help in providing additional information and can also help in applying for admission, etc. He or she can also give you a further insight into the "personality" and particular characteristics that are so important to these various schools.

Finally, the reader should bear in mind that tuition, like other costs, will be 5 to 10% higher each year to keep pace with inflation. Every effort has been made to show the correct figure for the 1989-90 school year.

STUDENT BODY					ACADEMICS			ENVIRONMENT		FINANCIAL AID			COSTS		
Size	Boys	Girls	Board	Day	%tile	Seniors	SATs	Urban	Suburban	Total	%	Avg.	Tuition	Extras	Total
EXAMPLE: ANDREW JACKSON					10 FEDERAL ST.			AKRON, OH.		30475			(404) 267-1246		
300	200	100	250	50	60%	85	1050		✓	500,000	25%	6500	14,500	500	15,000

STUDENT BODY					ACADEMICS			ENVIRONMENT		FINANCIAL AID			COSTS		
Size	Boys	Girls	Board	Day	%tile	Seniors	SATs	Urban	Suburban	Total	%	Avg.	Tuition	Extras	Total
EXAMPLE: ANDREW JACKSON					10 FEDERAL ST.			AKRON, OH.		30475			(404) 267-1246		
300	200	100	250	50	60%	85	1050		✓	500,000	25%	6500	14,500	500	15,000

The Campus Visit

First, remember that this guide contains 40 or more essential facts on each of the schools being visited, including many that are not necessarily found in the school catalogue.*

Therefore, the relatively short time in the interview and on the campus can be better utilized in finding out other information, mostly of a personal nature, and what else might be unique about that school.

Some General Suggestions for the Student:

1. Avoid, if possible, visiting over 2 schools a day.
2. Eat lunch at a school whenever it can be scheduled.
3. Take a written list of questions that otherwise might be overlooked.
4. Ask the Admissions Director these and others that come to mind.
5. In turn, answer his questions with more than a "yes" or "no."
6. Quiz the student guide. He or she is a good source of information.
7. Carry home all printed material available and offered, e.g., school papers, magazines, sport schedules, faculty profiles, etc.
8. Ask to observe a class in session and/or to meet a teacher.
9. Bring along copies of any transcripts not yet sent ahead.
10. Remember to relax and enjoy the visit.
11. Immediately afterwards, write down what has been learned and observed. It's easy to confuse schools even a day after the visit.
12. Finally, write a "thank you" note to the school interviewer.

*e.g., size of classes, student-teacher ratio, single rooms available, number and percent of day students, of foreign students, average financial aid per student, mean percentile of entering class, application and acceptance rates, average SAT scores, number and support of alumni, financial resources (endowment), college admission statistics, etc.